AF570765

Needs and Opportunities in the History of the Book: America, 1639–1876

A Publication of the
American Antiquarian Society's Program
in the History of the Book
in American Culture

Needs and Opportunities in the History of the Book: America, 1639–1876

edited by

David D. Hall and John B. Hench

WORCESTER
AMERICAN ANTIQUARIAN SOCIETY
1987

Library of Congress Cataloging-in-Publication Data

Needs and opportunities in the history of the book.

"A Publication of the American Antiquarian Society's Program in the History of the Book in American Culture"—half t.p.

1. Books and reading—United States—History—Research. 2. Book industries and trade—United States—History—Research. 3. Bibliography—United States—History—Research. I. Hall, David D. II. Hench, John B. III. American Antiquarian Society. IV. American Antiquarian Society. Program in the History of the Book in American Culture.

Z1003.2.N43 1987 028′.9′0973 86–28694

ISBN 0–912296–87–9

Printed in the United States of America
by Meriden-Stinehour Press

Table of Contents

Preface

THIS VOLUME reprints six essays and two commentaries prepared for a conference on needs and opportunities in the history of the book in American culture held at the American Antiquarian Society November 1–3, 1984. The pieces that appear here were first published in four successive issues of the *Proceedings of the American Antiquarian Society* (volume 94, part 2 through volume 96, part 1). Typescript copies of other papers prepared for the conference are available in the library of the American Antiquarian Society and some will be published elsewhere.* Major funding for this conference was provided by the Division of Research Grants of the National Endowment for the Humanities, with a matching grant from the Earhart Foundation, Ann Arbor, Michigan. Other contributors included ABC-Clio, Inc., Houghton Mifflin Company, and Macmillan Publishing Company. The American Antiquarian Society is grateful to these funding sources for their crucial assistance.

This conference occurred as part of the Society's Program in the History of the Book in American Culture, which was formally established in 1983 as a means by which AAS could assume leadership in stimulating and giving direction to a developing field of scholarly inquiry, the history of the book. Much of what we know of the potential richness of this field for illuminating past culture has come from French and German practitioners of what the former call *l'histoire du livre*, or *livre et société*. Although the primary focus of the Society's Program is on the impact of printing on American society during the period in which the Society specializes (i.e., from the begin-

* For example, Roger Stoddard's essay, 'Morphology and the Book from an American Perspective' will appear in issue no. 17 of *Printing History* in June 1987, and Robert Gross's paper has been expanded into a forthcoming book *The Authority of the Word: Print, Culture, and Society in America* (Hill and Wang).

nings of European settlement in America through 1876), the Program has always been open to learning from the methodologies pioneered by our colleagues abroad and attentive to the implications of this research for understanding the twentieth century. The Program in the History of the Book in American Culture has been deliberately international, as shown by the inclusion of several European scholars in the 1984 needs and opportunities conference and in the presence of several Europeans on the Program's Advisory Board.

This Program is a natural outgrowth of the Society's 175-year history. Founded by the leading publisher, printer, and bookseller of the late eighteenth century, Isaiah Thomas, the Society has assembled collections and developed programs that have made it a major center for the study of early American bibliography. Those collections garnered over the generations provide rich and deep sources for understanding the social and cultural life of America before the twentieth century. A purpose of the Program is to provide the means whereby the study of books as artifacts can be wedded to the analysis of how those artifacts actually operated in a past society. Such studies as the history of libraries and newspapers, the book trade and book distribution, and literacy, for example, are essential components for a wider understanding of the place of books in American Society.

A key figure in the 1984 conference was Stephen Botein, professor of history at Michigan State University. Deeply involved in the activities of AAS and its Program in the History of the Book, Steve Botein died on June 24, 1986, the last day of the AAS summer seminar which he was leading. That untimely and tragic death prevents our having him as the major contributor to the collaborative history that he would have been. We dedicate this volume to his memory.

John B. Hench
American Antiquarian Society
November 4, 1986

A Report on the 1984 Conference on Needs and Opportunities in the History of the Book in American Culture

DAVID D. HALL

ON NOVEMBER 1–3, 1984, the American Antiquarian Society convened a conference on 'Needs and Opportunities in the History of the Book in American Culture.' The purpose of this conference was to take advantage of a particular moment, the maturing of a field of study that bears the name 'the history of the book.' As envisioned in a proposal to the National Endowment for the Humanities requesting NEH support, this conference would 'stimulate and give direction to an emerging field of inquiry.' Via commissioned papers, the proposal went on to declare, the conference would 'systematically review the present state of scholarship and formulate agendas for future research.' Referring to the Society's newly founded Program in the History of the Book in American Culture, the proposal declared that the larger ambition was to 'suggest interpretative frameworks that link the history of the book to social and cultural history.'

I want to begin this report on the Worcester conference by thanking NEH, The Earhart Foundation (which made a matching grant), and other donors[1] for the support that made it

[1] Other donors include ABC-Clio, Inc., Houghton-Mifflin Co., and Macmillan Publishing Co.

possible. Conferences come and go in great abundance, and their consequences may seem modest or elusive. Because the Worcester conference is resulting in a series of published papers (several of them in issues of the *Proceedings of the American Antiquarian Society*),[2] its effects will grow as scholars absorb the points of view and information so richly spread before those in attendance. What follows is a brief summary of accomplishments, a review of the papers and discussion that may serve to introduce the present state and future prospects of the history of the book in America.

Starting from the goals enumerated in the NEH proposal, the conference organizers invited eleven scholars to present papers on topics in the history of the book. Four of these topics concerned the 'communications circuit' (to borrow a phrase from Robert Darnton) that books follow as they move from author to printer, and from bookseller to reader: printing, publishing, distribution, readers.[3] Two others concerned the artifact itself, the physical book as bibliographers describe and interpret it. The scope of the conference was, however, all of print (or printing), and not merely 'the book' in any narrow sense; thus, there was a paper on the nineteenth-century newspaper, and another on the religious press, which had an extraordinary importance in the nineteenth century. In the search for wider contexts and connections, other papers were solicited on the kindred topics of popular and elite culture. To conclude, a paper was commissioned on the general subject of social history and the history of the book. It may be useful to mention

[2] All of these papers, in the form in which they were prepared for the conference, are on deposit at the American Antiquarian Society. This journal is publishing some of these papers over three issues. That of David Grimsted, 'Books and Culture: Canned, Canonized, and Neglected,' with a commentary by Roger Chartier, appeared in volume 94, part 2 (Oct., 1984): 297–335. In this issue is G. Thomas Tanselle's essay on 'The Bibliographical and Textual Study of American Books,' with a commentary by Norman Fiering. Scheduled to appear in the next issue will be the essays by Michael Winship, James Gilreath, and William Pretzer. It is likely that other papers will appear in other journals.

[3] Robert Darnton, 'What is the History of Books?,' in *Books and Society in History*, ed. Kenneth E. Carpenter (New York, 1983), pp. 3–28.

some of the topics that were deliberately omitted, though only because any conference has to work within limits of time and energy: authors and the author-marketplace relationship; libraries and schools; the printed image, or illustration; censorship; governments and printing; literacy. In keeping with the scope of the American Antiquarian Society and its collections, the papers surveyed American book history from the beginnings of settlement to the year 1876.

The NEH proposal contained one other statement that deserves repeating. Referring again to the Program in the History of the Book in American Culture, the proposal spoke of its 'international outreach' and promised that the conference would 'bring to America a number of European scholars who have made the history of the book into a central field of study.' Accordingly, the conference would function to 'transmit themes and methods from one side of the Atlantic to the other,' and in so doing enrich several of the disciplines that converge on the history of the book. Indeed, the conference benefited from the presence of historians of the book in Europe; Roger Chartier (École des Hautes Études en Sciences Sociales), Michael Turner (Bodleian Library), Erdmann Weyrauch (Herzog August Bibliothek, Wolfenbüttel), themselves Europeans, and others such as Robert Darnton and Elizabeth Eisenstein, whose proper field is printing and book history in early modern Europe.

The conference opened with a paper on 'The Printing Trade and Allied Crafts: Technologies and Labor Practices.' William Pretzer (then at Winterthur Museum, now at the Henry Ford Museum), proposed that the 'history of the book trades should be seen as a part of the general history of American labor and technology.' Drawing on concepts arising within labor history, Pretzer focused his discussion on the history of work. Accordingly, he engaged in a careful reconstruction of the actual work processes in a series of crafts: printing, papermaking, typefounding, inkmaking, and bookbinding. In the course of this description he raised and helped to answer such major questions as the transatlantic transfer of technology, the process of technological diffusion, the role of capital investment, and the ideological consciousness of those who worked as journeymen and master craftsmen. The commentator was Rollo Silver, a distinguished historian of printing.

Michael Winship, who serves as editor of the *Bibliography of American Literature*, followed with an essay on 'Publishing in America.' The very term 'publishing,' as Roger Chartier remarked in the discussion afterwards, is confusing since its meaning changed sharply as functions in the book trade became differentiated. Taking note of these complications, Winship focused on the nineteenth century, 'when American publishing first became an independent and fully developed activity,' on the publishing of books in particular, and on the publisher as 'playing the central entrepreneurial role—that is, the person or office that organized and coordinated its main components.' Throughout his essay, Winship indicated that strategies and decisions in the practice of publishing grew out of certain basic relationships. He called attention in particular to capital, credit, and markets. Publishing was a business, though nineteenth-century entrepreneuers sometimes invoked an ideology of publishing as an art. The audience and his commentator, Michael Turner, seconded his plea that we seek more information about the economic costs and benefits of publishing.

The conference turned next to distribution. James Gilreath (Library of Congress) reviewed with care and precision the historiography. He called attention to certain interpretations, or alternatives, and assessed the merit of these different positions in the light of more recent research. A theme of Gilreath's paper was the persistent focus on American imprints and the ignoring of imported books, a tendency he deplored. Reflecting on the several channels by which books became available to readers, Gilreath emphasized the role of private collectors in the eighteenth century, and of tract societies and state and federal governments in the nineteenth. He reminded us that significant communication often happened via other means than books, a case in point being Benjamin Franklin's initial knowledge of electricity. A corollary observation was that a great many Americans never entered a bookstore, and may have owned or used but very few books. Distribution in the colonial period and the early republic was hampered by social, economic, and technological conditions; yet as Gilreath, Winship, and others pointed out, some books and pamphlets broke free of these restrictions—Paine's *Common Sense*, Stowe's *Uncle Tom's Cabin*—in ways that suggest it may have been demand that lagged, not supply.

Robert Darnton (Princeton University), the commentator, proposed a four-part structure—marketing, trade routes, intermediary service functions, and sales—as a way of grasping the importance of distribution, a neglected but, in his words, 'great' subject in the history of the book. The thrust of his commentary was to emphasize the role of the distributor as 'middleman,' a role that, as historians learn to describe it, helps us understand how books actually got into the hands of readers. Turning to comparisons between Europe and America, Darnton noted many parallels between German and American book history.

One parallel development was a 'reading revolution' that occurred as the eighteenth century gave way to the nineteenth. So William Gilmore (Stockton State College) argued in his essay 'The "Mystic Chords of Memory": Needs and Opportunities for a History of Reading.' Gilmore adopted the concept of a reading revolution from the German historian Rolf Engelsing, enriching it with the fruits of his own research on the print culture of the Upper Connecticut River Valley. By the early nineteenth century, he argued, reading had become a 'necessity of life,' an essential vehicle of information. Within this same span of time, literacy increased from lower levels to become nearly universal. Elsewhere in his essay, Gilmore reflected on the ambiguity of much of the evidence about what people read. In effect, the evidence is often indirect, as in the case of books that were owned but quite possibly not opened. Drawing again on his own research, he insisted, however, that books appearing in probate inventories should be understood as books that the owner read.

Discussion benefited from comments by Roger Chartier and Robert Darnton, both of whom have helped bring about a history of reading that construes it as an active process whereby readers impose themselves upon the text, interpreting it according to their basic social and intellectual situation. As the commentator on Gilmore's wide-ranging paper, I suggested that we temper the concept of a reading revolution, a point made more forcefully by Darnton. There were pleas on the part of historians that bibliographers—those who study the 'materiality' of the book—inform us about the relationship between differences in material form and mode of reading.

Turning from the 'communications circuit' to questions drawn from social and cultural history, the conference took up the related subjects of popular and elite culture. David Grimsted offered a masterful critique of popular culture studies in America. Roger Chartier, speaking from the perspective of the social historian of early modern Europe, followed with a thoughtful commentary. Chartier and Grimsted both argued that the historian of popular culture must avoid two facile extremes: the one of denouncing the 'popular' as inferior, degraded, or escapist; the other of embracing the popular as though it were genuinely democratic or 'of the people.' Enthusiasm and snobbery are equally useless. Grimsted devoted much of his essay to demonstrating that popular texts embody complexities of various kinds. He called attention to certain theories of culture, or theories of the relationship between society and culture, that had brought new energy to the field, and at the same time, new difficulties, as in the effort to separate the culture of the working class from that of owners or employers.

Indeed, Grimsted and Chartier were unhappy with the assumption that texts can be equated with any one social level. As Chartier has made clear in his essays on the *bibliotheque bleue*, a cheap form of book that began to appear in seventeenth-century France, certain items deemed 'popular' circulated widely, finding readers among the bourgeoisie and the peasants, the urban and the rural classes.

In the wake of popular culture came an essay on 'high' or 'elite' culture. But Stephen Botein (Michigan State University) and David Jaffee (Smithsonian Institution and Georgetown University) preferred the term 'expertise' to these older categories. In their essay, 'Printed Expertise in Eighteenth- and Nineteenth-Century America,' they presented four case histories of the 'process by which print media transmitted . . . craft and professional knowledge.' One of these case histories concerned the role of Blackstone's *Commentaries* in the acquisition of legal expertise. Botein and Jaffee demonstrated that American publishers made the *Commentaries* widely available in the early national period, and by doing so 'helped to keep the legal profession quite accessible to large numbers of middle-class Americans who were located at a considerable distance from the great urban centers of practice.' Botein and Jaffee concluded that print culture played a more ambiguous and complex role in relation to the professions than historians had suspected. The commentator was Edwin Wolf, 2nd (Library Company of Philadelphia).

The conference moved from these broad questions to the more specific subject of the nineteenth-century newspaper. John C. Nerone (University of Illinois) offered a critique of journalism history as it has been written in America, in which he argued that most of this work ignores the relationships—political, social, intellectual, and economic—that impinge upon the newspaper. Nerone traced the limitations of journalism history to its 'occupational' purpose of enhancing the status of journalists. Hence, he concluded, there arose the concentration on 'professional journalists' and the attitude that journalists are heroes. Yet Nerone also described recent scholarship that broke free of these limitations. By way of a conclusion, he sketched a number of themes and interpretative possibilities. The commentator, Ronald P. Formisano (Clark University), felt that Nerone had been too critical of the older historiography.

'The Religious Press in America' was the subject of an essay prepared by Harry C. Stout (University of Connecticut) and Nathan Hatch (Notre Dame University). They argued that the religious press was crucially involved in the emergence of a 'democratic' print culture that made available a veritable flood of inexpensive publications. One reason for the great activity of the religious press was an ideology, originating with the Reformation, that 'reading was a spiritual necessity, a sacred rite at the heart of personal religion, and that the printed page was itself efficacious.' At the outset of their essay, Stout and Hatch emphasized the importance to colonial Americans of a means of communication, the sermon, that reached the colonists via speech as well as through the printed word. Responding to their essay, Catherine Albanese (Wright State University) argued for an even broader view of the religious press than that which Stout and Hatch had taken. Evangelicalism—the movement on which they concentrated—may indeed have been numerically the most significant tendency in nineteenth-century America; yet Albanese reminded us of the many alternatives, such as spiritualism, that flourished in the same period. She criticized the emphasis Stout and Hatch placed on the occasional sermon, pointed out that statistics on press runs and book ownership from seventeenth- and eighteenth-century New England indicated the dominance of devotional literature. She pointed out, finally, that we know more about authors than about readers, and suggested that historians of the book concern themselves with the readership of the religious press.

Two essays, Roger Stoddard's on 'The Morphology of the

Book' and G. Thomas Tanselle's on 'The Bibliographical and Textual Study of American Books,' returned the conference to the artifact itself and its 'materiality,' to use a term familiar to historians of the book in France. Stoddard (Houghton Library), offered a series of reflections on the physical form of the printed book; the commentator was Marcus A. McCorison (American Antiquarian Society). Tanselle developed two lines of criticism, one of bibliographers of American imprints for failing to perform signature counts, the other of historians for failing to use bibliographical evidence in studying the texts on which they rely. Tanselle's starting point was the axiom that no two copies of any text can be presumed identical without careful bibliographical scrutiny of surviving copies. Responding, Norman Fiering (John Carter Brown Library) argued that an ideal standard of bibliographical control, while suited to some circumstances, was unsuited to others. Historians, he suggested, should adopt a standard of control adequate to the task at hand. Otherwise, Fiering prophesied that the burden of textual criticism would impede, if not overwhelm, every other stage of historical study.

Robert Gross (Amherst College) brought the Worcester conference to a close with an essay on 'The Authority of the Word: Print and Social Change in America, 1607–1880.' Exploring the connections between book history and structures of authority in society and culture, Gross began by observing that historians of colonial America have proposed competing 'democratic' and 'elitist' interpretations. In *The Americans: The Colonial Experience* (New York, 1958), Daniel Boorstin argued that printers and printing in America broke with European patterns; on this side of the Atlantic, said Boorstin, 'print lost its exalted status as the companion of privilege, adapted to necessity, and took on a more pragmatic, democratic purpose as a community-oriented vehicle of useful information.' The theme of Americanization, or the emergence of a pluralistic, democratic culture, had its counterpoint, Gross argued, in two other interpretations: one suggesting that the print culture of early New England 'sustained a deeply conservative social order, where consensus on fundamental values held sway,' the other arguing that in eighteenth-century Virginia books belonged to the privileged few, and were emblems of hierarchy. As for historians of nineteenth-century print culture, Gross pointed out that some argue that culture became democratized as literacy increased and more books were published, while others insist that the ethos of competitive capitalism became dominant. Gross moved to reconcile the historiography via an interpretation of his own, in which he stressed the emergence of a gentry in eighteenth-century America that sought wide control over books and culture. Responding, Bernard Bailyn (Harvard University) questioned how effective or established such a gentry was.

Formal papers and commentary are like the skeleton of the human body, a basic structure that achieves amplitude in the give-and-take of debate and discussion among the entire group of participants. Some of the points raised during the course of the conference deserve reiterating, as do one or two observations that arose in discussion or in the papers.

Thus, it seems worthwhile to recall James Gilreath's observation that in studies of eighteenth-century Virginia and of literary culture in early New England we encounter 'a seamless web of readers in which books appeared magically and circulated without regard to class, region, profession, or any other variable.' This criticism has wide application beyond the two examples that Gilreath specified. Generalizations about readers, distribution, publishing, and printing no longer satisfy unless they pay close attention to context. One context, as described from the floor by Alfred Young (Northern Illinois University), was economic and social inequality; referring to artisan and urban worker cultures in cities such as Boston in the Revolutionary period, Young suggested that certain forms of print culture should be understood as means of protest and self-assertion.

Indeed, many of the papers for the conference touched in one way or another on power. If we consider printing (or print culture) as synonymous with information, then it seems axiomatic that information is a form of power to which some have greater access than others. Similarly, the ability to read and the ability to write (especially the latter) are forms of empowerment that were unevenly available. Yet the thrust of discussion, and perhaps even more so of the formal papers and commentaries, was to reemphasize the connections between printing and pluralism or democracy. An explicit theme of Stout and Hatch's survey of the religious press, the democratic structure —or, if one wishes to speak of *process*, the democratization—of print culture in America, emerged implicitly in Grimsted's essay on popular culture and Botein and Jaffee's on expertise. With the exception of Gilmore, no one found it useful or necessary to speak of 'underground' printing (as Darnton has done so ably for eighteenth-century France) or of the role of the state in limiting freedom of the press.

Debate on these issues did not always conclude in agreement. The most explicit disagreement concerned texts and their transmittal: to what extent should historians undertake bibliographical research before they can proceed in confidence? Meanwhile, it was suggested that bibliographers put their skills to work answering questions of importance to historians, for example, the relationship between 'mis-en-page' and the ways in which a given text was read or appropriated. This exchange of expectations may not have satisfied either party, but it was exactly in keeping with the purpose of the Worcester conference. Similarly, it was in keeping with the purpose of the conference that it entertained pleas for progress on an improved national bibliography of American imprints and on preserving the records of American publishers. The southerners in our midst complained of an imbalance of references to other sections of the country, a complaint any westerner could have voiced as well. A conference may avoid situations of risk and fall back to the safety of familiar ground. This was not the case at Worcester. The legacy of this conference includes a number of provocative arguments and interpretations—Pretzer's fusion of labor history and the history of technology, Gilmore's argument for a 'reading revolution,' the theme of authority as unifying social history and the history of the book, the broad rethinking of elite and popular culture, the possibilities and limitations of bibliographical methods, to name several.

In between the lines, as it were, two other assertions emerge from the papers and commentaries. The first is that texts elude restrictions. Print culture is singularly open-ended. For that matter, so are the boundaries that we try to draw around printers, publishers, or communities of readers. I conclude with this paradox: books, though products of specific material and social formations, can never be equated with any one interpretation, social group, or form of power. Like the Cheshire cat in *Alice in Wonderland*, the printed book teases us with its tangibility, while remaining just beyond our grasp or comprehension.

The Quest for Autonomy and Discipline: Labor and Technology in the Book Trades

WILLIAM S. PRETZER

THERE IS MUCH to be learned about the history of labor and technology *in* the book trades. There is also much to be learned *from* the history of labor and technology in the book trades. Understanding the production of printed goods and their components will not only help us understand the changing nature of demand, distribution, circulation, and impact of print, but these investigations will also increase our knowledge of general aspects of the American Industrial Revolution. Indeed, the history of the book trades should be seen as part of the larger history of American labor and technology.

Much of this larger history is composed of the evolving character of conflict and conciliation in the workplace. And while the role of the plebeian classes as participants in the culture of the printed word is a topic well worth exploring, the focus here is on the role of the producers of printed culture. Continuing through the third quarter of the nineteenth century, two themes stand out in this history. First is the quest for autonomy pursued by master artisans and capitalist employers in terms of their control over raw materials, product markets,

This is a revised version of a paper presented at a needs-and-opportunities conference on the history of the book in American culture held at the American Antiquarian Society, November 1–3, 1984. I am grateful to Rollo G. Silver and Steven Rosswurm for their comments and to Kevin S. Baldwin for his research assistance.

and labor practices. We must also consider the quest for autonomy that was pursued by workers in terms of their control over craft knowledge and the labor process. The second theme is the attempt by employers to discipline their work forces and to maintain that subordination against workers' assertions of independence, while workers themselves sought to impose some discipline over an increasingly unruly economic system. Technology was both a weapon used in these contests and an arena in which these struggles occurred. In the contrasting pursuits of autonomy and discipline, freedom and order, we will find much of the meaning of the development of the book trades.

Pairing labor and technology suggests that the history of work, per se, is our central focus. Printing is not merely a method of communication; it is a form of production.[1] Our attention to labor and technology must ultimately raise questions about the sources and impact of the changing work experiences of men and women in printing offices, bookbinderies, papermills, and typefoundries. Asking questions about work and the factors that condition that experience and its interpretation allows us to investigate a wide range of issues. Rather than peering ever more intently at the esoteric concerns of engineers and inventors, we should begin with the experience of the worker and move both backward into the technologies themselves and forward toward the social and political implications of particular work structures, conditions, and experiences.

Following upon this coupling of the topics of labor and technology, a fruitful way to approach the history of work in the book trades is to pair five sets of social processes that encompass economic, technical, and cultural aspects of the trades. A developmental scheme of contrasting processes seems appropriate. Such a scheme might be organized along the following lines:

[1] Raymond Williams, 'Means of Communication as Means of Production,' in his study *Problems in Materialism and Culture* (London, 1980), pp. 50–63.

1. The transfer of Anglo-European goods and techniques and the creation of American traditions.

2. The expansion of established methods and the encountering of constraints (economic, cultural, technical, structural) to production or profitability.

3. The search for alternative production methods (be they organizational or technical) and the subsequent alteration of the labor process.

4. The restructuring of work and industrial organization and the diffusion of new methods that inevitably accompanied such reorganization.

5. The expansion of production and the subsequent creation of new production traditions, ultimately giving rise to new constraints to further expansion.

Although no single chronology is appropriate for all of these trades, it is possible, based on current knowledge, to suggest that the limits of Anglo-European technologies had been reached by the 1790s and that the first major crisis of reformation of the labor processes in printing, papermaking, and bookbinding came in the 1820s and 1830s, with typefounding lagging behind by about a decade. Papermaking reached the limits of mechanization before 1870 and experienced a profound reorganization by 1900. Typefounding, of course, also reorganized its industrial structure in the 1890s, largely as a response to the challenge of the Linotype machine as well as to the problems engendered by competition. Social relations in the printing trade were transformed in the 1830s and remained highly unstable for the next five decades. While presswork became more minutely subdivided and mechanized, composition remained handwork. But it was so thoroughly subdivided as to severely dilute skills and workers' autonomy.

Indeed, each of these five trades experienced some combination of the major transformations in social relations associated with the industrial revolution in the workplace: the rise of nonpractical, capitalist ownership and management; the mechanization of production and the move to factory organization; the subdivision, dilution, and feminization of skill; and the transition from customary to deliberate workplace regulation. During this era, tensions between differing definitions of autonomy and discipline were constantly at work. Thus, the essential questions are wide in scope:

1. What was the relationship between the expansion of printing and the rise of capitalism in America? How did the book trades come to be competitive capitalist trades, with their specific industrial structures? By what process did ownership of technology and control over productive processes come to reside in certain hands during the course of the nineteenth century? And in what ways did the expansion of the press contribute to bourgeois domination? This is baldly stated, simply because it seems to me that we must first and foremost recognize that we are discussing the epoch of the development of American capitalism. Issues of the control of technology and alterations of labor practices are at the heart of this historical transformation.

2. By what process did certain technologies become preeminent in their fields? What combination of technical difference, product superiority, marketing strategy, capital cost, ease of manufacture or use, and labor requirements or control recommended one technique over competing ones?

3. What was the changing relationship between technology and the work process? How did new technologies interact with work culture and discipline, the organization of work, labor market structure, workers' organizations, and employers' strategies? Why were some processes mechanized before others?

4. What were the relationships between changing product markets or audiences and technological-labor change? For instance, how did changes in typographical designs influence new methods of typecasting, thus altering the work and, ultimately, the technology of typefounding? Conversely, how did

new technologies affect graphic design, typography, and communications?

5. What were the sources of uneven economic development within individual trades and between separate trades? What impact did this have on their subsequent technological-labor histories? For instance, how did the mechanization of paper-making affect typefounding and printing?

Answering these questions will require us to investigate a number of constituent issues whose importance is best seen in relation to these conceptual questions. It is obvious that these questions have subordinate parts that can be explored independently of the full complex. Indeed, so intricate and different are the trades' histories that they must be dealt with individually for many issues. Yet I have the impression that some of the most exciting work in the next few years will focus on the complex interrelationships between trades. We will surely only recognize the importance of much of what we find if we have a conceptual base from which to work. Reviewing some of the actual details of the history of the book trades before 1876 will highlight the importance of the larger questions and suggest the range of subordinate issues.

Printing is by far the best understood of the book trades. Its history will alert us to some conceptual issues encountered in other trades. Printing is a classic case of the subdivision of labor, which abetted the mechanization of tasks, which led, in turn, to further degradation of skill and the use of semitrained labor.[2]

The work process in printing remained essentially unchanged from Gutenberg's day to the early nineteenth century. Composing consisted of taking individual pieces of type from their

[2] See the discussions of the printing trade in a number of recent histories of the urban classes: Sean Wilentz, *Chants Democratic: New York City and the Rise of the American Working Class, 1788–1850* (New York, 1984), pp. 129–32; Steven J. Ross, *Workers on the Edge: Work, Leisure, and Politics in Industrializing Cincinnati, 1788–1890* (New York, 1985), pp. 107–12; W. J. Rorabaugh, *The Craft Apprentice: From Franklin to the Machine Age in America* (New York, 1986), pp. 76–96, 146–54; Robert M. Jackson, *The Formation of Craft Labor Markets* (Orlando, Fla., 1984).

compartmentalized cases, placing them in a three-sided composing stick held in the left hand, and filling out each line with spacing pieces so that the lines were of equal length. When the stick was full, the composed matter was transferred to a table where it was arranged in proper order. It might be placed in a long tray and a proof taken to insure accuracy or immediately divided into pages and locked into place in a metal frame for placement on the press. The second operation in printing, called imposition, involved the correct ordering of the pages and their precise alignment within the frame. The matter was held tightly in the frame by the use of wooden strips and wedges knocked firmly into place. The frame, or chase, now weighing many times its weight when empty, was carried to the press and locked into place on the press bed. As the predominant method of composing matter, this process did not change substantially until the very end of the nineteenth century.

Presswork on a common handpress involved preparing the ink and wetting the paper, locking the chase onto the bed and insuring its alignment, performing all the tasks known as 'making ready' to prepare the press for even impressions, inking the form, positioning the paper, and creating the impression by forcing the heavy platen down. The common press was a large frame with crosspieces holding the screw that drove the platen down and a railing, along which ran the bed holding the form of inked type and the paper. The essential elements were the platen and screw, the bed on rails that could be winched in and out from under the platen, and the hinged frames that held the paper and positioned it over the inked type. This essential technological paradigm remained unchanged until the end of the eighteenth century.

The substitution of iron for wood frames in the early nineteenth century provided greater strength to the press, allowing a larger platen and greater stability. The substitution of a series of levers for the screw eased the work of the pressman. Still, in 1810 the iron handpress looked very much a member of the same family as the sixteenth-century wooden common press. And the processes of typesetting, imposition, and presswork were carried out in a routine, traditional fashion.

Mechanization of presswork began in England in the early nineteenth century with the development of the cylinder press by Frederick Koenig. The general principle of the cylinder machine consisted of the notion that a cylinder onto which the paper adhered could be revolved over the form holding the inked type more rapidly than the meeting of two parallel planes, as in the platen press. Keonig's machine was especially useful for newspapers, where time was essential but printing quality could be compromised because the product was meant to be ephemeral. The most noteworthy introduction of Koenig's machines came at *The Times* in London in 1814. Other manufacturers evolved their own style of cylinder presses; the first imported to the United States was a Napier press purchased by two New York City newspapers in 1825. These presses rapidly became the most popular for urban newspaper and periodical work.[3]

Other men, however, were convinced that the cylinder principle could not provide an absolutely precise impression. Also, many offices did not need the speed nor could they afford the expense of a cylinder press. Development of a machine bed-and-platen press occurred just after the invention of the cylinder press. This time, however, it was an American who developed the first successful innovation. Daniel Treadwell of Boston had become interested in printing presses as an application of mechanical principles to human movement, and by 1820 he had conceived of several improved presses. By 1830, two other New Englanders, the brothers Seth and Isaac Adams,

[3] Rollo G. Silver, 'An Early Time-sharing Project: The Introduction of the Napier Press in America,' *Journal of the Printing Historical Society* 4(1968):29–36; Frank E. Comparato, *Chronicles of Genius and Folly: R. Hoe and Company and the Printing Press as a Service to Democracy* (Culver City, Calif., 1979), pp. 13–15, 37–47; James Moran, *Printing Presses: History and Development from the 15th Century to Modern Times* (Berkeley, Calif., 1973), pp. 116–17.

had shifted their press-building operations from handpresses to bed-and-platens. They set the standard for the next three-quarters of a century. The Adams press moved its bed up and back from a stationary platen, the paper being taken to the point of impression by a frisket. Bed-and-platen presses became standard for all good bookwork by the 1840s, although some publishers preferred the iron handpress for fine work, and many smaller printers continued to use only handpresses. By the late 1830s, the increasing demand for commercial ephemera and the obvious financial and technical restrictions on the use of large power presses called for a small, flexible press. The platen jobber, often operated by foot treadle, with easily altered forms, and usually worked by a boy or woman, was the answer.

Within the era under consideration, there was one more thorough renovation of the conception of presswork. Iron handpresses, bed-and-platen, and cylinder presses all carried their type form on a flat plane. Pressmen retained much of their control over skilled adjustments of the press, gained in stature as machine technicians, and turned over the unskilled work to assistants. In the 1840s, the English press manufacturer Augustus Appelgath developed a press that had the type forms attached to a revolving cylinder. Placed around this cylinder were additional impression cylinders, which carried the sheets of paper to the central cylinder and made the impression. In 1847, the preeminent American press manufacturer, R. Hoe and Company, of New York, installed a new version of the type-revolving press. The Hoe press also used regular printing type, but rather than attaching flat plates to the type cylinder, the Hoe press used specially designed, wedge-shaped column rules to hold the type to a detachable part of the cylinder called a 'turtle.' The Hoe press had the additional advantage over the Appelgath of an automatic 'fly' to remove each sheet after printing. The final elaboration was the substitution of a roll of paper feeding directly to the press in place of individually fed sheets, a development of the late 1860s. These developments emphasize the importance to employers and inventors alike of such unskilled work as feeding and taking off. The type-revolving and web-fed presses were appropriate only for the largest metropolitan newspapers, but they constituted the epitome of fast printing in the nineteenth century.[4]

Two other technological developments influenced the work of printers. Stereotyping and electrotyping allowed the duplication of typeset forms. These processes allowed the storage of vast amounts of matter without the lost investment of storing foundry type. They permitted the duplication of material once set and the simultaneous multiple printing of matter. Stereotyping was first practiced in the United States in 1814, and electrotyping in the 1840s. The technologies had an indirect impact on the work in the printing office; they replicated the compositor's work, and denied him the opportunity to be paid for it, while increasing the profit opportunities for employers.[5]

Changes in the work routine and the organization of offices preceded and conditioned the impact of technological change. Master printers were dividing the work between compositors and pressmen, so that those became essentially separate occupations by the late eighteenth century. In the 1820s, the introduction of specially designated men as 'makers-up' broke the connection between these two work processes and denied many men the opportunity to learn this skilled aspect of the trade. Increasingly, distinctions were drawn between straight matter and more complex or artistic work. Different product markets grew for book and periodical work, job or commercial work, and newspapers. Out of this differentiation of products devel-

[4] Moran, *Printing Presses*, pp. 113–71, passim; Comparato, *Chronicles of Genius and Folly*, pp. 4–109, passim; Elizabeth F. Baker, *Printers and Technology: A History of the International Printing Pressmen and Assistant's Union* (New York, 1957), pp. 3–30.

[5] Michael Winship, 'Printing with Plates in the Nineteenth-Century United States,' *Printing History* 10(1983):15–26.

oped different types of offices, each with its own technology and work routine. Increasing competition among master printers sent many of them looking for cheaper sources of labor, and the use of partially trained, apprentice-aged boys and women increased dramatically in the first half of the century.

Compositors are generally considered to have enjoyed more control over their work than many other kinds of workers, and many enjoyed better-than-average wages. Their craft customs have received a certain amount of attention and are usually linked both to Anglo-European traditions and to the continuity of the work process. The separation of pressmen from compositors is often considered the major division of labor within the trade, but little attention has been paid to the type of work culture invented by pressmen, who were also among the most highly paid of nineteenth-century workers but whose labor was the product of new technology.

The interpretation of the impact of the structural differentiation of the printing trade on labor and technology is only just beginning. But it is clear that by the late 1820s, before the introduction of cylinder or bed-and-platen presses, the printing trade was no longer the artisan workshop of the early modern era. Technology altered the requirements for workers in the office and demanded new skills for pressmen, but it did not obviate the skill of the compositor. The separation of composing, imposing, and printing into different skills performed by different individuals in the larger offices allowed employers to pay for only the single skill a worker possessed rather than to encourage the 'all-around' printer. Technology contributed to, but it did not cause, a number of changes: the separation between employer and worker, increased capital requirements, reduced upward mobility, more complete division of labor, a flood of underemployed compositors, and increasing profit rates. The late 1820s and 1830s were the crucial era. For the next several decades the trade expanded but generally experienced only elaborations on these themes.

Press manufacturing and printing make interesting examples of the impact of uneven economic development. As competition increased among manufacturers in the 1830s, each one strove to acquire a secure yet growing share of the market. Their efforts included aggressive marketing, credit and patent policies, as well as manufacturing improvements and technical innovations. Individual manufacturers sought to establish market control through product differentiation. Thus, competition fueled technological change in the printing trade, increased the diversity of presses available, contributed to the specialization of labor, and encouraged both the expansion of and competition within the printing trade.

Still, the role of technological change in the evolving structure of the printing trade is not fully understood. We can focus on the important offices that first adopted innovative presses, but we have little concrete sense of when and where those presses next appeared. The diffusion of printing techniques has yet to be thoroughly explored. The relationship between the growth of newspaper readership and faster presses is often asserted but seldom analyzed. Alteration of the work process and the extent to which compositors, pressmen, and foremen influenced those changes is still not adequately appreciated. Printers were among the most highly organized tradesmen in the nineteenth century. The history of the union movement has been told several times, but we are only beginning to ask questions that move beyond institutional history and into the social and political origins and implications of union policies.

While printing offices preceded papermills in North America, papermaking was a much older craft. By the early eighteenth century, papermaking techniques were fairly standardized in the Western world and the craft was well understood. Papermakers guarded their secrets for procuring whiter paper, but there was in fact little variation among the recipes. Papermaking required lots of clean water, rags, some bleaching agents, and a minimum of machinery; but it also required specially made hand molds, and highly skilled workers. During the nineteenth century, social relations within the trade were radically altered and mechanization totally transformed the production process.

Before pulping, rags were sorted into piles of clean and white pieces for white paper and dirty and colored rags for less expensive or colored paper. The rags were soaked, bleached with an alkaline solution, and then beaten by hand with a mortar and pestle, beating machine or, after about 1750, a Hollander machine. The rags were mixed with water to create a pulpy mass called 'stuff.' A skilled vatman dipped a wire-bottomed mold into the stuff and allowed water to drain, meanwhile shaking the mold to interlace the fibers and form them into a uniform thickness. After removing the top of the mold, or 'deckle,' the vatman passed the mold to another worker, the 'coucher,' who inverted it, dropping the moist sheet of paper onto felted cloth. The coucher covered this sheet with another piece of cloth and dropped the succeeding sheet of paper onto that. A stack of cloth and paper sheets was then placed into a screw press and the water squeezed out. Individual sheets were later hung to dry in another room, preferably a well-ventilated loft. After drying for several days, the sheets were dipped in sizing made from animal bones and hooves, pressed, and dried again. Finally, they might be passed through a pair of rollers in a calendering process.

The equipment for such a hand-operated mill was minimal. The screw press was a basic form dating back centuries. The Hollander (if there was one) was a pulping machine, usually water powered, consisting of a vat with one set of knives mounted on the vat floor and another set on a wheel rotating past them, which tore and shredded the rags. Molds were two-piece affairs: a wire-bottomed mold and a detachable frame or 'deckle' that was used to form the edges of the paper. Not many Americans practiced the complex business of making wire molds. English and French molds were imported to America well into the nineteenth century. Mills approximated the appearance and the size of most textile mills of the era and were situated near water, markets, and sources of rags and labor. The mill buildings themselves were separated into a rag room, a beating room, a vat room, a drying loft, a size room, and a finishing room.

The hierarchy of the work force approximated the division of the mill's rooms. The sorting room and drying loft were occupied by low-paid women and boys, while the beating and vat rooms, where the stuff was prepared and the sheets actually made, was the domain of the skilled papermaker and his assistants. The coucher was in a responsible position, since his carelessness or clumsiness could destroy the vatman's products. The layboy, on the other hand, simply was trusted with moving moist sheets of paper and assisting the coucher and vatman. Early in the nineteenth century, vatmen and couchers might receive on the order of three to five dollars a week, layboys seventy-five cents and women sixty cents plus board. The owner of a small mill in Massachusetts paying these typical wages allowed himself nine dollars weekly.[6]

Paper production expanded rapidly during the early decades of the nineteenth century. The number of mills grew from eighty or ninety at the end of the Revolution to just one-hundred at the turn of the century, then doubled in the next decade. The two hundred mills in operation in 1810 produced perhaps four hundred thousand reams of paper yearly. Still, American papermakers could not keep up with demand and much paper was imported from England, France, and Holland. American mills remained small, using at most three or four vats, and employing twenty or so workers.[7] Eighteenth-century efforts to import skilled workmen generally failed, leaving

[6] Norman B. Wilkinson, *Papermaking in America* (Greenville, Del., 1975), p. 26; see also Jane L. Carter, *The Papermakers: Early Pennsylvanians and Their Water Mills* (Kennett Square, Penn., 1982).

[7] Wilkinson, *Papermaking*, p. 23; Isaiah Thomas, *The History of Printing in America*, ed. Marcus A. McCorison, 2d ed. (New York, 1970), pp. 26–28.

paper manufacturers to train local talent. Nineteenth-century expansion and the location of the industry enticed foreigners, especially Irish and Scottish artisans. Throughout the century, papermaking had a higher proportion of foreign-born workers than any other book trade. Capital investment, machinery, and annual production remained limited in many mills, although papermaking was and is still the most capital-intensive of all the book trades.

It was not merely capital or labor that perplexed manufacturers. Raw materials presented a major obstacle to consistent production. By the turn of the nineteenth century, Americans were searching far and wide and paying high prices for clean, white rags with which to make the whitest paper. The development of chlorine in the 1770s by French chemists reduced some of the necessity for white rags, but it was still no simple chore to obtain one and a half pounds of rags for every pound of paper produced. Moreover, the price of rags constituted the paper manufacturer's greatest cost and fluctuated violently, as did the availability of rags. The search for rag substitutes was a century-long concern of the paper trade and the elaboration of nineteenth-century techniques continued into the twentieth century. It was, of course, wood pulp that came to the rescue of papermakers in the 1860s, creating new technological questions for the paper industry and opening entirely new ecological issues.

However, the search for a mechanical means of papermaking began with labor problems. Nicholas Louis Robert was a clerk entrusted with improving productivity in a French papermill in the 1790s. His greatest problem was the workers' intransigence; they wanted nothing to do with his discipline and efficiency. Robert set out with his employer's blessing to devise a method of displacing the skilled workmen who controlled the labor process. After several years' work and a number of improvements on his original model, Robert patented a machine in 1798 for his employer, Didot. Didot lacked the financial resources to market the machine for a profit and ended up selling the rights to the English papermakers Henry and Sealy Fourdrinier. The Fourdriniers' mechanic, Bryan Donkin, improved Robert's machine in several ways, and in 1807 it was offered for sale to papermakers. Only a few Fourdrinier machines were sold during the subsequent fifteen years, but by midcentury there were hundreds worldwide.[8] A Fourdrinier machine was first imported to the United States in 1827, a full decade after the first American-developed papermaking machine was introduced by the Gilpin brothers of New Castle County, Delaware.

Joshua Gilpin opened his first papermill on Brandywine Creek in northern Delaware in partnership with his uncle in 1787.[9] He was later joined by his brother Thomas, and by 1800 the Gilpin's mill was using one hundred thousand pounds of rag and producing one thousand reams of paper annually. The Gilpins expanded their operations considerably during the next few years, establishing mill villages that included housing for workers and jobs for several members of individual families. Just how these villages compared to New England mill villages is a matter for further research.[10] Joshua Gilpin visited England and the Continent for two extended periods between 1795 and 1815 to obtain technical and industrial information. During two years of outright industrial espionage between 1814 and 1815, he obtained sufficient data to allow his brother to construct a papermaking machine. Modeled after an English machine developed by John Dickinson in 1809, the Gilpin machine operated on principles quite different from the Fourdrinier machine.

[8] R. H. Clapperton, *The Papermaking Machine: Its Invention, Evolution, and Development* (Oxford, N.Y., 1967), pp. 247–49.

[9] Harold B. Hancock and Norman B. Wilkinson, 'The Gilpins and their Endless Papermaking Machine,' *Pennsylvania Magazine of History and Biography* 81(1957): 391–405.

[10] See Anthony F. C. Wallace's comments on papermaking in *Rockdale: The Growth of an American Village in the Early Industrial Revolution* (New York, 1978), pp. 11, 80, 125, 162, 284.

The Fourdrinier was a web machine: the pulp poured onto a continuously moving web of wire screen that ran over rollers. The paper passed to a belt of felted material, where it moved through more rollers that squeezed out much of the water. The paper was finally rolled onto a cylinder. The Dickinson/Gilpin machine involved a copper-mesh cylinder that revolved while partially submerged in the vat of stuff. A suction device in the cylinder's center made the pulp adhere to the cylinder's outside. The paper was then passed to a felted belt, carried through a series of rollers on the belt, then separated from it, and finally wound onto a roll.

Scholars disagree on the actual rate at which papermakers adopted the machines. The cylinder machine cost much less than the Fourdrinier and was easier to operate, but it produced a generally lower-quality product. Opinions about the relative merits of the two machines changed over time. The cylinder seems to have been more popular until the final two decades of the century, when the Fourdrinier became increasingly dominant.[11] Research into the actual diffusion of these technologies will undoubtedly show great regional differentiation, a fact not unique to papermaking, although it was perhaps accentuated by the trade's particular requirements for raw materials.

Both machines dramatically increased mill productivity, decreased labor costs, and transferred the knowledge, skill, and control of the work process from the handcraftsman to the mill owner. Mechanization increased the employment of women and required the reskilling of many vatmen and couchers. It also vastly increased the use of steam engines and the capital investment required to establish a mill. By 1880, the average papermill in the United States (of which there were 692) was capitalized at sixty-six thousand dollars, more than three times the average capitalization of a printing office or ink manufactory, and ten thousand dollars more than the

[11] Lyman H. Weeks, *A History of Paper Manufacturing in the United States, 1690–1916* (New York, 1916), p. 296; Clapperton, *The Papermaking Machine*, passim.

average typefoundry. Papermills employed the second highest proportion of women (31.2 percent of the total 24,422 workers) but the lowest percentage of children (2.7 percent) of all the book trades.[12]

Judging by patent activity, it is evident that papermaking processes were constantly revised. While there were only ninety-two American patents in the paper trade before 1838, they included the basic mechanization of the production process, along with improvements in felting materials and the drying apparatus. After 1840, there were an average of thirty patents a year, centering on methods of improving the speed of the basic process and in using new fibers. Innovations in calendering, sizing, and cutting the paper product increased both quality and productivity in the middle decades of the century. By midcentury, the search for new fibers had produced a number of substitutes, but it was the creation of the mechanical means of producing usable wood chips that turned the tide. Ground wood pulp was first used for commercial newsprint in 1868 and gradually came to supply the bulk of paper stuff. The final quarter of the nineteenth century saw massive changes in the structure of the industry. Manufacturers increasingly adopted the corporate form, vertical and horizontal integration increased, and mill size expanded along with the use and size of Fourdrinier machines. The 1870s marked the end of the traditional, mechanized paper trade.

American typefounding was the third book trade most influenced by changes in the division of labor, mechanization, and internal factory organization. Typefounding consisted of several distinct and very precise operations. Although many have noted that early printers engaged in all aspects of the book trades, typefounding probably was removed from the printing

[12] U.S. Department of the Interior, *Report on the Manufactures of the United States at the Tenth Census* (Washington, D.C., 1883), p. 12. These and subsequent statistics from this source are presented merely to suggest the magnitude of these trades. Any analytical work must depend on manuscript sources and will undoubtedly show immense regional and urban-rural differences.

office by 1585. After that time, it was the unusual printer or the odd job that required casting in the printer's office. At least this was true in Europe. In colonial America, there was more overlap among trades, and printers occasionally engaged in typefounding. Still, most eighteenth-century type was imported from foreign commercial foundries, since domestic production only began in earnest after the Revolution.

The first step in typefounding was the most artistic. The letter cutter designed and cut the letter into the end of a soft steel shank. After hardening, the punch, as it was called, was driven into a blank piece of copper to create the matrix. This matrix, squared and precisely finished, was fitted into one of the more remarkable achievements of the fifteenth century, the adjustable type mold. The mold was composed of two pieces of wood with a slot for holding the matrix absolutely square and a channel with a mouthpiece for introducing the molten metal. The mold held constant the depth and height of the type but was adjustable for different width sorts. Cutting the letter, creating the matrix, and fashioning the mold to precise configurations were demanding operations, representing the typical unity of conception and execution in artisan production.

Once the matrix was set in the mold, the caster prepared a mixture of lead, tin, and antimony. The proportions changed with the size of type to be made. Smaller type contained a higher proportion of tin and antimony in order to produce a free-flowing alloy that hardened completely. The caster held the mold in his left hand, ladled the molten metal out of a crucible, and poured it into the mouth of the mold. Simultaneously, he jerked the mold upwards, forcing the metal to the very face of the matrix to create a full impression of the letter without any air holes. The metal solidified quickly, the mold was opened, and the type thrown out. The caster closed the mold and repeated the process, casting perhaps four hundred to five hundred sorts per hour.

The type came from the mold with a long, extraneous piece

of metal attached. This 'jet' was broken off by an unskilled boy or woman, who passed the type to another unskilled boy or woman known as a rubber. The rubber quickly and deftly smoothed the type's two broad sides by passing it rapidly over a grindstone that lay flat on a table. The type was quickly placed in long wooden frames and taken to a dresser, a man who used a planelike device to square the narrow sides and then cut a groove where the jet had been attached at the bottom of the type body. He then inspected the type for any imperfections and wrapped them in page-sized bundles. Printers could order special amounts of individually needed sorts, full fonts of type, or type by weight.

There were few technical changes in this process, but those that did occur were profound. In 1811, the American founder, Archibald Binney, patented and popularized an improvement of the hand mold. Binney attached a small spring lever to the matrix that the caster depressed as he opened the mold. This had the effect of 'popping' the type out as the mold opened and increased the speed of the process. Until the 1820s, despite several attempts to create a casting machine, the process of typefounding remained unchanged.

In the 1820s, continual attempts to increase productivity and the need to cast newly popular, fine-lined faces encouraged more experimentation with pumps to force the molten metal into the mold. Several pumps were developed both in England and the United States, one of the most successful by David Bruce, Jr., an important New York typefounder. The pump was the first interruption of the traditional hand process, beginning the shift away from the 'workmanship of risk' to the 'workmanship of certainty,' to use David Pye's instructive terms.[13]

In the late 1830s, Bruce developed a commercially successful machine to cast type. The pivotal caster, so called because the mold and matrix pivoted back and forth up to the spout that

[13] David Pye, *The Nature and Art of Workmanship* (Cambridge, Eng., 1968).

delivered the metal, became the standard typecasting machine for the rest of the century. The machine caster increased productivity by a factor of ten and subsequently increased the employment of unskilled breakers and rubbers. Hand-cranked, the pivotal caster removed the skilled aspects of the work of casting (although not that of cutting punches or making matrices). But it left the remaining, less-skilled work processes unaffected. Large type and ornaments continued to be cast by hand, although both stereotyping and electrotyping cut into their production. Attempts to mechanize the cutting of punches and rubbing the cast type were generally unsuccessful in this era.

Eighteenth-century America lacked the materials and men with skills to produce type. The first attempt to commercially cast type came in 1769, but successful foundries were only established after the Revolution. John Baine immigrated from Scotland and established a foundry in 1789 in Philadelphia. Benjamin Franklin purchased and imported an entire typefoundry from France in 1786. Adam Mappa, an experienced typefounder, moved himself and his equipment to New York four years later. Archibald Binney and James Ronaldson arrived from Edinburgh in 1797. Binney, an established typefounder, brought his equipment with him. Another pair of Scotsmen, David and George Bruce, also immigrated to New York in the mid-1790s. Binney and Ronaldson had the only operating foundry in the country in 1800, but by 1810 the industry was well established. By 1820, domestic demand could be fully met by the five foundries operating in Baltimore, Philadelphia, New York, Boston, and Cincinnati.

We have only scattered data on the operations of these and subsequent foundries. Most seem to have employed several workmen and a dozen or more women. However, one of the largest utilized thirty casting machines in 1850.[14] Every foundry accepted orders from around the country, although each hoped

[14] *Godey's Ladies Book* 53(1856):301.

to dominate its regional market. Typefounders competed in choice and execution of design as well as in quality, timeliness, and cost of production. By 1880, the forty-eight foundries, capitalized at $2.8 million and producing $2.3 million in type annually, employed just under two thousand persons, including 400 women and 250 children.[15] By this time, typefounders were beset by the problem of cutthroat competition and declining prices. Soon, the Linotype's popularity would reduce demand for foundry type. The perceived solution to this lay in the formation of the consolidated American Typefounders Company in the 1890s. Typefounding thus presents almost stereotypical examples of the crises accompanying the transitions from petty commodity production to corporate capitalism.

Most early modern European printers made their own ink or purchased it from fellow printers who produced a surplus. After the fifteenth century, much of this ink was of very poor quality, since master printers often retailed their poorest-quality ink. Purveyors of paints also made ink, again, often of poor quality. There really were few secrets in the basics of inkmaking, although some printers did add special ingredients for specific effects. To boiled linseed oil was added some rosin for thickening, which was then combined with lampblack. Manganese was often added to speed drying and 'resin soap' added to form a distinct impression. The quality of linseed oil, the judgment in boiling it for the proper time, and the quality of the lampblack largely determined the quality of ink.

By the early eighteenth century, some master printers, publishers, and customers were fed up with inferior ink. Several master printers in England and on the Continent began experimenting with methods of producing ink that was darker and more stable in color, less liable to create brown, oily halos around letters, and less likely to turn to powder upon drying. This fostered a sense of competition with other printers and inkmakers. By the late eighteenth century, commercial ink-

[15] U.S. Department of the Interior, *Report on Manufactures,* p. 14.

makers were plying their trade throughout England and Europe, although a few master printers still preferred to make their own.

European and English inks were imported to America throughout the colonial era and well into the nineteenth century. There were several ill-fated attempts to establish commercial ink manufactories in America in the eighteenth century, but only three makers were in business at the beginning of the American Revolution. Several firms founded in the very early nineteenth century became leaders in the field and prospered through much of that century. By 1880, there were sixty-three commercial ink manufacturers employing only 480 persons and capitalized at just $1.25 million. Their annual product ran to $1.63 million, more than enough to supply American printers and authors.[16]

Technological change is not a major theme in the history of ink production. There occurred only one important development and several minor innovations involving the production process itself. On the other hand, major changes in ink production have come from the use of different raw materials, especially pigments for the production of colored inks, utilized in traditional processes by ink manufacturers. Boiling linseed oil, producing lampblack, adding some agents for specific effects, mixing and grinding the whole to a uniform, pastelike consistency remained the essence of the process. The major technological change was the introduction of a steam-powered grinding machine used to reduce the mixture to a homogenous whole. Even this did not require alteration of the common batch system of production.

The use of steam-powered mixers and grinders reduced much backbreaking labor but did not eliminate all of the onerous aspects of working in an ink factory. Boiling linseed oil and producing lampblack in large furnaces were still hardly congenial chores. Nor did the introduction of machinery reduce the skill required to boil the linseed oil just right or to add the

[16] Ibid., p. 11.

proper quantity of other materials to produce the desired consistency, viscosity, color, and drying rate.

A review of patents issued in England and the United States shows that most proposed changes in inkmaking were in the actual composition of the inks themselves rather than in any processing machinery or production techniques.[17] Many patents involved the development of oil substitutes or the use of new materials as pigments. The introduction of refinements in the composition of inks and their processing were important for the reproduction of fine woodcuts and lithographic printing. Various natural pigments were commonly used until the introduction of coal-tar colors in the middle of the nineteenth century. Coal-tar pigments vastly increased the range of colors readily available to inkmakers but did not greatly alter their production process or commercial operations, although colored inks required extremely fine grinding and the application of steam-powered rollers was an immense advantage.

We know very little about the actual labor process, as opposed to technical descriptions, of the production process of inkmaking. We know next to nothing about the sources, organization, work routines, or customs of American labor. For example, Anglo-European master printers made a ritualistic excursion out of the need to move to open ground to boil and 'flame' the linseed oil to produce ink. Pieces of bread and sometimes onion were placed in the boiling oil to absorb the excess grease. This fried bread was considered a great morsel when consumed hot, and journeymen and apprentices considered it a perquisite of their occupation. Also, Moxon noted that journeymen invited the 'typefounder, smith, joiner, and inkmaker' to the annual wayzgoose, or festival, expecting each of them to contribute money for the merriment.[18] The journeymen could expect a donation because it was they who decided which

[17] C. Ainsworth Mitchell and T. C. Hepworth, *Inks: Their Composition and Manufacture* (London, 1904).

[18] Frank B. Wiborg, *Printing Ink: A History with a Treatise on Modern Methods of Manufacture and Use* (New York, 1926), p. 97; Joseph Moxon, *Mechanick Exercises on the Whole Art of Printing* (1683; repr., Oxford, 1958), pp. 82–86, 327.

suppliers would provide the printing office with needed services and materials. How did such traditions influence American laborers? In nineteenth-century America, it was the office foreman who made most of these decisions. Since foremen were often charged with accepting bribes from the agents of inkmakers and typefounders, attitudes had obviously changed. One of the great needs in the cultural history of work is the investigation of how widely accepted notions of 'right' and 'obligation' were transformed between the sixteenth and nineteenth centuries by concepts of property, theft, and influence. It would be useful to examine how commercialization of ink production affected the nature and composition of workers' rituals, customs, and controls over the labor process.

The demands made of ink were and are great: it must be the proper color and tint and stay that way; it must not 'powder' off or 'bleed' into paper; it must dry quickly but not too quickly; and it must come off the type cleanly without smearing, and wash off the type easily. The various methods of obtaining these desired results were a combination of knowledge of the proper ingredients and their properties, and skill and dexterity in manipulating the physical processes of boiling, 'flaming,' and mixing. No wonder early printers attached a ritualistic aura to the occasion. Scientific advances did not contribute significantly to inkmaking until the application of coal-tar pigments in the mid-nineteenth century. The use of external power sources, especially the use of power rollers to grind the ink in the 1820s, was the major technical change in the trade. Power printing presses with automatic inking required uniformly finer ink than could be handground. Bloy notes that power grinders were further stimulated by their difficulty in obtaining workers willing to engage in the arduous and noxious work of hand grinding.[19] The development of colored inks was greatly stimulated by the introduction of another printing process, lithog-

[19] Colin Bloy, *A History of Printing Ink, Balls, and Rollers, 1440–1850* (London, 1967), pp. 51–52.

raphy. Printers who used typographic methods found lithography a serious competitor very soon after its commercial development in the 1820s, and they soon demanded more and better colors for letterpress printing.

The introduction of finer-quality inks as well as composition ink rollers was stimulated by the introduction of machine presses. A great stumbling block to faster printing was the limitation on the speed with which the form could be inked. Leather-covered cylinders were tried, but the inevitable seam down the length of the cylinder prevented uniform inking. At least one claim is made that printers derived the idea of a molasses-and-glue composition roller from the Staffordshire potters, who used similar rollers to apply designs to their ceramic wares. The new printing presses worked at such rapid speeds, and without the intervention of human judgment in the application of ink, that a more finely ground, uniform, and quicker-drying ink was needed. Frederick Koenig, the developer of the first cylinder press, developed his own ink to meet the needs of the press. The Hoe Company did essentially the same in the nineteenth century. Thus, developments in other book trades as well as techniques known in other industries contributed to the demand for technical change in inkmaking.

Bookbinding reflects the impact of uneven development within the book trades, as large, factorylike binderies grew alongside custom-oriented artisan shops. The process of handbinding books with 'solidity, elasticity, and elegance' is conveniently divided into three stages, each with a number of subordinate operations.[20] These stages are preparing, forwarding, and finishing. The sheets delivered from the printer had to be prepared, that is, gathered into piles, each comprising a whole work. The piles were then folded, collated to ensure the proper arrangement of pages, and, if necessary, plates were added. Well into the twentieth century, this low-skilled, low-paying

[20] John Hannett, *Bibliopegia; or, The Art of Bookbinding*, 4th ed. (London, 1848), p. 13.

work was performed by hand by women. After preparation, the book was beaten with a hammer to flatten and compress the folded sections. It was then placed into a sewing press and its sections sewn together, again, a task done by women. In many binderies, the preparation was accomplished in a separate room sometimes called the 'girls' room' or 'sheet room.' From here the book went to the forwarder.

The forwarder first beat the book again to ensure uniform thickness. Then he used a round-headed hammer to create the familiar rounded back. Next, the book was placed between boards in a vicelike press and the forwarder used another hammer to form the shoulder and groove, which held the millboard covers. The boards were then attached to the book by tying the cords running across the back of the book through holes punched in the boards. If the book was simply to be put in boards, this ended the work process.

Leatherbound books, however, required further highly skilled work. A book to be bound in leather was first trimmed on three sides using a plough, the bookbinder's essential edge-cutting tool. The plough consisted of two pieces of wood, called cheeks, that were linked by a wooden screw, with a pointed knife attached perpendicularly to the inside of one cheek. The book was placed in a vise with just as much of the edge exposed as was to be trimmed. The plough was placed over the book with one cheek running in a groove in the vise. The plough was run back and forth to trim a few sheets; then the screw was tightened to draw the knife across a few more sheets and the plough run back and forward again, and so on until the entire edge had been trimmed. This was repeated for the other sides. Higher-quality binders required that the book be trimmed 'in-boards,' meaning that the boards were already attached. The cover of calfskin (usually) was pulled over the boards, folded over, and held by end sheets pasted to the inside of the boards. From here, the book passed to the finisher who prepared and decorated the leather using a variety of heated tools to impress designs. The finisher was the most artistic member of the bindery. Using a number of heated rolls and fillets, the finisher tooled designs into the leather. These designs could simply be impressed, in which case it was 'blind-tooling,' or gold leaf could be affixed to the designs in the case of 'gold-tooling.'

In the mid-eighteenth century, minor changes were made in this process that changed the appearance and construction of the book. Preparers sawed grooves into the back of the book, so that the cords of the binding would lie flat against the back once they were sewn to the sections. By the early nineteenth century, many books were being bound 'out-of-boards,' that is, they were trimmed before the boards were attached. This reduced individual attention to specific volumes, allowed for more rapid trimming because books were trimmed in batches, and permitted a division of labor. Such changes in the details of construction and process encouraged flexibility in what a bound book meant and led the way to further changes in bookbinding methods.

Preparing, forwarding, and finishing remained the essence of decorative bookbinding just as they were in the sixteenth century. Several changes, however, made the processes mean something different for the majority of books placed between the covers after the early nineteenth century. These changes altered traditional hand practices without introducing new technologies. One new method was the out-of-boards technique, which reduced the cost of a bound book, even though it was substantially the same in construction and appearance as a book bound in-boards. Another important change was that of pasting the cords to the boards rather than punching holes in the boards and tying the cords to them. The cords were frayed at the ends, pasted to the boards, and endpapers pasted over them for appearance and further solidity. The introduction of cloth to replace the much more expensive leather as a covering for the millboards was a singularly important substitution. Accompanying these changes to the traditionally bound book was the introduction of yet another type of protection for the book. This involved the use of high-quality marbled or colored paper in place of leather or cloth as a covering and the use of printed labels with author and title data in place of impressions in leather. These techniques spread almost sequentially between 1800 and 1835. All of these alterations, involving new materials and processes, were efforts to cheapen the cost of binding. They opened the door to the notion of 'casing.'

Casing was simply the production of covered boards into a unit that could then be attached to a sewn book. Casing was introduced into the United States from England between 1825 and 1835 and has become the chief distinguishing characteristic of edition binding as opposed to handbinding. However, even the cases themselves were handmade until the 1890s. Initially, the cases were attached to the book by use of a piece of paper pasted to the back of the book and then to the case. By the 1860s, a piece of linen fabric, called a 'crash,' was commonly used. The cords then served only as the common bond to which the signatures were sewn. The use of cases allowed yet another division of labor, increased the productivity of binderies, and reduced the cost of a book.

Technological changes were widespread in the actual work of bookbinding during the nineteenth century. In the early 1820s, a rolling press was introduced to replace the burdensome process of handbeating during preparation. The use of this press stirred several hundred London journeymen binders to sign a petition protesting the unemployment caused by the machine, but, as far as we know, no similar protests were launched on this side of the Atlantic. In 1832, an embossing press was developed that allowed the creation of designs on cloth-covered boards, something unattainable before cloth was sized so that it would hold the impression. The sized cloth and embossing press allowed binders to offer the public cloth-bound books that approximated the look and feel of leather. The embossing machine did not displace any labor, since it was introduced just as cloth was becoming a common covering in America. One of the most skilled aspects of forwarding, the process of rounding and backing, attracted inventors' attention, and by 1845 there was a patented backing machine. But it provided little more than a method of holding the book while giving a guide for forming the groove for the cover. The binder still used his hammer to round and back the book. These machines reduced the amount of judgment and dexterity exercised by the binder and were standard equipment for nearly half a century. It is worth mentioning that none of these machines relied upon steam power.

The first machine that made a real difference in the work performed by women in binderies was the folding machine, developed by Cyrus Chambers, Jr., during the 1850s. The Chambers folder was a truly ingenious translation of the hand's motions into mechanical movements. The folder used a series of dull blades to force the paper through a pair of rollers to create a fold. By adding blades and rollers, the number of folds could be increased. The Chambers folder and others like it tripled productivity, folding 1,500 octavo (three-fold) sheets an hour, compared to a handfolder's five hundred sheets. Women operatives fed this and other folding machines, and thus lost their control over pace and routine.

David Smyth developed a mechanical sewing machine to replace the handsewers sitting at their bookpresses, but he did not successfully introduce it commercially until the 1880s. Women continued to be predominant in the preparation stage of binding even after the introduction of machinery, making up an increasing proportion of bindery workers between 1870 and 1900. The decade from 1875 to 1885 was a transitional one, as wire-stitching machines used for pamphlets, sewing machines, and folders proliferated. The quarter-century after 1876 was destined to be a period of intense labor struggle in the bookbinding trade, as in other trades, as employers sought to exploit fully the technologies introduced earlier in the century.

It is worth mentioning that binderies produced more than just bound, printed volumes. The eighteenth-century hand-binder provided stationery and blank books, periodicals and pamphlets, rebound books and publishers' editions, as well as the individually bound volume. His nineteenth-century successor often produced a similar range of items. But technical changes in one area were not necessarily applicable to other aspects of the binder's work. A stabbing machine used to perforate holes in signatures prior to sewing and a wire stitcher introduced in the 1820s were important changes in pamphlet work but were unsuitable for bookwork. Ruling machines introduced in the 1840s produced the parallel lines in ledgers, account books, and stationery. Binders thus had to keep abreast of changes in several different technologies. Binderies displayed the mechanical marvels of the age, even though much of the work of bookbinding remained handwork and the journeyman binder retained much of the skill and autonomy of his eighteenth-century predecessor.

Nineteenth-century bookbinding resembled printing in that the sizes of offices varied greatly and the industry's structure included dominant large shops with a plethora of small operators. Some offices specialized while others took in all kinds of work, and while there was a combination of custom and standardized work, each job presented its own idiosyncracies. Further, both trades were distinctly local-market oriented and illustrated a great deal of regional variation. By 1880 the 588 binderies enumerated in the census of manufactures employed some 10,600 people (45.5 percent of them women) and $5.8 million in capital. Binderies employed the highest proportion of women among all the book trades and paid them about what the others did, one-third to one-quarter of men's average wages.[21]

This said, however, we need to know much more about the changes in the economic and structural nature of the book-

[21] U.S. Department of the Interior, *Report on Manufactures*, p. 9.

binding trade during the eighteenth and nineteenth centuries. This is especially true if we ever want to reach a better understanding about the larger question of how consumers bought and saved books for personal pleasure. Before the 1870s, mechanization in bookbinding did not require massive reskilling as it did in the papermaking and typefounding trades. Still, we know too little now to gauge the interaction of technological change and work routine, labor organization, gender relations, or workers' customs. Both master and journeymen bookbinders organized local trade societies during the 1820s and afterward. What they have to tell us about trade conditions and labor history is still unknown. We know little about bindery management or the relationships between master binders, capitalist investors, and inventors. Nor has anyone explored issues involving the rate of technical change and factors such as market and trade structure, labor organization, or capital investment. The trade's history has been sketched, but it has been barely analyzed.

It should be evident from this review that the invention, introduction, diffusion, and impact of technologies compose a large, untold story in the book trades. This is especially true of the diffusion process, where we may know the end points but not the process itself. We know something about the prominent individuals and companies, but not nearly enough about the broad social and economic effects of innovation. Also, each of the trades has its own history, its own set of continuities and changes, its own conflicts and convergences. There is no universal pattern to be seen in the book trades. Yet, broadly speaking, each of the trades experienced changes in the structures of competition, work, composition of labor, and ownership that enlarged and solidified the wage-labor system. Indeed, it was the expansion of wage labor, the division of labor, and the separation of craft knowledge from execution that affected the workers' lives far more than the uneven mechanization process in the book trades.

The 'big questions' in the history of technology and labor in the book trades prior to 1876 have to do with how technology contributed to the development and consolidation of wage labor and its specific conditions in the United States. How did changes in the work process, whether linked to technical advances or not, contribute to the formation, elaboration, and reformation of the class structure? In order to approach this question, the experience of work must be placed in the context of the broader social and political cultures in which workers were immersed.

How was technology combined with work processes to delineate certain forms of control and conflict? How did workers and employers adopt methods for dealing with change and come to accept new work routines imposed on both groups? What impact did this have on workers' social and economic views? Conversely, of course, we should be asking how technology was shaped and directed by larger social processes such as capital accumulation, class formation, and workplace conflict.

A much-needed approach to technological and labor history is the study of industrial health, hygiene, and safety. Type-rubbers, rag sorters, lampblack makers, and newspaper compositors were continually exposed to the most unhealthful conditions. Pressfeeders and paperfolders endured hours of stressful attention to demanding yet boring work routines. Vatmen in hand-operated mills suffered from deformed hands, and handpress operators were known by their overdeveloped right shoulder and foot; technological changes should have made these kinds of deformities anachronistic. Attention to these details, which should be approached as issues in labor history, may open new vistas on work and technological change.

Policies of local trade societies toward technology should be closely scrutinized, keeping in mind that these societies and, later, unions often preserved the privileged status of skilled, male workers to the detriment of subordinate male and female workers. We need to incorporate more fully discussion of these other worker groups into our explorations of technology and work. We need to consider systematically trends in wage ratios between skilled and unskilled workers. We need to know more about the sources and recruitment methods of unskilled workers, their wages, working conditions, and response or reaction to technological change.

We need to focus on capital accumulation more broadly in all the trades. We need a better understanding of credit arrangements and the role of supply firms and typefoundries, as well as political and social organizations, in providing credit for the establishment of printing offices.[22]

Historians could profit by asking any number of questions implied in the currently debated themes in the history of technology. By what methods and to what effect were Anglo-European technologies transferred to North America? What impact, if any, did scientific experimentations and ideas have on technology? What kind of decision-making process was involved in the choice of technologies by entrepreneurs? It is important to emphasize the fact that this was a process of human choice. For example, we need to understand how papermakers obtained information about the cylinder and Fourdrinier machines, how they interpreted that data and made decisions. We need to interpret their thought processes, calculations, and biases, without applying neoclassical economic constructs to the information.[23] Similar questions should be posed of typefounders, bookbinders, and printers.

There is every reason to value investigations of the technologies of the book trades as case studies of more general aspects of the history of technology. Thus, the Napier cylinder

[22] A promising start in this direction has been made by Carolyn Stewart Dyer in 'Economic Dependence and Concentration of Ownership Among Antebellum Wisconsin Newspapers,' *Journalism History* 7(1980):42–46.

[23] At the very time I first penned these words, Judith McGaw was (unbeknownst to me) preparing an article addressing just these questions. See her provocative 'Accounting for Innovation: Technological Change and Business Practice in the Berkshire County Paper Industry,' *Technology and Culture* 26(1985):703–25.

press and the Fourdrinier papermaking machine make illuminating examples of the transatlantic transfer of technology. They are all the more interesting in that their stories emphasize the importance of the actual machines themselves rather than the plans or ideas for these machines, and also because they highlight the importance of the American mechanics who were called upon to assemble the machines once they were imported. Similarly, the examples of Gilpin's tour of Europe in search of papermaking techniques and Bruce's inquiring after methods of stereotyping are interesting instances of other methods of transfer. Further, what we today call 'industrial espionage' was rather commonplace throughout the eighteenth and nineteenth centuries.

To state the obvious, invention is not an ahistorical process; it occurs in a particular time and place. It is only reasonable to assume that motivations differ from epoch to epoch, as well as from individual to individual. Some societies foster certain types of inventions and prove particularly fertile for particular types of innovations. Part of our investigation should be directed toward examining why and with what consequences Americans became known for inventing certain kinds of technologies, while Europeans focused their inventive energies in other directions. Thus, we need to understand the international division of labor more precisely. Why did capital support some types of inventive work and not others?

We should consider technology as a debate, sometimes an argument, and not infrequently, a street fight. More than merely a body of knowledge, it is a contest over knowledge, usually involving a particular division of knowledge, skill, power, and labor. Any individual machine, process, or technique is the product of a historically-specific process in which various participants (inventor, manufacturer, employer/capitalist, worker) share roles. Their contributions are, however, unequal, and the result is also unequal. In addition, any new technology expands the socially accessible body of information and constitutes itself as a new debate, a continuing contest over knowledge and power.

This new debate includes new participants and can focus on internal or external aspects of the hardware or process. It can lead to improvements in the operations of the process or to the elaboration of its operations. It might consist of the inventor's quest for perfection, the manufacturer's desire for simplicity or easy replicability, the employer's need for reliability or cost effectiveness, or the workers' desire for safety, ease of operation, or increased control over the workaday world. This new conversation might focus on the use or social or economic impact of the new technology. In any event, conflict is an inherent part of the process.

Thus, it should not come as a surprise that technology had both its enthusiasts and its detractors. Technology was seldom considered in the abstract, except by literary pundits. For most people, technology was or was to become a tangible presence, and their involvement with it and its transformations influenced their responses. For some, it allowed a larger market, greater profits, fewer problems. For others, it provided new products that seemed important or reduced the cost of items already desired. The new technologies were forces to be celebrated. For still others, technology meant dislocation, unemployment, or the opportunity for low-paying, repetitious work, with little or no opportunity for job mobility. It could hardly stimulate rapturous reminiscences or descriptions. Technology was reported secondhand by many but experienced firsthand at the point of production, and therefore it elicited different responses precisely because it was experienced differently by those on opposite sides of the labor process.

The responses to technology of journeymen and master artisans varied. When the Bruce brothers wanted to begin stereotyping, fellow typefounders refused to supply the needed type for fear of reducing future demand for foundry type. Daniel Treadwell was forced to establish his own printing office in

Boston in the early 1820s after master printers refused to accept the superiority of his machine press. His office was subsequently burned down, reportedly by 'irate pressmen who feared for their jobs.' In 1854, George Sanborn had to escape out of a window after being threatened by skilled bookbinders when he attempted to introduce his rounding and backing machine. When a papermaking-machine tender heard that his machine was to be altered to increase its speed by ten feet per minute, he charged that 'when a machine was run faster than a man could walk, it was time to quit,' which he promptly did. A newly installed Hoe type-revolving press was subjected to such abuse and minor sabotage in the Government Printing Office in Washington in 1863 that the Hoe Company was required to remove it. David Bruce, Jr., succinctly explained the attitude of skilled workers toward the introduction of the mechanical typecaster: 'There seemed to exist among the casters a certain *esprit de corps* which held it disgraceful to descend to the turning of a crank, and upon the "turnspit" principle, thus annihilate all their acquired science of "throwing" for faces.'[24] Similar considerations of craft culture and skill no doubt motivated other craftsmen.

It may be true that America did not see an antimachinery movement equivalent to the Luddites, but that does not mean that technologies were automatically endorsed. There was anti-machinery sentiment in various forms in nineteenth-century America. Violence, however, was isolated, sporadic, and not highly publicized. Its full dimensions and consequences remain to be investigated. It is worthwhile to remember in this discussion of the book trades that one of the best-known twen-

[24] For sources of these anecdotes, see *The Printer* 1(1859):258; Comparato, *Chronicles of Genius and Folly*, p. 16, and *Books for the Millions* (Harrisburg, Penn., 1971), p. 110; *The Progress of Paper* (New York, 1947), p. 91; Stephen D. Tucker, 'History of R. Hoe and Company, 1834–1885,' edited by Rollo G. Silver, *Proceedings of the American Antiquarian Society* 82(1972):416; *Inland Printer* 6(1888):206; and David Bruce, Jr.'s manuscript 'The Progress of Typography,' Typographic Library, Columbia University, n.p.

tieth-century examples of antimachinery violence was the 1975 attack on the presses of the *Washington Post*.[25]

Looming over the issues of technological change and work experience is the history of the book trades as a metaphor for the development of American society during its industrial transformation. In the separation of the manual and intellectual, mechanical and artistic, employed and employer, the book trades are emblematic of bourgeois America. Since communication is a form of production, we should not be surprised to find that the book trades represent specific forms of production and reproduction. It is also true that the choice of production techniques conveys images of authority and value, and thus represents a form of communication. The book trades illustrate the contest over bourgeois values and forms of order and discipline (or disorder and anarchy) that many saw as representative of American society in 1876.

Primary Sources

The primary sources for such studies as I have outlined here are spread far and wide. One might begin with the trade journals and technical manuals for each trade. Such nineteenth-century trade journals as *American Bookmaker* (New York, 1885–), *American Printer and Lithographer* (New York, 1874–), *Inland Printer* (Chicago, 1887–), *The Printer* (New York, 1858–), *Printers' Circular*, (Philadelphia, 1866–), *Proof Sheet* (Philadelphia, 1867–), *Rounds' Printer's Cabinet* (Chicago, 1857–), *Typographic Advertiser* (Philadelphia, 1855–), and *Typographic Messenger* (New York, 1865–) should be used more extensively and carefully. The fact that many items appear after the era under consideration should not prejudice them. These journals contain many letters, reminiscences, and essays of considerable historical value. The published and unpub-

[25] Andrew Zimbalist, 'Technology and the Labor Process in the Printing Industry,' in A. Zimbalist, ed., *Case Studies on the Labor Process* (New York, 1979), pp. 103–26, esp. pp. 117–21; David Noble, 'Present Tense Technology: Part Three,' *Democracy* 3(1983):71–93, esp. pp. 73–76.

lished diaries and reminiscences of workers in the book trades are very useful, as Rollo Silver and others have demonstrated.

The essential archival collections in the book trades are well known, although often their specific holdings are less understood and even less used. The American Typefounders Library at Columbia University is the preeminent collection of book trades materials. Still, has anyone exhausted the Binney and Ronaldson papers and ledgers there, or the Bruce family letters? The collections of the American Antiquarian Society are, of course, unparalleled. The Newberry Library has tremendous holdings of published materials, trade journals, and type specimen books. The Kemble Collection at the California Historical Society, San Francisco, offers great opportunities for the study of the Western expansion of the book trades. For instance, the Towne and Bacon Papers, the records of an important San Francisco printing and binding firm, have yet to be mined. The Rochester Institute of Technology has a major collection of bookbinding materials.

Judith McGaw has made intelligent use of paper company records still held in the hands of papermaking firms in Berkshire County, Massachusetts. Local historical societies often contain the ledgers, account books, or papers from local printing offices, newspapers, mills, or manufactories. For example, the payroll book of the St. Paul *Dispatch Pioneer-Press* from 1862 to 1865, in the manuscript division of the Minnesota Historical Society, provides a rare look at the attendance, daily production, and earnings of ten piecework compositors during the Civil War. Local typographical union records are held in several local libraries or historical societies such as the Rhode Island Historical Society, Cornell University Labor-Management Center, the Bancroft Library at the University of California-Berkeley, and the Pennsylvania Historical Society. The International Typographical Union office in Colorado Springs still has some material. Since national unions in the other trades did not emerge until after the period under discussion, one will have to be content with finding local trade society materials, if they exist.

Despite Rollo Silver's imaginative use of them, the importance of the Patent Office Records, Record Group 241, in the National Archives, still has not been recognized. Not only do the original applications and drawings contain much technical data, but the patent extension records offer much social and economic information. Moreover, we might begin to look more deeply into the role of the patent system in the nineteenth century. As with technology, patents were both weapons and sources of conflict. State and local records should be examined for contracts relating to printing and other services for government agencies.

Museum and library collections offer even more underutilized material. Major collections of printing technology can be found at a number of small, special-interest museums, as well as at the Smithsonian Institution's National Museum of American History, the Henry Ford Museum, the Sacramento (Calif.) Historical Society, and the privately owned Lindner Collection in Los Angeles. It may be that historic archaeology will answer questions concerning the use of new machinery and power sources in rural papermills and urban printing offices. Of course, libraries contain the physical products of the book trades. Books, paper, type specimens, and ink samples all contain evidence of past practices. The kinds of questions that material culture studies raise and answer are only now becoming a major topic for discussion among historians. The methods and concerns of analytical bibliography are a useful beginning. The machines and products of the book trades remain plentiful and await further consideration.

Bibliography

General histories of the printing trade that deal with business, labor, and technology include Isaiah Thomas, *The History of Printing in America*, ed. Marcus A. McCorison, 2d ed. (New York, 1970), Lawrence C. Wroth, *The Colonial Printer* (1938; rpt., Charlottesville, 1964), Milton Hamilton, *The Country Printer, New York, 1785–1830* (New York, 1936), and Rollo G. Silver, *The American Printer, 1787–1825* (Charlottesville, 1967). There is no comparable history exploring the middle and later parts of the nineteenth century.

Essential guides to printing history are the *American Dictionary of Printing and Bookbinding* (New York, 1894) and J. Luther Ringwalt, ed., *American Encyclopedia of Printing* (Philadelphia, 1871). Technical manuals, starting with Joseph Moxon, *Mechanick Exercised* (1683; new ed., London, 1958), should be used carefully to trace technologies, trade conditions, and methods of doing and teaching. That boys and girls could learn the rudiments of printing from printed matter is in itself an interesting connection between knowledge, printing, and labor studies.

Unfortunately, few journalistic or business histories of newspapers or publishing houses have much to say about labor or technology. There is important data on smaller master printers in Leona M. Powell, *The History of the United Typothetae of America* (Chicago, 1926), and Charlotte Morgan, *The Origin and History of the Employing Printers' Association* (New York, 1930), and a recent revision of some of Morgan's ideas in Irene Tichenor, 'Master Printers Organize: The Typothetae of the City of New York, 1865–1906,' in Stuart W. Bruchey, ed., *Small Business in American Life* (New York, 1980).

Histories of printing labor begin with Ethelbert Stewart, 'A Documentary History of the Early Organization of Printers,' in U.S. Department of Labor, 11, bulletin #61 (Washington, D.C., 1905). George A. Stevens, *New York Typographical Union #6* (Albany, 1913), and George A. Tracy, *History of the Typographical Union* (Indianapolis, 1913) are extremely useful conventional institutional histories. George E. Barnett's *The Printers: A Study in American Trade Unionism* (Cambridge, 1909) is the most thorough and original interpretation of the growth of the national union. Elizabeth Faulkner Baker's *Printers and Technology: A History of the International Printing Pressmen and Assistants' Union* (New York, 1957) is an important interpretation of the split between the typographers and pressmen and the subsequent developments within the pressmen's union. *A Study of the History of the International Typographical Union*, 2 vols. (Colorado Springs, Colo., 1964), by the executive council of the ITU, is a very useful 'official' history of the union that quotes at length from convention proceedings and other contemporary materials. Seymour M. Lipset, Martin A. Trow, and James S. Coleman, *Union Democracy* (Garden City, N.Y. 1952), is a path-breaking sociological study of the internal politics and craft culture of twentieth-century printers, and it should be read for its questions and methods. Helpful for comparative purposes on organized labor are A. E. Musson, *The Typographical Association* [England] (Oxford, 1954), J. Hagan, *Printers and Politics: A History of the Australian Printing Unions, 1850–1950* (Canberra, 1966), and Sally F. Zerker, *The Rise and Fall of the Toronto Typographical Union, 1832–1972: A Case Study of Foreign Domination* (Toronto, 1982). We badly need a study of the German-American printing trade and labor union movement.

Recently, historians have begun to look beyond the union hall and the organized worker to the workplace itself and, conversely, to the wider structures of class and community. Henry P. Rosemont's 'Benjamin Franklin and the Philadelphia Strikers of 1786,' *Labor History* 22(1981):398–429, reassesses the wage action that led to the first strike and subsequent association of Philadelphia journeymen. Wayne Roberts argues that printers retained much of their artisanal culture, control, and attitudes right into the twentieth century in 'The Last Artisans: Toronto Printers, 1896–1914,' in Gregory Kealey and Peter Warrian, eds., *Essays in Canadain Working Class History* (Toronto, 1976); pp. 125–42. Gregory Kealey presents a more modest assessment of the journeymen's autonomy in 'The Honest Workingman and Workers' Control: The Experience of Toronto Skilled Workers, 1860–1892,' *Labour/Le Travailleur* 1(1976):32–68. William S. Pretzer argues that the tramping system for which printers (as well as papermakers, typefounders, and other skilled tradesmen) were so well known was a crucial link between economic structure and craft culture in 'Tramp Printers: Craft Culture, Trade Unions, and Technology,' *Printing History* 12(1984):3–16. Leonard Walloch has traced the divisions within the journeymen's ranks to a dual labor market and to cultural differences found in the Philadelphia working class in general in 'The Limits of Solidarity: Philadelphia's Journeymen Printers in the Mid-Nineteenth Century' (a paper presented to the Organization of American Historians, Los Angeles, April 1984). Pretzer focuses on the concepts of 'artisan republicanism' and the shift from informal to formal work controls in reinterpreting one of the more famous nineteenth-century labor disputes in his essay ' "The British, Duff Green, the Rats, and the Devil": Custom, Capitalism, and Conflict in the Washington Printing Trade, 1834–36,' *Labor History* 27(1986):5–30. Ava Baron has presented a provocative thesis on the relationship between gender, labor process, and class development in 'Women and the Making of the American Working Class: A Study of the Proletarianization of Printers,' *Review of Radical Political Economics* 14(1982):23–42. An informative comparative study is J. Hagan and C. Fisher, 'Piece Work and Some of its Consequences in the Printing and Coal Mining Industries in Australia,' *Labour History* (Canberra) 25 (1973):19–39. Natalie Z. Davis, *Society and Culture in Early Modern France* (Stanford, 1975), and Robert Darnton, *The Business of Enlightenment* (Cambridge, Mass., 1979) offer stimulating and important observations on the workshop practices, customs, and ideology of French journeymen printers. Their numerous essays should also be consulted.

On the technological history of printing, we have several 'biographies' of individual presses, that is, histories dealing with the technical and commercial development of presses common in the eighteenth or nineteenth centuries. Elizabeth Harris's study (with drawings by Clinton Sisson) *The Common Press* (Boston, 1978) is a unique artifactual analysis of an early eighteenth-century hand-press. Milton Hamilton, *Adam Ramage and his Presses* (Portland, Me., 1942) is very useful. Ralph Green was an amateur historian with great technical experience and knowledge. His technical descriptions and drawings are unsurpassed. His *The Iron Hand Press in America* (Rowayton, Conn., 1948), 'Early American Power Printing Presses,' *Studies in Bibliography* 4(1951):143–53, and *A History of the Platen Jobber* (Chicago, 1953) are the best short histories available. Jacob Kainen, *George Clymer and the Columbian Press* (San Francisco, 1950), is a general discussion of the first American iron-made press. Rollo G. Silver has published two articles dealing with the invention and introduction of specific models of power presses: 'An Early Time-Sharing Project: The Introduction of the Napier Press in America,' *Journal of the Printing Historical Society* 4(1968):29–36, and 'Efficiency Improved: The Genesis of the Web Press in America,' *Proceedings of the American Antiquarian Society* 80(1970):325–50. Frank Comparato has included much of the data presented in these case studies in his history of the Hoe Company entitled *Chronicles of Genius and Folly* (Culver City, Calif., 1979). More comprehensive and more reliable is the authoritative *Printing Presses: History and Development from the 15th Century to Modern Times* (Berkeley, 1973), by James Moran.

The series 'The Printing Press' by Stephen McNamara in *The Inland Printer* (1884–87) is full of insight and bias, as is Robert Hoe's *A Short History of the Printing Press* (New York, 1902). Stephen Tucker's reminiscences in Rollo G. Silver, ed., 'History of R. Hoe and Company, 1834–1885,' *Proceedings of the American Antiquarian Society* 82(1972):351–453, is a superb introduction to nineteenth-century machine shop practices and the processes of press development. These studies can be supplemented by Comparato's *Chronicles of Genius and Folly*. As a business history, *Chronicles* may be serviceable, but it does not exhaust the story of labor and technology in the Hoe Company's history. For a comparable history of an important British firm, see Charles Wilson and William Reader, *Men and Machines: A History of D. Napier and Sons Ltd., 1808–1958* (London, 1958).

A standard and thorough chronological survey of American papermaking is David C. Smith, *History of Papermaking in the United States, 1691–1969* (New York, 1970). Smith's knowledge of sources is virtually encyclopedic. Edwin Sutermeister's *The Story of Papermaking* (Boston, 1954) focuses more on the economic and technical aspects of papermaking. An older survey, less scholarly but full of useful information, is Lyman C. Weeks, *A History of Paper Manufacturing in the United States* (New York, 1916). No one can afford to miss Dard Hunter's *Papermaking: The History and Technique of an Ancient Craft* (New York, 1947), *Papermaking by Hand in America* (Chillicothe, Ohio, 1950), or *Papermaking in Pioneer America* (Philadelphia, 1952). A short and extremely useful survey that carries the story into the nineteenth century and emphasizes the mid-Atlantic region is Norman B. Wilkinson, *Papermaking in America* (Greenville, Del., 1975). Joel Munsell's *Chronology of the Origin and Progress of Paper and Papermaking* (Albany, 1876) is little more than a list of events and statistics.

By far, the best technical history of papermaking machinery (or any book trade technology, for that matter) is R. G. Clapperton, *The Paper-Making Machine: Its Invention, Evolution, and Development* (Oxford, 1967). Clapperton's is the quintessential 'internal' history of a technology written by an insider with extensive practical experience in the trade. It illustrates in no uncertain terms the difference between the original invention, the patent, and the commercially successful machine. For our purposes, it is marred only by its emphasis on England and Europe and its lack of documentation. For the American scene, Clapperton must be supplemented by Eugene S. Ferguson, ed., *Early Engineering Reminiscences (1815–40) of George Escol Sellers* (Washington, D.C., 1965), Harold B. Hancock and Norman B. Wilkinson, 'The Gilpins and their Endless Papermaking Machine,' *Pennsylvania Magazine of History and Biography* 81(1957):391–405, and Judith McGaw, 'The Sources and Impact of Mechanization: The Berkshire County, Massachusetts, Paper Industry, 1801–1885, as a Test Case' (Ph.D. diss., New York University, 1977). The latter is the only available full-scale study of the relationship between labor and technology in nineteenth-century papermaking. James N. Gross's 'The Making and Shaping of Unionism in the Pulp and Paper Industry,' *Labor History* 5(1964):183–208, should also be consulted.

The literature of typefounding focuses on two general issues. One is the aesthetics and legibility of typefaces; the other is the business history of typefoundries. Neither tradition pays enough attention to technology or any attention to labor. The single outstanding exception is the magisterial *Typographical Printing Surfaces: The Technology and Mechanism of their Production* (London, 1916), by Lucien A. Legros and John C. Grant. Daniel B. Updike's *Printing Types: Their History, Forms, and Use*, 2 vols. (Cambridge, Mass., 1922), is seminal on issues of comparative aesthetics and the sources of designs. A. F. Johnson's revised edition of T. B. Reed's *A History of the Old English Letter Foundries* (London, 1952) is the best general history of nineteenth-century typefounding. Orginally published in 1887, it is technical/business history at its narrative best.

Two works of great distinction on the American side are Lawrence C. Wroth, *Abel Buel of Connecticut: Silversmith, Typefounder, and Engraver* (Middleton, Conn., 1958), and Rollo G. Silver, *Typefounding in America, 1787–1825* (Charlottesville, Va., 1965). Both are as concerned with the personalities as they are with the structures of early typefounding. In a similar vein are James Eckman's essay on Marder, Luse and Co. in *Printing and Graphic Arts* 7(1959):69–83, 112–24, and on Barnhart Bros. and Spindler, ibid. 9(1961):1–28, 100–15, and Steven L. Watts, 'The Pelouze Family of Typefounders,' ibid. 4(1956):29–35. One should also consult Stephen O. Saxe, 'The Type Founders of New York City, 1840–1900,' *Printing History* 3(1980):4–19, and his 'A Brief History of Golding and Company,' ibid. 6(1981):13–19.

Perhaps the epitome of this concern with the family and business connections of American typefounders is found in Maurice Annenberg, *Type Foundries of America and their Catalogues* (Baltimore and Washington, D.C., 1975). David Bruce, Jr.'s, 1874 manuscript, *The History of Typefounding in the United States*, was published with an introduction by Douglas C. McMurtrie (New York, 1925.) It is an essentially accurate statement of the technological changes of the nineteenth century, with some understandable emphasis on the Bruce family's contributions. Richard L. Hopkins, *Origin of the American Point System for Printers' Type Measurement* (Terra Alta, W. Va., 1976), highlights the problems experienced by founders and printers prior to and during the adoption of the standardized system of type measurement. His analysis of the competition and antagonisms among the founders themselves, and between founders and printers, is a salutary addition to the basically sterile portrait of nineteenth-century business conditions presented elsewhere.

For actual foundry descriptions, see *Godey's Ladies Book* 53 (1856): 299–305, and *The American Bookmaker* 1 (1885):77. Founder's specimen books, listed in detail in Annenberg (above), are useful as guides to styles and ornamentation and also to technical and economic details. Stereotyping, electrotyping, and the production of large ornamental or wooden type are distinct yet related trades not dealt with in this essay. But see Michael Winship's essay (footnote 5), and Rollo G. Silver, 'Trans-Atlantic Crossing: The Beginning of Electrotyping in America,' *Journal of the Printing Historical Society* 10 (1974).

The literature on the history of printing ink is rather slight. Joseph Moxon's *Mechanick Exercises* is a starting point for the early details of ink recipes and techniques. M. D. Fertel, *La Science Practique de l'Imprimerie* (Saint-Omer, 1723), is representative of slightly later European practice, as is (for a later period) W. Hasper, *Handbuch de Buchdruckerkunst* (Karlsruhe, 1835). William Savage, *Practical Hints on Decorative Printing* (London, 1822), is extremely helpful on contemporary practices, as is his later *On Printing Ink, Both Black and Coloured* (London, 1832). American printers' manuals, such as those of Van Winkle, Adams, and McKellar, all contain descriptions of inkmaking. A technical treatise that includes important historical information, including a review of English patents, is C. Ainsworth Mitchell and T. C. Hepworth, *Inks: Their Composition and Manufacture* (London, 1904).

A modern history of ink is found in Colin Bloy, *A History of Printing Ink, Balls, and Rollers, 1440–1850* (London, 1967). This slim volume surveys the major developments, individuals, and companies associated with ink and inking. Frank B. Wiborg, *Printing Ink: A History with a Treatise on Modern Methods of Manufacture and Use* (New York, 1926), skips too quickly to the twentieth century to be of much help. A good, if all too brief description of American ink manufacturing at the Jersey City factory of George Mather's Sons is found in 'Concerning Printing Inks,' *The American Bookmaker* 1 (1885):25–28.

Hellmut Lehmann-Haupt, ed., *Bookbinding in America*, (1941; rev. ed., New York, 1967), contains seminal essays by Hannah D.

French and Joseph W. Rogers, as does the recently published edition of a number of Hannah French's essays, *Bookbinding in Early America: Seven Essays on Masters and Methods* (Worcester, Mass., 1986). These works, along with Douglas Leighton, *Modern Bookbinding: A Survey and a Prospect* (London, 1935), form the base from which all discussions of the nineteenth-century trade begin. Frank Comparato's *Books for the Millions* (Harrisburg, Penn., 1971) is a wide-ranging account of the mechanization of bookbinding that contains much useful historical information and a good bibliography. The best general introduction to the processes and history of binding is Bernard Middleton, *A History of English Craft Bookbinding Technique* (London, 1963). Sue Allen presents a convincing if brief analysis of the technical and stylistic traditions in American machine-stamped binding in 'Machine-Stamped Bookbindings, 1834–1860,' *Antiques* 115(1979):564–72. For an analysis using the extant artifacts as primary evidence, see her 'Floral-Patterned Endpapers in Nineteenth-Century American Books,' *Winterthur Portfolio* 12(1977):182–224.

Some technical manuals are worth reading, both for their descriptions and analyses of technical processes and machines and for their historical trade data. These include James B. Nicholson, *A Manual of the Art of Bookbinding* (Philadelphia, 1856), and Edward Walker, *The Art of Book-Binding, Its Rise and Progress; Including a Description of the New York Book Bindery* (New York, 1850). One will also find much useful information in W. Salt Brassington, *A History of the Art of Bookbinding with Some Account of the Books of the Ancients* (New York, 1893), and Edith Diehl, *Bookbinding: Its Background and Technique*, 2 vols. (New York, 1946).

The description of the New York bindery presented in Walker (above) should be compared to the description of the Lippincott bindery in *Godey's Ladies Book* 45(1852):402–12. And both of these should be contrasted with the impressions of a small Hartford, Connecticut, bindery of the 1830s that is presented by apprentices and young journeymen in Newton C. Brainard, ed., *The Andrus Bindery: A History of the Shop, 1831–38* (Hartford, 1940). This is especially important for evidence of informal work controls, resistance to the imposition of a work discipline, conflict between apprentices, journeymen, foremen, and employers, and the origins of 'stents.' There is no history of labor in the American bookbinding trade, but one should look at Mary Van Kleeck, *Women in the*

Bookbinding Trade (New York, 1913), and Ellic Howe, *The London Bookbinders, 1780–1804* (London, 1950).

Helpful historiographical discussions that include suggestions for thematic approaches to technological history are found in the following: Brooke Hindle, *Technology in Early America* (Chapel Hill, 1966); Eugene S. Ferguson, 'Toward a Discipline of the History of Technology,' *Technology and Culture* 15(1974):13–30, and his 'The American-ness of American Technology,' *Technology and Culture* 20(1979):3–24; Thomas P. Hughes, 'Emerging Themes in the History of Technology,' *Technology and Culture* 20 (1979): 697–711; Carroll W. Pursell, Jr., 'History of Technology,' in Paul T. Durbin, ed., *A Guide to the Culture of Science, Technology, and Medicine* (New York, 1980), pp. 70–120; David Hounshell, 'On the Discipline of the History of American Technology,' *Journal of American History* 67(1981):854–65; David Hounshell, ed., *The History of American Technology: Exhilaration or Discontent?* (Wilmington, Del., 1984). More narrowly focused, but still very helpful, is Paul Uselding, 'Studies of Technology in Economic History,' in Robert E. Gallman, ed., *Research in Economic History, Supplement 1: Recent Developments in the Study of Business and Economic History: Essays in Memory of Herman E. Kross* (Greenwich, Conn., 1977), pp. 159–219.

The current state and future directions of American labor historiography are assayed in David Brody, 'The Old Labor History and the New: In Search of an American Working Class,' *Labor History* 20(1979):111–26; David Montgomery, 'To Study the People: The American Working Class,' *Labor History* 21(1980): 485–512; and Sean Wilentz, 'Artisan Origins of the American Working Class,' *International Labor and Working Class History* 18 (1981):1–22.

Publishing in America: Needs and Opportunities for Research

MICHAEL WINSHIP

> The publisher's calling is not, in truth, a mere trade. He is the dispenser of knowledge to the community, and even his material interests are best served by whatever excites and appeals unto that desire for knowledge which it is his lofty mission to satisfy.[1]

> One day when we were playing golf at St. Andrews, Mr. Carnegie turned to me and asked in his modest Scotch way: 'How much money did you make in your book business last month?'
>
> I told him I could not tell—that no publisher made up his books more often than once a year, and it was impossible to figure profits month by month.
>
> He said: 'Do you know what I would do if I were in a business in which I couldn't tell the amount of monthly profit?'
>
> 'No,' I replied; 'what would you do?'
>
> 'I would get out of it,' he said.[2]

I

IN THIS PAPER I plan to investigate the history and impact of publishing in the United States through 1876 and to suggest

I would like to thank my colleagues Hugh Amory and Roger E. Stoddard for their help and encouragement in preparing this essay. My students at Columbia University's Rare Book School in the summer of 1984 provided a test for the usefulness of many of the ideas contained in the essay, including the diagrammatic model of the book trade, and I thank them for their input. Richard S. Tedlow, assistant professor at the Harvard Business School and editor of the *Business History Review*, was kind enough to take time to discuss with me some of the economic aspects of publishing; it was he who pointed me to the anecdote about Carnegie and Doubleday quoted at the head of this essay.

[1] Extract from an editorial statement in *American Publishers' Circular and Literary Gazette* 1(1863):2.

[2] Frank N. Doubleday, *The Memoirs of a Publisher* (New York, 1972), pp. 58–59.

some of the important needs and opportunities for research into publishing that should contribute to our understanding of the role of the book in American culture and society. I believe that the publisher was the central, indeed indispensable, figure in the book trade and I intend here to illuminate the role of the publisher and to show how his relationships with other segments of the book trade came into being and developed.

In the past, general histories of the American book trade have tended to take the role of publishing for granted without investigating its precise nature. Indeed, Isaiah Thomas in his pioneer work *The History of Printing in America* (Worcester, 1810; 2d ed., Worcester, 1874; 3d ed., New York, 1970) preferred to concentrate on manufacturing, particularly printing, and to ignore its necessary corollary, publishing. Hellmut Lehmann-Haupt and his collaborators in *The Book in America: A History of the Making and Selling of Books in the United States* (New York, 1939; 2d ed., New York, 1951) give a still-unmatched overview of the American book trade, but again the role and nature of publishing is implied rather than made explicit. Two more recent works—Charles Madison's *Book Publishing in America* (New York, 1966) and John Tebbel's massive, four-volume *A History of Book Publishing in the United States* (New York, 1972–81)—have, as their titles suggest, concentrated their attention on publishing, but the approach of both authors has been generally that of a chronicler rather than a historian. I am aware of no work that attempts to analyze the role of publishing in the early American book trade or to provide a historical analysis or interpretation of its importance in American culture and society.[3]

Fortunately, it is unnecessary to burden this essay with a long bibliographical list or description of publications and pre-

[3] An exception might be Sheila McVey, 'Nineteenth-Century America: Publishing in a Developing Country,' *Annals of the American Academy of Political and Social Studies* 421 (Sept. 1975):67–80. However, this attempt to relate early American publishing to the situation in modern developing countries remains too general to be very helpful.

vious research relevant to the study of American publishing, since that function is admirably served by G. Thomas Tanselle's indispensable *Guide to the Study of United States Imprints* (Cambridge, Mass., 1971). I do intend, however, to describe briefly the major categories of material available to us. Many specific works will be referred to throughout this essay or will be found listed in Tanselle's *Guide*.

The largest group of publications relating to American publishing are those that have been prepared under the auspices of the different publishing firms and are most often published by these firms. These include firm histories, anniversary volumes and anthologies, autobiographies and memorial biographies of leading publishers and editors, and a great variety of other promotional material. In spite of the self-congratulatory and propagandistic nature of many of these publications, as a group they remain the major source of information about many publishing houses. Samuel G. Goodrich's *Recollections of a Lifetime* (New York, 1856) and Ellen B. Ballou's *The Building of the House: Houghton Mifflin's Formative Years* (Boston, 1970) are among the best, which are often full of important information, insights, and sound scholarship.

Scholarly studies of publishers and publishing are comparatively rare. There are studies of particular periods: Lawrence C. Wroth's *The Colonial Printer* (New York, 1931; rev. ed., New York, 1938) and Donald Sheehan's *This Was Publishing: A Chronicle of the Book Trade in the Gilded Age* (Bloomington, 1961). There are also studies of particular places: Walter Sutton's *The Western Book Trade: Cincinnati as a Nineteenth-Century Publishing and Book-Trade Center* (Columbus, 1961) and Milton W. Hamilton's *The Country Printer, New York State, 1785–1830* (New York, 1936); and there are studies of particular publishers: Clifford K. Shipton's *Isaiah Thomas: Printer, Patriot and Philanthropist, 1749–1831* (Rochester, 1948) and David Kaser's *Messrs. Carey & Lea of Philadelphia: A Study in the History of the Booktrade* (Philadelphia, 1957).

All of these investigate narrow areas of the book trade and shed much light on publishing practices. However, no matter how thorough and authoritative these studies may be, they are generally lacking in depth of historical perspective and analysis and tend to focus on publishing in much the same fashion as the general studies mentioned above.

In one area, the publication of a particular genre, these scholarly studies can be particularly sophisticated and useful. In a few cases these genre studies are little more than a memorial history of a dominant firm in that field, for example, William Arms Fisher's *One Hundred and Fifty Years of Music Publishing in the United States: An Historical Sketch with Special Reference to the Pioneer Publisher, Oliver Ditson Company, Inc., 1783–1933* (Boston, 1933). But in other cases—Richard Crawford and D. W. Krummel's 'Early American Music Printing and Publishing,' in *Printing & Society in Early America*, ed. William L. Joyce et al. (Worcester, 1983), pp. 186–227 and Richard J. Wolfe's *Early American Music Engraving and Printing: A History of Music Publishing in America from 1787 to 1825* (Urbana, 1980)—they provide an excellent base for future studies of publishing. This approach to publishing has been most extensively developed in the field of periodical publishing, best represented by Frank Luther Mott's marvelous five-volume *A History of American Magazines* (Cambridge, Mass., 1930–68), as well as in numerous works on newspapers.

Following the lead of French scholars of the *Annales* school, and learning from many publications of European scholars over the past twenty-five years, American scholars of the book are beginning to approach their field with new questions and a new set of models and analytical tools. It is important to keep in mind, however, that the bulk of European work has concentrated on periods before the nineteenth century. But the nineteenth century was the period when American publishing first became established as an independent institution, and it is a century that presents special problems because of the tremendous expansion of the book trade brought on by mechanization, expanding markets, and increased literacy. Two European studies—Ilsedore Rarisch's *Industrialisierung und Literatur: Buchproduktion, Verlagswesen und Buchhandel in Deutschland im 19. Jahrhundert* (Berlin, 1976) and Frédéric Barbier's 'The Publishing Industry and Printed Output in Nineteenth-Century France,' in *Books and Society in History*, ed. Kenneth E. Carpenter (New York, 1983), pp. 199–230—are cited here because they present general statistical surveys of nineteenth-century publishing in Germany and France and suggest the direction that future American studies in the field might take.

II

For the purposes of this essay I have found it useful to define publishing in functional rather than occupational or business terms.[4] Specifically, I intend to separate out a particular set of activities from all those involved in the manufacture and distribution of books and other printed matter and to refer to these activities as publishing. It is important to remember, however, that any particular individual or firm that used the term publisher may not have been responsible in every instance for all of these activities, and almost certainly engaged in other activities that I have chosen to exclude from my consideration of publishing.

The position of publishing within the book trade is indicated in the attached diagram, which is meant to provide a model of

[4] A useful insight into the development of the concept of publishing can be gained by examining the usage of the term *publishing* and related words as documented in the *Oxford English Dictionary* and the *Dictionary of American English*. In England in the seventeenth and eighteenth centuries, the *publisher* was that individual whose name appeared in the imprint of pamphlets (usually of a nature to make them suspect to authorities) that he undertook to distribute, although they had been printed at the expense of others; see Michael Treadwell, 'London Trade Publishers: 1675–1750,' *Library*, 6th ser. 4(1982):99–134. The modern meaning of the term seems to have become current only at the beginning of the nineteenth century. An interesting contrast is provided by the German term *verlegen*, which, as early as the sixteenth century, carried the sense of the entrepreneurial aspects of publishing; see Rarisch, *Industrialisierung und Literatur*, p. 35.

the book trade as a whole.[5] As with publishing, each square in the diagram represents a function or set of activities, though again in any particular case a single individual or firm might be responsible for many of these, or many different individuals or firms might be involved in a single function. *Creation* is taken to represent the activities of authors, editors, annotators, illustrators, and designers, among others. *Manufacturing* includes such activities as composition, platemaking, printing, and binding. *Supply* covers both suppliers—for example, the dealers and importers of paper, type, book cloth, binder's board, etc.—and the producers of the materials required in manufacturing—such as typefounders, paper mills, die cutters, machine and press manufacturers. On the vertical axis, *financing* is that function, perhaps involving bankers or silent partners, that provides the capital for publishing firms and ventures. *Distribution* includes the activities of a variety of businesses and institutions, such as book shops, jobbers, auction houses, and libraries. Finally, the *audience* represents the ultimate consumers in the book trade: the individual readers, who, as we

MODEL OF THE BOOK TRADE

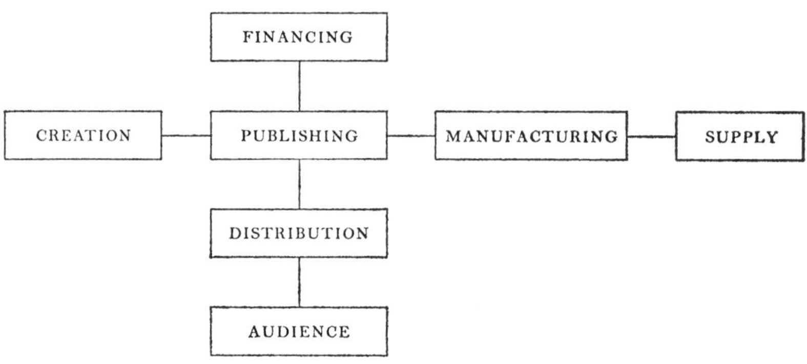

[5] This model was developed from one proposed by Robert Darnton in 'What Is the History of Books?' in *Books and Society in History*, p. 6. A similar scheme is used by John P. Feather in 'The Commerce of Letters: The Study of the Eighteenth-Century Book Trade,' *Eighteenth-Century Studies* 17(1984):407. Darnton's model has the advantage of showing the circular nature of the book trade and of emphasizing the influence of earlier publications on authors and the book trade.

are now learning, read their books in a variety of ways, or other consumers, who may have acquired or purchased their books for any number of reasons and uses that did not involve reading.

The position of *publishing* in this diagram makes clear what the functions of publishing are. Publishing is that set of activities that connect the production or manufacturing activities of the book trade, here laid out on the horizontal axis, with the commercial or distribution activities, laid out vertically. In a sense, the publisher is the entrepreneur of the book trade, making the decisions that bring together all the other activities and arranging for the coordination and credit—always important in a business where income realized from the sale of a product often comes months or years after the expense of production—and taking the risks necessary to make the whole book trade function.

This diagram is intended to be a model of the book trade that helps to separate the different functions or activities, but it is clearly too schematic to account for the actual relationships, even in the simplest cases. During the eighteenth century, individual booksellers might have been responsible for the costs of at least part of an edition of a particular book. They might also have bound it for the customer in their own shops. Thus, they were involved in finance, publishing, manufacturing, and distribution. Although the nineteenth century saw more specialization in the book trade, this pattern of taking responsibility for multiple functions remained common. A hypothetical example might be a town history published by a local historical society, for which the historical society took responsibility for creation, finance, publishing, and distribution but would also have been the main audience, thus leaving only manufacture and supply outside its direct control in the publishing venture.

At this point, a brief digression to discuss publishing as an occupation or business is useful. Clearly, as I have defined it here, publishing has always been an important, indeed central, part of the book trade and cannot be said to have a separate origin or development. However, as the book trade expanded and became more complex, the different functions within it became more defined, and it became possible for an individual or a firm to specialize in a particular set of activities. Thus, it became possible in particular cases for a publisher to be named who was distinct from the manufacturer, distributor, or creator; and eventually it was possible for a firm to specialize in this activity. In North America, these developments seem to have depended on the expansion of the book trade, signaled by the expansion of productive capabilities and of book-consuming audiences. Although some major eighteenth-century figures—such as Benjamin Franklin, Isaiah Thomas, and Mathew Carey—were certainly beginning to specialize and to see themselves primarily as publishers, it was not until the first decades of the nineteenth century that it became feasible for publishing to exist as a separate specialized activity within the book trade. The further development of publishing into even more distinct functions, such as editing or promotion, carried out by a professional staff or managers responsible to the owners or stockholders, does not seem to have become possible or common until the end of the century. It is important to note that, although it became possible at the beginning of the nineteenth century to concentrate on publishing as a specialized and distinct activity, this was not necessarily the normal or preferred pattern. Indeed, many successful firms—Harper and Brothers of New York, and Houghton Mifflin and Company of Boston are two prominent examples—continued to maintain a variety of manufacturing and distributing functions. The question of the possibility and advantages of specialization as against diversification is a complicated one, and much further work will be necessary before any clear patterns or criteria for these developments can be suggested or established.

For the remainder of this essay, I intend to restrict my discussion to the narrower functional and entrepreneurial aspects of publishing. I will also focus on the nineteenth century, since this is the period when American publishing first became an independent and fully developed activity. Implicitly, the origin of publishing in America in the eighteenth century is an important part of our work, but this study belongs in large part to European publishing history of the period. There is much to be learned from a comparative study of other colonial publishing (especially that of Ireland) during that century. Finally, I will concentrate on the common ground between different types of publishing, in an attempt to expose and clarify a general concept of publishing. Most of my examples will come from the publishing of books, especially literary ones, since this is the area I am most familiar with. An investigation into the distinctive features of specialized branches of publishing—such as periodical, medical, children's, Catholic, or music publishing—will be necessary and informative, but much more so when seen in contrast to a general model that illustrates normal patterns of publishing.

III

To begin my discussion, I will explore the relationships of publishing to each of the other functions of the book trade depicted in my diagram, in the hope of sharpening this concept of publishing as the central entrepreneurial activity of the book trade. In investigating these relationships, I will concentrate on how they affected and formed the several activities of publishing. I will attempt to summarize the important work of earlier scholars in the field and the lessons we can learn from that work, as well as to suggest the many further areas of research that should add to our knowledge in important ways.

The relationships between publishing and creation are particularly complex. This is an area that has attracted many excellent scholars, particularly from the field of literary studies. In this regard, the unequaled work of William Charvat—*Lit-*

erary Publishing in America, 1790–1850 (Philadelphia, 1959) and *The Profession of Authorship in America, 1800–1878*, ed. Matthew J. Bruccoli (Columbus, 1968)—should be mentioned, although the work of other scholars—for example, Carl J. Weber's *Hardy in America: A Study of Thomas Hardy and His American Readers* (Waterville, 1946) and C. Harvey Gardiner's *Prescott and His Publishers* (Carbondale, 1959)—have made thorough studies of the relationships of a single author to his publishers. These works have already provided a good analysis of the types of agreements and contracts that were typical between authors and their publishers, as well as of the delicate negotiations involved in soliciting and editing manuscripts, and of the variety and amounts of royalties and other payments that were made to authors. Much further information is readily available in the many published memoirs and biographies of authors, publishers, editors, and other literary figures, as well as in their published and unpublished journals, diaries, correspondence, and other papers. Hamlin Hill's edition of *Mark Twain's Letters to His Publishers* (Berkeley, 1967) is an example in which this kind of raw material has been brought together in a single published volume. In my work, I have frequently been struck by the amount of untapped information there is to be found in the papers of writers of the second rank, who were certainly more numerous than the major literary figures and whose experiences were probably more typical and thus potentially more informative. Literary scholars have understandably concentrated on writers whose literary standing has survived intact to the present and who are still studied and read in graduate departments of American literature, but I believe that it is part of our work to look at minor authors as well.

Further work remains to be done in this area, particularly in investigating the boundaries between creation and publishing. Authors were commonly required to act also as publishers by assuming at least part of the risks of publication and also by providing credit and perhaps some input into design and editorial decisions. As the book trade expanded during the nineteenth century, there seems to have been a general trend toward separating the functions of creation from those of publishing. In many cases, authors managed to gain a certain autonomy and to force their publishers to assume the risks and to make credit arrangements on their own. At the same time, a new role evolved for literary editors, publishers' readers, professional book reviewers, and vanity publishers (and, at the end of the century, for literary agents),[6] who acted as mediators between authors and publishers. These remain shadowy figures and it would be fascinating to know more about their relationships with publishers, what their exact responsibilities, obligations, input, and rewards were, and how these relationships developed and changed over time. For example, I wonder which of their functions came to be controlled by authors and which by publishers.

Another area where our ignorance remains large is that of the design of books. We know very little about how design decisions, whether conscious or unconscious, were made and who exactly was responsible for them. Undoubtedly, authors were very concerned about how their books looked; this is made clear by the care that William Hickling Prescott took with the appearance of his histories, which appeared in a magnificent quarto format, and the disappointment of Richard Henry Dana, Jr., when his *Two Years before the Mast* (New York, 1840) appeared in the smaller, less elegant format of *Harper's Family Library*.[7] Nonetheless, I suspect that design

6 See James Hepburn, *The Author's Empty Purse and the Rise of the Literary Agent* (London, 1968) and Linda Marie Fritschner, 'Publishers' Readers, Publishers, and Their Authors,' *Publishing History* 7(1980):45–100. Although these works are primarily concerned with the British book trade, the former briefly discusses the American book trade.

7 See Gardiner, *Prescott and His Publishers* and Eugene Exman, 'Before the Mast with Dana,' in *The Brothers Harper: A Unique Publishing Partnership and Its Impact upon the Cultural Life of America from 1817 to 1853* (New York, 1965), pp. 124–40. Both studies discuss these authors' concern with the design of their books. Interest-

decisions remained in large part the responsibility of the publisher. I wonder, though, if it is not possible to trace the origins of book design as a distinct activity of publishing.

A related field of inquiry is that of book illustration. Here we have at least some guides, notably Sinclair Hamilton's *Early American Book Illustrators and Wood Engravers* (Princeton, 1958; suppl. 1969), which provides us with the names of illustrators and a list of their works. But, again, much remains to be discovered. How were illustrators paid? What were their wages? Clearly, illustrators developed special relationships with particular publishers, but what exactly were these relationships? What was the input of the publisher in the creation and execution of book illustration? To what extent were the illustrations a more important part of a book than the text itself? A particularly interesting study would be to examine the development and importance of the stable of notable illustrators at Harper and Brothers after the Civil War who worked under the direction of Charles Parsons. Their work, which was certainly important to the success of Harper's periodicals, also appeared in many other publications.[8] To what extent is the importance of Harper as a publisher responsible for the present fame of these illustrators?

The ties between publishing and manufacturing were particularly strong; in fact, many publishers started their careers as printers and maintained their own printing establishments, often with binderies attached, long after their efforts were concentrated on publishing. Occasionally, members of other branches in book manufacturing also became involved in publishing, as in the case of the Philadelphia binder Henry S.

---

ingly, in the contract between John Lothrop Motley and Harper and Brothers for the publication of *The Rise of the Dutch Republic* (New York, 1856) and *History of the United Netherlands* (New York, 1861–68), it is stated that they should appear 'in good style, similar to the Editions of Prescott's works'; see *The Archives of Harper and Brothers, 1817–1914*, microfilm edition (Cambridge, Eng., 1980), A1: 251, 378–79.

[8] Eugene Exman, 'Charles Parsons and His School of Artists,' *The House of Harper: One Hundred Fifty Years of Publishing* (New York, 1967), pp. 102–20.

Altemus and the New York stereotyper J. S. Redfield. On the other hand, some successful publishers—Ticknor and Fields of Boston, for example—never became directly responsible for book manufacturing, apparently choosing different printers and binders as the occasion arose. Still other publishers, such as the Century Company of New York, seem to have established a special relationship with a particular printer or binder, and we find that the majority of that publisher's publications were manufactured at this establishment. The publishers of daily newspapers were a special case; their dependence on speed meant that they were forced to control their own manufacturing facilities, which were dedicated to their needs. Indeed, these publishers provided the major incentive for the development of the larger and speedier printing machines that we associate with the nineteenth century.[9]

An investigation of the relationship between manufacturing and publishing will shed much light on our understanding of the place of the publisher in the book trade. Although the expansion of the book trade made it possible for a firm to concentrate on publishing, many apparently chose to remain or to become intimately involved in book manufacturing. What exactly were the advantages and incentives for this choice? Whatever these may have been, they were clearly not simple, since many publishers who maintained their own facilities for manufacturing would still have some of their publications produced elsewhere or would take on work for other publishers. In investigating these relationships, the different nature of the two activities must be kept in mind. Whereas publishing remained a high-risk activity, where freedom to expand or contract allowed a firm to take full advantage of a particular set of circumstances, manufacturers were restricted by the necessity of making decisions based on having their capital tied up in expensive plants and machinery; to a lesser extent, manufacturers

9 See Frank E. Comparato, *Chronicles of Genius and Folly: R. Hoe & Company and the Printing Press as a Service to Democracy* (Culver City, 1979).

were also restricted by the responsibility of maintaining a sufficient staff of skilled and semi-skilled employees. Another element of the relationship between manufacturing and publishing that needs investigation is the question of credit and payment. Although the manufacturers were dependent on publishers for work, the latter often could not have received their return from the manufactured product, the book, until long after the work had been completed. How is this situation reflected in the financial arrangements between the two enterprises?

The distinction between manufacturing and supply is a complicated one, since many suppliers—papermakers, typefounders, ink manufacturers, printing and binding machine suppliers—were manufacturers themselves. For the purposes of this essay, it is important only to investigate those situations in which the publishers were directly responsible for the arrangements between suppliers and manufacturers. Through the end of the nineteenth century, some of the materials required for book production continued to be imported, and publishers may have been in a better position to deal with foreign suppliers and manufacturers than were individual printing firms or binderies. On the other hand, publishers may have insisted on materials of American origin for patriotic reasons, especially during the first decades of the new nation. Surviving publishers' records strongly suggest that it was common for the publisher to be responsible for deciding on and ordering the paper stock for his publications.[10] Again, it would be interesting to know more about how these decisions were made, which papermakers and suppliers dealt with which publishers, and what the financial arrangements for credit and payment were. It also seems probable that the publishers were responsible for some of the arrangements involved in supplying cuts and dies

[10] Warren S. Tryon and William Charvat, eds., *The Cost Books of Ticknor and Fields and their Predecessors, 1832–1858* (New York, 1949) and David Kaser, ed., *The Cost Book of Carey & Lea, 1825–1838* (Philadelphia, 1963).

that were intended to decorate and illustrate particular publications.

Much less certain is the relationship between the suppliers of binding cloth and publishers. Once publishers were in a position to offer a particular publication in a uniform publisher's binding, which used a specific color and grain of book cloth, were they also responsible for arranging for the shipment of that cloth to their binders? This situation may well have held for Ticknor and Fields, who in the 1840s and 1850s established a characteristic house binding in a deep brown ribbed (T grain) cloth that seems to be distinctive to their publications. Did they make special arrangements with the British book cloth manufacturers for its supply to the several Boston binderies that they employed?

The financing of publishing activities has barely been touched upon by previous scholars of American publishing. The very nature of publishing as a business, with the returns from a particular publishing venture almost impossible to predict—usually they must have been low, but in some cases they were spectacularly high, and not available until long after the date of publication—underscores the importance of maintaining an adequate supply of the capital and credit that publishers needed to stay in business and to keep the book trade working. A variety of approaches to this problem seem to have been common: in some cases, the author was required to provide capital or credit in the form of delayed royalty payments to cover the costs of their publications; in certain types of subscription publishing, the subscribers, the audience, either provided capital when they paid for their copies in advance or else offered a type of credit by promising to pay for their copies on delivery; in still other cases, some sort of sponsorship was sought by the publisher from a governmental body or other institution in order to help cover the costs of publication. Also, arrangements between publishers and their printers and binders, which specified that the notes paying for work performed would not come due for an extended period of time, must have helped in financing the activities of publishers. Nonetheless, much ordinary publishing must have relied on the availability of risk capital. Who provided this capital? Under what conditions was it provided? What were the risks and the returns, normal or otherwise, from such investments?

A start in answering these questions will come from an investigation of the frequent changes in the names of publishers in the imprints of their publications. Surely a change in the style of an imprint reflects a new financial relationship or arrangement within the firm. Further evidence must be sought in the surviving archives of particular publishing houses, in the records of a variety of financial institutions such as banks and credit reporters, and in the probate court files relating to bankruptcies in the trade and to the estates of publishers. In this regard, the records of the credit-reporting firm of R. G. Dun and its predecessors, roughly covering the years 1841 to 1890, now housed at the Harvard Business School's Baker Library, seem particularly promising.[11] In using these records, however, we must remember that they represent a single source and that the information contained in them must be verified elsewhere when possible. We must also recall that any conclusions based on a credit report will reflect the reliability of the original informants and the purposes for which the record was compiled.

The relationships between publishing and distribution, like those with manufacturers, are particularly close and complicated. Again, many publishers began in business with a book-

[11] These are briefly described in Florence Bartoshesky, 'Dun Credit Ledgers at Baker Library,' *The Book* 3(1984):5–6. See also Roy A. Foulke, *The Sinews of American Commerce* (New York, 1941) and James Madison, 'The Evolution of Commercial Credit-Reporting in Nineteenth-Century America,' *Business History Review* 48(1974): 167–68, 174–76, 184; also see James D. Norris, *R. G. Dun & Co., 1841–1900: The Development of Credit-Reporting in the Nineteenth Century* (Westport, Conn., 1978). In surveying these records, I have found that the coverage of publishing is incomplete, perhaps because publishers did not rely on normal commercial channels for credit, or because they tended to operate small businesses in large business centers and were overshadowed by larger commercial concerns.

shop and maintained their own retail outlet, which handled both their own and other publishers' publications, long after this was a minor sideline to their publishing activities. At the same time, the expansion of the book trade in the nineteenth century, together with the development of the railroads and other improved means of communication that opened up access to the expanding markets in the South and the West, created a need for wholesalers and jobbers to take charge of the mass distribution of printed materials. The importance of these distributors is suggested by the increasing number of popular bestsellers, though I confess that I am at a loss to explain exactly by what means a particular book—for example, 300,000 copies of Harriet Beecher Stowe's *Uncle Tom's Cabin* (Boston, 1852) in a single year,—passed in such large quantities from publisher to reader.[12] This is an extreme but not an isolated example, and clearly the means of distributing printed material were well established by 1852 and were capable of handling such large numbers of books. Fortunately, another essay will deal with this problem, and I look to that discussion for some of the approaches that will serve to explain this phenomenon. In this essay, I intend only to discuss a few of the aspects of publishing's relationships with distribution and the final audience that seem to me to present important insights into the nature and development of publishing in America.

A need for cash to meet obligations and notes coming due seems to have been a regular feature of publishing and called for some means of liquidating stock to raise this cash. The trade sale auction served this purpose and became a regular and important, though often maligned, institution in the nineteenth-century book trade.[13] Much research remains to be done before

[12] See Frank Luther Mott, *Golden Multitudes: The Story of Best Sellers in the United States* (New York, 1947) and James D. Hart, *The Popular Book: A History of America's Literary Taste* (New York, 1950).

[13] Trade sales are described in Edward Hazen, *The Panorama of Professions and Trades; or Every Man's Book* (Philadelphia, 1836), pp. 196–97; Sutton, 'The Cincinnati Trade Sales, 1838–77,' *The Western Book Trade*, pp. 262–76; and Lehmann-Haupt et al., *The Book in America*, 2d ed. (1951), pp. 258–63.

we understand exactly how trade sales worked, who participated in them, and their role in disposing of remainders and other stock, including printing plates and stationery, no longer of use to the consignor, as well as their role in providing a normal means of distribution for new publications and a publisher's backlist. A first step in studying this aspect of publishing will be to search out surviving copies of trade sale catalogues, especially any that are annotated by purchasers with the prices that they paid, as well as contemporary accounts of the sales in letters, trade journals, and newspapers. A full study of the trade sale should provide invaluable insights into the business of publishing and distribution.

The relationships between publishers and bookstores and other distributors also need to be investigated and analyzed. Discount schedules, responsibility for the costs of shipping, policies on credits and returns, and agreements for exclusive rights to distribute a publication in an area have not yet been the subject of any systematic scholarly study. Such a study could be based on surviving publishers' and book dealers' records and correspondence, as well as on evidence that can be found in the advertisements, catalogues, and publications that publishers aimed at distributors. A particular need is for a list of publishers' catalogues, many of which have been stamped or printed with the name of an individual distributor or wholesaler, and for a list of the variety of leaflets, posters, newsletters, and other printed ephemera produced by publishers to advertise their publications.

Another area where investigations into distribution patterns should teach us about publishing are those cases where the publisher sold his product directly to the individual consumer. One wonders what role the post office played in allowing individuals with no access to bookstores to purchase books from the publisher through the mails. This distribution method may have been encouraged by the frequent practice of inserting publishers' advertisements in publications, as well as by the distribution of a variety of periodicals through the mails, which served to advertise, review favorably, and publish excerpts from a publisher's current list of publications. Such periodicals not only served literary publishers—notable examples are *Harper's New Monthly Magazine*, founded by Harper and Brothers in 1850 and *The Atlantic Monthly*, which was founded by Phillips, Sampson & Company in 1857, but which after 1860 became the organ of Ticknor and Fields—but were probably more important for more specialized publishers. Examples of these periodicals are the *American Phrenological Journal* for Fowler and Wells, the *Medico-Chirurgical Review* for J. B. Lippincott's medical list, and *The American Agriculturist* for Orange Judd & Company. The answer to the question of the role of direct distribution may be found in surviving publishers' archives, but further evidence will come to light through an investigation of the style and wording of the advertisements that publishers placed in the newspapers that reached a local audience on a regular basis. It may also be useful to investigate postage schedules and the congressional debates, reports, or hearings involved in revising these rates. Certain publishing schemes—such as the use of the periodicals just mentioned that tied in with a publisher's current list, and the publication of cheap series, which maintained the fiction of regular publication in order to take advantage of cheaper postage rates for serials[14]—seem to have been designed to allow for the direct distribution of publications to the consumer, and one wonders what role these schemes had in a publisher's overall strategies. The rise of a special form of subscription publishing after the Civil War, which was based on door-to-door canvassing and sales, may also have been an attempt at direct distribution.

[14] James J. Barnes, *Authors, Publishers, and Politicians: The Quest for an Anglo American Copyright Agreement, 1815–1854* (London, 1974), pp. 17–28, describes such ventures in the 1830s and 1840s. A superb example of the fictional aspect of regular publication of dated series is provided by *Nye and Riley's Wit and Humor* (New York, 1896), which, although issued under the date January 15, 1896, contains an obituary of Edgar Wilson Nye, who died on February 22, 1896.

However, I suspect that the canvassers probably offered the publications of several publishers at the same time and were in fact agents for specialized distributors, who in turn dealt with the individual publishers.[15]

The development of a characteristic and readily recognized house style, which was aimed at encouraging a consumer to purchase a particular book by a particular publisher, is another instance where aspects of distribution have an important influence on publishing decisions. A house style was not only dependent upon specialization in particular genres or subject fields, with a list of consistent quality, but it also depended on packaging the publications in a distinctive fashion. This house style could be defined by a particular typographic style, size, and format, but in the nineteenth century it was also often marked by a uniform style of edition binding. For example, the Boston publishers Ticknor and Fields were particularly successful at establishing a house style: in the 1840s and 1850s their list contained an unmatched collection of the best literary writing of contemporary American and British authors, all dressed in a familiar binding of brown ribbed (T grain) cloth, which seems to have been adapted from the London publisher Edward Moxon, and, as far as I know, was not copied by other American publishers. A later Ticknor and Fields house style, the smaller '*blue and gold*' editions of belle lettres first published in the late 1850s was very successful, although it was widely copied.

Another manifestation of this approach to publishing that was of particular importance in America was series publishing. Clearly, publishers hoped that by offering their books in a uniform style and binding as part of a series, often numbered, that the success and reputation of popular titles would boost the

[15] See Frank E. Compton, 'Subscription Books,' *Bulletin of the New York Public Library* 43(1939):879–94; Sutton, 'Henry Howe: Twenty Thousand Agents Wanted!' *The Western Book Trade*, pp. 215–35; and Michael Hackenberg, 'Hawking Subscription Books in 1870: A Salesman's Prospectus from Western Pennsylvania,' *Papers of the Bibliographical Society of America* 78(1984):137–53.

sales of the entire series. A particularly interesting and successful form of series publishing was used by Harper and Brothers in the 1830s and 1840s; their extensive *Family Library* and *School District Library* series was supplemented by a number of smaller, more specialized series. In fact, many Harper titles were recycled through a number of series.[16] Similar to series publishing was the practice of offering a collective edition of an author's writings in a uniform format and binding. Again, the goal was to sell the less popular titles along with the more popular ones. All of these types of publishing need to be investigated and analyzed, including the development of a publisher's series or house style, the ways in which publishers attempted to control and affect the decisions of the individual purchaser or reader, and publishers' efforts to control distribution patterns.

In our investigations of publishing, it is important to remember its central position in the book trade. It is not possible to study publishing in a meaningful way as an isolated activity, since the chief role of publishing is to connect the various branches of the book trade and to assure the smooth functioning of the trade as a whole.

IV

In this section I intend to discuss the relationships of publishers among themselves. These relationships were various; they ranged from friendly competition to outright hostility, or to attempts, usually short-lived, at some sort of cooperation for mutual advantages and benefits. Whatever these relationships were, our investigation of publishing will require that we analyze and understand them.

One important characteristic of the American book trade

[16] These series are discussed in Exman's *The Brothers Harper* and *The House of Harper*.

was a widespread commitment to the goal of producing printed materials at a low cost, aimed at a mass audience—the ideal of providing the most books to the most people at the lowest possible price. This commitment was based on an oft-stated ideological conceit that, in the great American democratic experiment, access to information was not only a requirement but also a right. Until very recently, printed materials were the main source for this information. Parallel to this conceit was a widely felt mistrust of any form of combination or special privilege and a belief in the correctness of laissez faire competition. These facts of American ideology were certainly reflected in the relationships of publishers to each other. Still, the economic realities of their business required that publishers to some extent coordinate their activities and learn to come to terms with each other.

Formal attempts at coordinating publishing activities resulted in the formation of a series of trade associations, usually restricted to a particular city. At the beginning of the nineteenth century, publishers participated in a variety of booksellers' and printers' associations, but as the book trade expanded and publishing became established as a separate activity, a number of specialized organizations arose that were dedicated to the needs of publishers. A history of these associations would be of great interest, for it would shed light not only on what their stated purposes were but also on how well they fulfilled these goals. My sense is that these associations were generally formed for the purpose of regulating publishing activities, and particularly, to establish standard discount schedules and maintain retail prices, often in reaction to a perception that trade sales had a damaging effect on publishing. Even trade sales required some sort of formal organization, however. I doubt that American publishers, unlike their colleagues in London, were able to maintain such controls for any period of time, and I suspect that their associations generally served merely a social function, providing for celebratory dinners and perhaps for funeral expenses or charity payments to a deceased member's family.[17]

The investigation of trade periodicals devoted to publishing is also worth further investigation. A German visitor to the United States in the 1840s noted the general disorganization of the American book trade and particularly the absence of any periodical that would serve to record new publications and provide a forum for discussions of publishing developments.[18] Even by that time, however, there had been a few hesitant attempts at filling this need; by 1876, *Publishers' Weekly* was firmly established as the chief, but by no means the sole, organ of the trade. We need to make a full list of American publishing trade periodicals and to locate and examine unbroken runs.[19] Although many of these periodicals—such as *Wiley & Putnam's Literary News-Letter* and *Appleton's Literary Bulletin*—were published by a particular house and were mainly dedicated to their own publications and affairs, others—such as the *Literary World* or *Norton's Literary Gazette and Publisher's Circular*—were much broader in scope. These periodicals are all an invaluable source of information on publishing activities; they also serve as a record of the relationships among publishers.

Another important field for further research is that of the various less-formal arrangements between publishers, arrangements that served to regulate their activities. During the eighteenth century, the exchange of lists between publishers was a well-established means of distribution, and I suspect that this pattern survived well into the next century. The most familiar arrangement in the nineteenth century, however, was what is

[17] The early history of book trade associations are discussed in Rollo G. Silver, *The American Printer, 1787–1825* (Charlottesville, 1967), pp. 78–89. The British situation is discussed in James J. Barnes, *Free Trade in Books: A Study of the London Book Trade since 1800* (Oxford, 1964).

[18] Hermann E. Ludewig, 'Die Organe der Erscheinenden Literatur,' *Serapeum* 7(1846):177–90.

[19] Adolph Growoll, *Book-Trade Bibliography in the United States in the XIXth Century* (New York, 1898), remains the best guide to these important periodicals.

known as 'courtesy of the trade.' This arrangement established a standard set of procedures that regulated the rights of publishers to reprint in America the uncopyrighted works of foreign authors.[20] A number of questions arise: How did 'courtesy of the trade' work in reality? Which publishers followed this convention, and for what periods of time, and with which types of publications? What sorts of pressure was used to maintain it? Were there practical reasons involving the costs and technology of book production that served to encourage the practice, in addition to more obvious means of coercion?[21]

A number of other informal arrangements between publishers deserve our attention. Although the practice of establishing congers of publishers to pool resources and share the risks of publishing a particular work never became as firmly established in the less-centralized book trade of America as it did in London, it was not an uncommon event during the first decades of the nineteenth century and needs to be investigated. I know of no American instance of the activity of trading in shares that was so characteristic of British publishing in this period, but such a practice may have existed.[22] We also need to investigate the arrangements that are reflected in multiple imprints on a single publication or in multiple issues, each with a different publisher's imprint. Were there not other concealed relationships between publishers—agreements for exclusive distribution rights to particular publications or for the exchange of lists—that need to be revealed and analyzed?

During the period that we are considering, the American book trade developed from a minor branch of the British book trade into an independent and highly successful business in its

[20] Exman, *The Brothers Harper*, pp. 52–59 and Ballou, *Building of the House*, pp. 70–84, both give examples of how this convention did and did not work.

[21] I have suggested this possibility in my 'Printing with Plates in the Nineteenth-Century United States,' *Publishing History* 5(1983):15–26.

[22] For an overview of the British situation see Terry Belanger, 'From Bookseller to Publisher: Changes in the London Book Trade, 1750–1850,' in Richard G. Landon, ed., *Book Selling and Book Buying: Aspects of the Nineteenth-Century British and North American Book Trade* (Chicago, 1978), pp. 7–16.

own right. This development is important for all of our investigations as we attempt to identify and understand the characteristics and contributions that are peculiar to the American book trade. For this investigation of publishing in America, it is particularly important to examine the relationships between American publishers and their foreign colleagues. A significant proportion of American books originated abroad, either as foreign texts reprinted here or as books produced abroad but imported and distributed here. In addition, many aspects of American publishing were copied from or influenced by foreign practices. Moreover, American texts and books were popular abroad and sold there, and their story is also part of our investigations. The ties between American and British publishers, who shared a common language and heritage, were particularly strong. A number of American publishers (Mathew Carey, for example) began their careers in Britain and in Ireland, and several American firms, such as Wiley and Putnam, established London branches to look after their interests in Britain. It would be interesting to know more about the role and activities of those individuals, men such as John Miller and Obadiah Rich, who served as agents mediating between American and British publishers.[23]

American publishers also established important relationships with Continental publishers that need to be investigated. America was populated by immigrants, who established their own ethnic and foreign-language publishing houses in their new homeland. To what extent did these publishing establishments build connections with the book trade of their country of origin, and to what extent did they remain independent? What were their relationships with other American publishers, and what was their fate as the immigrant population that they were

[23] See James J. Barnes, 'John Miller: First Transatlantic Publisher's Agent,' *Studies in Bibliography* 29(1976):373–79; Adrian W. Knepper, 'Obadiah Rich: Bibliopole,' *Papers of the Bibliographical Society of America* 49(1955):112–30; and Norman P. Tucker, 'Obadiah Rich, 1783–1850: Early American Hispanist' (Ph.D. diss. Harvard University, 1973).

designed to serve became assimilated into American culture and society? An interesting study would be that of the influence that the flood of German immigrants after 1849 had on American publishing. These immigrants brought with them their experience of the highly organized German book trade, centered on the Börsenverein of Leipzig, and it can be no coincidence that the names of Hermann E. Ludewig, Frederick Leypoldt, Nicolas Trübner, and later Adolph Growoll and Hellmut Lehmann-Haupt, are all associated with the beginnings of American book trade bibliography and history. In any case, we must avoid an isolated approach in our investigations; surely our understanding of the book in American culture and society will be more complete and richer when placed in this broader international perspective.

V

Thus far in this essay I have limited my discussion of publishing to the context of the book trade, though all publishing activities also took place within the larger matrix of American society and culture and were influenced by intellectual, economic, and political trends and forces. These too must be considered in our investigations of American publishing. Although it is beyond the scope of this essay to examine these cultural influences in all their variety and complexity, I do intend to note several of the more important ways in which they affected publishing activities and decisions and to suggest areas where further work is needed.

American society has always produced numerous intellectual and cultural movements that were reflected in and influenced by our published output. The attention that intellectual and literary historians have paid to transcendentalism and the publications that it produced illustrates this point, although such movements as abolitionism and religious revivalism were far more important in the quantity and range of publications that they spawned. The role of publishing in fostering and spreading awareness of such movements was considerable and provides an important incentive for our investigations. But more specifically, we need to discover and research the ways in which these movements and the social forces they represent influenced publishing decisions and activities. They certainly played an important role in providing new subject matter for publications and in opening up new audiences. We need to examine how a variety of organizations and institutions were responsible for sponsoring particular publications, series, and periodicals. In this regard, the role of governmental bodies—city, state, and federal—and religious organizations—tract, Sunday school, and missionary societies—is well understood and easily recognized, but the sponsorship role of a number of other organizations—such as educational, learned, and historical societies—is also relevant. The importance of official patronage in fostering the spread of printing on the American frontier has been well documented.[24] But what exactly were the arrangements that were made, and how did patronage encourage and restrict publishing activities?

In addition to formally sponsoring particular publications, the federal government undertook to encourage publishing activities in a variety of more general ways. A number of scholars have already examined the ways that copyright legislation and treaties, or rather the lack of the latter, affected publishing, although in general they have focused their attention on the influences of copyright on authorship and the earnings of authors.[25] Further work will be needed on the history of copyright legislation and treaties, and on their influence on other aspects of the book trade and publishing during the nineteenth century. The availability of a large pool of popular foreign works that were unprotected by copyright certainly played an important part in the expansion of the American book trade, for it allowed these works to be reprinted in very cheap edi-

[24] For example, see Wroth, *Colonial Printer.*

[25] The best study is Barnes, *Authors, Publishers, and Politicians.*

tions. I wonder, though, if it can be documented, as was frequently claimed, that the lack of international copyright actually discouraged the publication of copyrighted American works. Such works were indeed published and can often be found in editions every bit as cheap as the foreign works, but perhaps the cost of their publication was underwritten in part by the profits from the foreign works, on which no royalty payments were required. Federal legislation and policies also affected publishing through protective tariffs. The role of imported books in America during the seventeenth and eighteenth centuries cannot be overemphasized, but our knowledge of their importance in the nineteenth century remains incomplete. I suspect that imports were then largely limited to expensive technical and scholarly books aimed at a small audience, even though foreign books were certainly produced cheaply enough to be able to compete with the cheapest American publications. An investigation of tariff legislation and the accompanying debates, petitions, and reports would certainly provide useful insights into this question. A third area where federal action must have had a direct effect on publishing was through the control of postal rates and policies. I have already suggested the possible importance of the mails as a means of direct distribution of printed materials, and feel sure that an examination of postal regulations and rates will add to our understanding of publishing.

Another important field for investigation of publishing's relationship with society is the question of the censorship of seditious, libelous, blasphemous, and obscene materials. During the colonial period, government control of the press was not uncommon, as evidenced by the experiences of William Nuthead in Jamestown in 1683, of William Bradford in Philadelphia in 1693, and the Massachusetts law of 1662 that required that a text be approved by a licensing board before being published. In a few cases, the people took affairs into their own hands and plundered or burned printing offices. The celebrated libel case of John Peter Zenger of New York in 1734 may have established an important precedent for the freedom of the press, later reinforced in the Bill of Rights, but censorship continued to be practiced in America. For example, Ezra H. Heywood spent time in jail for distributing his curious free-love tract *Cupid's Yokes* (Princeton, Mass., 1876) through the mails, although the large number of copies of this work that were produced suggests to me that this was not a totally successful attempt at censorship. We need to investigate further the extent and effectiveness of formal censorship. Did the federal or state governments have other means of restricting the circulation of undesirable works than banning their circulation through the mails? We must also remember, however, that in addition to formal, legal censorship, a whole range of social forces could and undoubtedly did serve to remove or limit general access to certain printed materials that violated a community's moral, cultural, or political sensibilities. These forces could surface and influence the circulation of printed materials in many ways: the queasiness of backers or manufacturers when faced with certain works or ideas; the refusal of distributors, bookshops, or libraries to handle materials they deemed questionable; or, ultimately, a refusal by the consumers to purchase a publisher's products in reaction to what they regarded as a transgression of their standards of morality or propriety. All of these forces, which had the effect of censorship because they limited publishing activity and choices, deserve to be part of our investigation.[26]

VI

Any study of publishing must confront one important area that, for our period at least, remains barely touched upon: its nature

[26] Most studies of censorship in America underestimate the problem before the activities of Anthony Comstock at the end of the nineteenth century, although James C. N. Paul and Murray L. Schwartz cover the earlier period briefly in *Federal Censorship: Obscenity in the Mail* (New York, 1961).

as a business. Ultimately, the measure of any publishing venture depended on its economic failure or success, and we must begin to analyze how economic factors influenced publishing decisions in specific cases and how such factors affected the business of publishing in general.

The first step in such an investigation will be to analyze the costs of individual publications. Fortunately, publishers seem to have developed a rudimentary form of cost accounting early in the nineteenth century and some of these cost books survive. Building on the information recorded there, we must attempt to analyze the costs of publications and to establish what were normal patterns and ratios for the relative costs of paper, printing, binding, advertising, and royalties in comparison with the overall cost of a publication. We also might consider what the normal ratios were between production costs per copy and the retail and wholesale price. A more difficult problem will be to develop a sensible system for reckoning overhead—editorial and clerical salaries, rent, and interest on capital—and distributing these costs to the various publications in a publisher's list. These calculations will allow us to compare gross profits to net profits and to begin to judge in a quantitative way the profitability of particular publications and publishing strategies. We need to look for distinct patterns in these cost ratios between different types of publications, or between the lists of different publishers, and to analyze how changes in edition size, royalty rates, or advertising expenses affected these ratios and profitability. Were certain publishers more successful because they established and maintained more advantageous cost ratios for their publications? Were certain types of publications more profitable? Did cost ratios change over time as new manufacturing technologies and more sophisticated distribution networks became available? What were the optimum edition sizes? Were economies of scale arising from an increased edition size offset by increased risks and costs of venture capital? The answers to these and many other related questions will provide many important insights into the economics of publishing.[27]

A further step in this investigation of the economics of publishing will be to look at publishing in the larger business environment of the entire book trade. I have already suggested some aspects of this investigation—for example, in discussing the role of financing in publishing—but others remain to be investigated. We need to examine how economic factors were reflected in publishing activities and strategies. Is there evidence that the types of analysis suggested in the preceding paragraph were actually used in assessing past performance or planning future publishing programs? If not, what was the basis for such judgments? What were the economic forces that led to the concentration of publishing in urban centers and eventually led to the absolute predominance of New York City over several important earlier centers such as Philadelphia, Cincinnati, or Boston? What economic advantages encouraged the strategy of specializing in a particular genre or subject field, as opposed to the strategy of publishing a broad range of material? What sorts of organizational strategies, such as vertical or horizontal integration, did publishing develop to cope with and take advantage of our expanding and increasingly complex economic and technical environment? What role did publishing play in the evolution of this complexity? How did publishers react to and cope with the business cycles of boom and bust that have characterized the American economy? What economic forces encouraged or hindered the consolidation of publishers into large combinations, as opposed to their remaining small, independent entrepreneurs? The opportunities for research into the economic aspects of publishing are many, and the results should be fruitful.

The final stage in this investigation, possible only after our

[27] Leonard Shatzkin, *In Cold Type: Overcoming the Book Crisis* (Boston, 1982), provides concrete examples of how the economics of publishing can be usefully analyzed, although he is concerned exclusively with modern-day publishing.

understanding of the economics of publishing has reached the stage where we have begun to postulate the answers to many of these questions, will be to compare publishing with other American business enterprises. To what extent was publishing similar to and how did it differ from other businesses? What sorts of strategies and structures did publishing share with or borrow from other businesses? How does publishing compare with them in terms of risks and potential profits? Was publishing typical in its reactions to the changing economic environment, or, if it was not, in what ways did it differ? Scholars have tended to consider publishing as a special activity and to emphasize its unique qualities, but I wonder whether it is not in reality much the same as many other business enterprises, such as the garment or shoe industry. These matters will only become clear after much further work in the field.[28]

In our investigations of the economic aspects of publishing, one interesting aspect of the field will become better understood. This is the curious perspective that publishing is a creative intellectual act only tangentially influenced by practical business considerations. This perspective is hinted at in the passages quoted at the head of this essay, but is made much clearer in the memoirs and biographies of American publishers. For example, James T. Fields's *Yesterdays with Authors* (Boston, 1872) and James C. Derby's *Fifty Years among Authors, Books and Publishers* (New York, 1884) emphasize the publisher's association and friendship with famous authors and literary figures but largely ignore their business activities or associates. Part of our study of publishing will be to investigate this ideology and to explore the self-image of publishing as a profession and the ways that this image inhibited and encour-

[28] General histories of American business that I have found helpful are Arthur H. Cole, *Business Enterprise in Its Social Setting* (Cambridge, Mass., 1959); Alfred D. Chandler, Jr., *Strategy and Structure: Chapters in the History of Industrial Enterprise* (Cambridge, Mass., 1962); Alfred D. Chandler, Jr., *The Visible Hand: The Managerial Revolution in American Business* (Cambridge, Mass., 1977); and the essays in Stuart W. Bruchey, ed., *Small Business in American Life* (New York, 1980).

aged the business of publishing. We will need to relate this self-image to the mercantilist ideology of the eighteenth century and the developing American business attitudes and ideals of the new republic.

VII

Before concluding this essay, I want to stress two basic needs that seem to me to be of the highest priority. Throughout this essay I have suggested many areas that need further research, and I have tried to point to new approaches that seem to me to be useful in increasing our understanding of publishing. The two needs discussed here encompass many of these more specific projects, but it strikes me that addressing our energies to them will be a basic step for all further investigations and research.

The first need is to identify, locate, and interpret the primary sources for publishing history. Although many specific archives and types of material are well known and have already been used by scholars in their work, there has not yet been a systematic attempt to uncover and make available the basic resources for our work. Surely we must begin here.

An important step towards this goal will be to identify as many different types of source materials as possible. Although certain classes of material come immediately to mind—memoirs, business records, archives, and publishers' and trade sale catalogues—others are not so obvious and have not yet been used to full advantage. The bankruptcy records kept in the Massachusetts probate courts have provided invaluable insights into the publishing activities of the Boston firms of Thayer and Eldridge, as well as of the Arena Publishing Company.[29] Are there not also insurance, banking, tax, and incorporation records that will also be useful? Shouldn't we look at

[29] Roger E. Stoddard, 'Vanity and Reform: B. O. Flower's Arena Publishing Company, Boston, 1890–1896,' *Papers of the Bibliographical Society of America* 76(1982): 273–337. I thank Rollo G. Silver and Madeleine B. Stern for bringing the Thayer and Eldridge bankruptcy records to my attention.

the mass of data contained in printed government documents and census records? Are there customs records that will document the import and export of books? Can we use library records and catalogues to analyze purchasing and distribution patterns of books? This search for source material is, in some sense, limited only by our imagination and ingenuity in discovering new data and new ways that the book played a role in American culture and society. It will be important, however, not to restrict our search to manuscript or archival materials, especially when we consider the intimate connection between publishing and printed objects.

Next, we will need systematically to locate the surviving examples of each type of source material. In America—in contrast with many foreign countries where legal requirements, more stable business environments, and a stronger sense of the importance of tradition have all encouraged the preservation of cultural and historical records—we have often been very profligate with such material. Very few publishing firms that existed one hundred years ago are still in business today, and it seems safe to say that even fewer publishing archives or records survive from that or earlier periods. This situation makes it imperative that we locate those records that do survive. But a finding list will not be sufficient. If we are to pursue our research, we will need to make sure that these sources are preserved for the future, made accessible to serious scholars (in cases where they remain in private repositories), and, in appropriate cases, made more available by being published in microform or print.

The final step will be learning to interpret and analyze the data contained in these sources. Only rarely has the exact data needed for our investigations been recorded, and, even in those cases where it is available, it is not necessarily organized in a way that is useful for our studies. Often, the meaning of the data preserved is anything but self-apparent. We need to develop a set of analytical methods and tools with which to interpret this data in useful and meaningful ways. In those cases where relevant data is missing, incomplete, or inadequate, we will need to develop strategies that will help us fill in the picture, such as through the manipulation of related information that does survive and by building and testing general models based on that information. It is particularly important that we bring a critical attitude to our use of these sources, and that we evaluate them in terms of the variety of functions—advertising, inventory, cost accounting, recording past agreements and future obligations, meeting legal responsibilities and requirements—that these materials were originally created to serve. We need to learn to interpret the data contained in these sources. Too often, work in our field has been marred by an uncritical use of sources; data has been accepted naively, without being verified by a study of related evidence, in much the same way that investigations of literacy have been based simply on signature counts, without a full appreciation of what exactly was being measured.

Given the primary importance of this need, an appealing project would be to address it in one all-encompassing guide. Unfortunately, this approach strikes me as impractical. The types of sources are too various and are preserved in too many different forms and places, and the meaning and usefulness of many of them remains obscure or has not yet been discovered. The very complexity of the materials makes it difficult to imagine how they could be brought together meaningfully in a single way. A more plausible approach would be to plan a series of guides, each limited to a distinct type of source or group of related source materials. Each guide would not only attempt to list all the surviving material within its scope, giving the present location of that material, but it could also describe the nature of the source and explain the meaning of the data it contains. In addition, each guide might suggest meaningful ways that the source materials could be used for research. Such guides will need to be compiled by scholars who understand

and have actually used the sources for their researches. Inevitably, the progress in creating such a series of guides would be dialectical: the publication of a list of surviving source materials will undoubtedly bring additional material to light, and, as our work in the history of the book in America progresses, new uses for the sources with which we are already familiar will probably be discovered, and new types of source materials will be found to be relevant.

Our second basic need is bibliographical. We must complete the work of establishing the record of the published output of the American book trade for our period. This output is the primary source for all studies of publishing, and the task of compiling and analyzing the imprint lists of individual publishers is an indispensable first step for further investigations. A book, by its very physical nature, provides the final test that will confirm our theories, models, and generalizations. This primary role of the book, and the great need for more bibliographical work, was recognized by G. Thomas Tanselle in his important essay 'The Historiography of American Literary Publishing' (*Studies in Bibliography* 18 [1965]: 3–39), published nearly twenty years ago. In this essay, Tanselle points to the importance of compiling imprint lists as a first step in our work, but thus far few scholars have accepted this challenge.[30]

Fortunately, work on this bibliographical task is well underway, however far from completion it remains. The monumental work of Charles Evans and his successors covers American publications through 1800, and is at present being supplemented by the North American Imprints Program here at the American Antiquarian Society. This coverage has been extended into the 1830s by Ralph R. Shaw and Richard H. Shoemaker and their successors. Particular genres and locations are

[30] Tanselle states in part: 'It should be a truism, but apparently is not, that a knowledge of the lists of individual publishers underlies all broader investigations into publishing history. Generalizations about the output of any publisher, about the characteristics of publishers in any period, or about the trends in American publishing from one period to another, must begin there' (p. 38).

the focus of many excellent bibliographies and checklists, many of which build on work sponsored by the WPA in the 1930s. Further lists of American publications are found in many types of sources, such as publishers' catalogues, book trade periodicals, copyright records, publishers' archives, and library catalogues. But none of these bibliographies or sources is comprehensive and, as the published output multiplied with the expansion of the book trade during the nineteenth century, coverage became less and less complete. Many kinds of important printed ephemera are scarcely recorded, and have frequently been excluded from the scope of past bibliographical work. Full bibliographical control of all these sources is an unattainable goal, but, nonetheless, it remains an important one.

For the study of publishing, it will be necessary to organize the bibliographical work into the form of imprint lists, that is, chronological lists of the publications of an individual firm. Compiling these lists will involve searching through many of the already existing bibliographies—a formidable task that will become easier as it becomes possible to make computer searches of large bibliographical databases such as OCLC and RLIN. This work will also involve discovering and identifying publications that have not yet been recorded or described but, are listed in publishers' advertisements, catalogues, and records. But bibliography is more than simply listing books. For our work, it will also be necessary to analyze the imprint lists in order to discover and document the characteristics of a publisher's list for a certain period and to identify trends and developments that arose. Until this bibliographical analysis is done, our conclusions will remain unproven and our discussions impressionistic. After the imprint lists have been compiled and analyzed, it will, for the first time, be possible to make definitive statements about a publisher's list, to assess the amount of specialization in his output, and to interpret how the published output reacted to or affected a whole range of intellectual, political, and cultural movements.

In doing this work, it will be of first importance to locate surviving copies and to examine and analyze them bibliographically. Although these printed objects are our primary source of information, the evidence they present is often hidden or confusing. Frequently, a title page is a false witness that, if accepted without question, will mislead us in our understanding of the nature or subject matter of a publication, its author or publisher, and the date and means of its publication. Only a careful and bibliographically informed examination of each publication, both of its text and its physical structure, will make it possible for us to interpret accurately and usefully the important, but often duplicitous, evidence it provides. For example, a single text discovered with a variety of imprints may signify a popular work frequently reprinted, a single publishing venture issued simultaneously for a number of distinct markets, or a failure that was remaindered several times with canceled title leaves. Only careful examination of the bibliographical evidence will allow us to discriminate between these possibilities.

These then are the two basic needs that I see as crucial to our investigations into the role of publishing in the history of the book in American culture and society. All of our theories and conclusions will ultimately be based on the evidence found in the surviving records of the book trade and its published output. The success or failure of our work will depend on our ability to meet the challenge of identifying, locating, and interpreting these basic source materials.

VIII

We find ourselves at a very exciting stage in the investigation of the history of the book in American culture and society. The history of the book is in the process of becoming established as an important field of research, and in the future we should find ourselves with the access to resources that will allow us to call on the expertise of a wide range of scholars and specialists. But this favorable situation is also a challenge for us to come up with approaches and results that satisfy the interest and the excitement that the history of the book is generating, results that help us interpret history in a meaningful and useful way.

In this essay I have attempted to explore and illuminate the importance of publishing to the study of the book. Future investigations should add to our understanding of the role of publishing in the book trade. But in pursuing these investigations we must avoid limiting ourselves to the perspectives of a chronicler or antiquarian, however useful and important these approaches may prove to be. Publishing is more than a branch of the American book trade or American business history. The greater value of publishing is inherent in the significance of printed materials, which for our period remained the major agent of communication and which document many important developments and changes. In marked contrast to many other material objects, such as furniture, tools, or shoes, books generated an intense amount of interest and excitement, as well as other reactions, both positive and negative. Books were the object of concentrated attempts to increase or limit their accessibility. Books were responsible for the spread of new ideas and for the survival of old ones. For all these reasons, our study of publishing will not only contribute to our understanding of the history of the book but will also add to our understanding of the role books played in significant intellectual, social, and cultural trends in American history.

Postscript

This paper was prepared for a needs-and-opportunities conference on the history of the book in American culture held at the American Antiquarian Society, November 1–3, 1984. It was not meant to be a definitive study of publishing in the

United States but rather to serve as the basis for discussion and to suggest questions and directions for further research. It is here offered as originally written in the hope that it may still usefully serve these functions.

After a year, I find no reason to alter the main points presented in the paper, but I believe that two further aspects of publishing might have been included. The first is the investigation of the social, religious, and political environments within which individual publishers found themselves. Which of their relatives were also involved in the book trade? Who were their neighbors? To what church did they belong? How did they stand on such issues as temperance, abolition, and women's rights? Did they participate in the activities of political parties? The answers to these and similar questions may go a long way to explaining publishing strategies and decisions. The second potential area for study is the recognition of the important connections between publishing and jobbing. Whereas publishers leave behind physical evidence of their activities in the imprints of the books that they published, wholesalers and jobbers often remain anonymous. It seems likely to me that this difference has meant that modern scholars have tended to underestimate the importance that distribution played in the emergence of publishing as a distinct activity in the nineteenth century. Several firms—D. Appleton & Co. of New York and Parry, M'Millan & Co. of Philadelphia come to mind—may have been more significant as jobbers than as publishers, and I feel sure that a closer investigation of the interplay between both activities will prove fruitful.

Both of these points became clear to me as I was working on the research for a paper on trade sales in nineteenth-century America, which was delivered at a conference on the book in nineteenth-century America held at the University of Chicago, October 18–19, 1985. Many of the papers delivered at this conference—which are to be published in a separate volume by the Library of Congress's Center for the Book—deal directly with problems or issues relevant to publishing that I have outlined in this paper and show that the present interest and activity in the field of book history in America is beginning to discover the answers to many of the questions that I have posed. In addition, Joshua L. Rosenbloom, a graduate student in the field of economic history at Stanford University, has prepared an excellent paper on the emergence of modern publishing in the United States during the first decades of the nineteenth century; his work brings new theoretical and analytical approaches to the topic that seem promising.

In the penultimate section of this paper, I suggest two needs that are of such priority that they seem basic to further investigations and research. The first of these, the need to identify and locate the primary sources for publishing history, is being addressed by the Bibliographical Society of America. Under its direction, a pilot project, funded by the H. W. Wilson Foundation, is now drawing to a close and should result in a concrete proposal for the compilation of a comprehensive guide to surviving book trade and publishing archives. Progress on the latter has not been so promising, and the need for bibliographical work on the output of American publishers cannot be overemphasized. Nevertheless, two relevant projects should be mentioned. William Clarkin's *Mathew Carey: a Bibliography of His Publications, 1785–1824* (New York, 1984) lists the output of one of the most important figures in the emergence of American publishing, although it leaves much to be desired in its accuracy and analysis. Robert Harlan of the University of California, Berkeley, is preparing a list of San Francisco imprints through 1869 that promises to add significantly to our understanding of publishing on the American frontier.

This work is encouraging, but the task at hand remains formidable. Although current work in the study of the history of the book in American culture and society has confirmed our convictions of the fruitfulness of the topic for our investigations, it is clear that much work remains before us and that many more questions remain to be posed than have yet been answered. The central role and function of publishing in the book trade cannot be questioned, and as our understanding of publishing increases, so must our understanding of the importance of the book in American culture and society.

American Book Distribution

JAMES GILREATH

A COMPREHENSIVE HISTORY of book distribution must be based on the recognition that the book is both an economic product of a press and a conveyer of culture and ideas. Each theme poses its own problems and promises its own rewards. Both concepts are difficult to keep in focus simultaneously, but when fused they can produce striking contributions to the history of the book.

Viewing the book as a commodity, with special attention to distribution, creates new dimensions for the history of American publishing, reorienting its current preoccupations with author-publisher relations and printing technologies towards a number of new concerns: retailing strategies, the diversity of markets, the effects of landscape and transportation, the influences of capitalization and industrialization, and the transformation of the industry from one built on family businesses to one based on corporate structures. Historians of the book are not alone in neglecting such subjects; business historians also have been more interested in production than distribution. Commenting on the historiography of the American department store, economic historian Peter Samson observes in the *Business History Review* that business historians have given little attention to the development of retailing operations and that chroniclers of retail institutions have not successfully set these organizations in the context of society as a whole. Samson writes: 'Of all facets of business, retailing is the most sensitive to its social surroundings. . . . We must begin by asking where, and in what manner, goods reached the ultimate consumer. The best histories of retailing would not be institutional history, but social and economic history broadly conceived' (p. 31).

As important as it is for historians to explore the social and economic milieus of the book trade, they must not forget that books are more than manufactured paste, paper, and leather goods. The gatherings of stitched signatures pressed between bindings contain ideas, a fact that sets the history of book distribution apart from that of other products. To fully appreciate the impact of the book on American culture, the study of book dispersal must be part of our intellectual and cultural history. There are significant difficulties in any such endeavor. Robert Skotheim's *American Intellectual Histories and Historians* and Gene Wise's *American Historical Explanations* describe talented historians who have been snared by the methodological traps awaiting those intrepid enough to place ideas in social environments. Historians of the book must be prepared to acknowledge that the culture of a country or even a small geographic area cannot be summarized by its book culture. To use one example, Brooke Hindle's *The Pursuit of Science in Revolutionary America, 1735–1789* convincingly illustrates that individuals receive information from a variety of sources such as newspapers, magazines, letters, spoken communications, and books. Benjamin Franklin first learned about electricity from the itinerant lecturer Adam Spencer long before he read about it in the pages of *The American Magazine*. The history of book distribution also may offer little to intellectual historians like Perry Miller who, to use Skotheim's terms, are concerned only with the internal structure of ideas removed from any social context. As a genus of the historical human species, literate man, like economic, political, and theological man, has limitations representing the diversity and richness of human experience. But it is the extent to which the field of study that has come to be known as the history of books—with its interests in the making, distribution, and readership of books and printed documents—sheds light on the character and influence of literate man in society that such study will produce insights valuable to all historical studies.

The history of book distribution can serve as a vehicle, as imperfect as any other, for discovering clues about the diffusion of ideas, attitudes, and values through specific geographic areas, periods of time, and segments of society. In 'Common Houses, Cultural Spoor,' Peirce F. Lewis traces the migration of patterns of house styles from the eastern seaboard into other parts of the country. For instance, he finds what he describes as the colonial 'I' house spreading in time from the Middle Atlantic states to the upper South and the lower Midwest. At the same time he plots the movement of the New England 'upright-and-wing' architectural design into the upper Midwest. It may be that similar rough formulas could be devised for certain books or the output of some publishers. On some happy occasions it may be possible actually to watch ideas being shaped in and by society through observing book distribution. The range of distribution activities can affect all states of the life of a book. Any clear picture of the history of the flow of books in American society can offer a contribution to what Merle Curti proposes as the central theme of his research in *The Growth of American Thought*: 'a social history of American thought, and to some extent a socioeconomic history of American thought' (p. xi).

American historians seldom make book distribution the sole focus of their research. It is usually subsumed as a minor facet of another subject such as printing or publishing, although recently this situation has begun to change. Histories of the book in America vary in the space they devote to distribution, roughly according to when the study was produced and the period of American history under consideration. The oldest secondary works pay little attention to distribution, but some modern studies make it centrally important. The seventeenth century is the dominant topic for historians of the American book in books and journals published before 1930; but unlike the study of general intellectual histories, this early period has almost ceased to hold any interest for historians of the book today. John Tebbel's summary of the secondary works on the seventeenth century, in part two of the first volume of *A History of Book Publishing in the United States*, cites only two works published after World War II, both of which were general studies not specifically related to the book trade. After the demise of seventeenth-century studies, the eighteenth century caught the interest of book historians between 1930 and 1950. And, of late, researchers are turning their attention to the period between the Revolutionary War and the third decade of the nineteenth century. With the exception of a small number of histories of nineteenth-century publishing houses, and surveys of fine printing—such as Joseph Blumenthal's *The Printed Book in America*—that emphasize the twentieth century, relatively few attempts have been made to assess the history of the book in America after 1800, a period when the country's geographic boundaries, population, and publishing activities rapidly expanded. Despite their limited numbers, writers taking the nineteenth century as their subject are the most imaginative and encompassing in their appreciation of the significance of the book and book distribution in America.

Scholarship about book distribution in seventeenth-century America divides into two traditions that are not antithetical but deal with different facets of the trade. The first tradition is exemplified by George Littlefield's *Early Boston Booksellers, 1642–1711*, published in 1900, and the second by Thomas Goddard Wright's *Literary Culture in Early New England, 1620–1730*, issued in 1920. Littlefield's and Wright's works are radically different, despite the fact that the subject of the first is books sold in seventeenth-century New England and that of the second is books read in the same place and time. Each author bases his conclusions on different primary sources and discusses different books, which leaves the reader with the perplexing impression that what was being sold in seventeenth-century New England bookstores was not the same as what was being read in New England homes of the day.

The divergence between the two books comes about because the two authors define their topics in ways that exclude different parts of the book trade during the seventeenth century. Notwithstanding that the title of his book states that it is a history of bookselling, Littlefield is not interested in what booksellers sold but rather in what printers produced. Littlefield equates the book in America with the book printed in America and the history of bookselling with biographies of printers strung together in genealogical fashion. Wright, on the other hand, ignores New England's printers and the product of their presses and analyzes probate records that mention books, catalogues of libraries, and letters exchanged between colonists that included book titles. Since he deals only with booksellers who were printers, Littlefield omits the enormous number of books imported from England and France by the colonies that were, if Wright's research is any guide, read by many New Englanders. Wright's description of seventeenth-century New England culture emphasizes the books of educated settlers in contrast to Littlefield's highlighting of New England's native popular literature of sermons, manuals, almanacs, and broadsides. Wright makes New England seem like a small English university town in which there was no place for John Eliot's books for the instruction and conversion of the Indians. Referring to American imprints in *The Literary Culture of Early New England, 1620–1730*, Wright apologizes for their inferiority and quickly moves on in the text to those books that the colonists published in Great Britain. In contrast to Wright's attitude, Littlefield seeks to give the literature produced in New England a more important place in history and closes his book with the observation that 'whatever was the burning question which occupied the public mind, the bookseller was able to supply the literature relating to it by publishing the latest opinions of the prominent critics and wisest commentators' (p. 231).

For the purposes of this essay I stress contrasts between *Early Boston Booksellers, 1642–1711* and *Literary Culture in Early New England, 1620–1730* and how each deals with only a portion of the history of the book in America. I should add that Littlefield helps to begin the twentieth-century discussion of the book as an economic product as does Wright for the book as a participant in the socioeconomic history of ideas. Littlefield's interest in printers and the practice of printing is essential to any understanding of the economics of the book trade because the number of copies printed and the manner in which books are put to press are partly business decisions. Thomas Wright's research into private and institutional book collections in seventeenth-century New England forms a foundation for studying the relationship between book distribution and the diffusion of ideas and culture. However, implicit in both Littlefield's and Wright's endeavors is the assumption that the presence of even a single example of a title stood for the presumed distribution throughout the entire society. Their New England is a seamless web of readers in which books appeared magically and circulated without regard to class, region, profession, or any other variable. Books were a perfect reflection of literary taste and interest, without their availability ever becoming a problem. Littlefield freezes the book in time on the printer's platen, and Wright isolates it on the library shelf of one class of readers. They both ignore the evidence that a study of distribution points such as bookstores could have provided, evidence that could alert them to the variety of readers and books circulating in seventeenth-century New England.

Regrettably, there have been few methodological advances in studies dealing with book distribution in seventeenth-century America since the publication of Littlefield's and Wright's books. Henry Boynton's *Annals of American Bookselling, 1638–1850*, published in 1932, follows Littlefield's lead by including only booksellers who also were printers. That bookseller-printers constituted a majority of the colonial book trade is disputed by John Winterich's findings in *Early American Books and Printing*, which reveal that only a few of the thirty booksellers in Boston during the seventeenth century also printed books. The significance of the transatlantic book trade in the distribution of books in the colonies is largely missed by historians writing before 1930. Worthington Chauncey Ford in *The Boston Book Market, 1679–1700* uses invoices of books sent from England in his research; but he still organizes his study on themes related to production technology such as bookbinding rather than on terms more appropriate to the import-export trade. Without a balanced view of the available evidence, a historian runs the risk of presenting a skewed picture of society. On the one hand the reader is offered a country that is almost cut off from its transatlantic roots, while on the other he is shown a community that is in close and constant contact with England. Such a theme is not an isolated problem of a specialist historian of the book trade but directly involves one of the central questions of all seventeenth-century American studies: how did Americans begin to form a unique national identity that eventually led them to fight a war to separate from Great Britain? Tracing the problems represented by the contrasts in the work of Thomas Wright and George Littlefield helps illuminate the curiously segmented nature of American studies of the role of books in culture.

Wright's use of books available in personal and institutional collections to measure regional cultural maturity foreshadowed the post–World War II methodological approach among southern cultural historians. If pre–World War II historians like Wright marshaled evidence to counter the view that seventeenth-century New England was culturally interior to Great Britain, so have many southern historians since World War II argued that southern colonial culture was not inferior to New England's. Louis Wright's *The First Gentlemen of Virginia* and *The Cultural Life of the American Colonies, 1607–*

1736 and Richard Beale Davis's massive *Intellectual Life in the Colonial South, 1585–1763* are foremost proponents of this school of thought. Although Louis Wright's and Davis's books are significant contributions to American cultural studies, both writers think of books as being uniformly distributed throughout southern culture without regard to social class or geography. Neither Louis Wright nor Davis provides us with a clear view of how books arrived in the colonies and who purchased or read them. In a revealing passage, Davis concludes his essay 'Books, Libraries, Reading, and Printing,' in *Intellectual Life in the Colonial South, 1585–1763*, by weaving together all classes of readers into a southern seamless web. He states, 'Out-of-doors men these southern colonials were indeed, but they also spent many hours in the chimney corner of paneled Georgian library or of rough log-walled greatroom taking delight in their books' (p. 626). It will never be possible to be quantitatively precise in discussing the distribution of books in seventeenth-century America, but it is necessary to acknowledge that varied readers acquired different books in numerous ways. Students of the American book could benefit from some methodological handwringing about distribution and readership similar to that found among general cultural historians during the 1970s about the possibility of profiling a national character.

The narrow views of the book trade in the works of Littlefield, Thomas Wright, and their colleagues, and the subsequent lack of research, leave us knowing relatively little about American book distribution during the seventeenth century. The many bibliographies of imprints, library catalogues, reading lists, and related documents that appeared during the first three decades of this century in journals such as the *William and Mary Quarterly* and the *Proceedings of the Massachusetts Historical Society* need to be reexamined and related to general historical trends. Charles Laugher's *Thomas Bray's Grand Design* describes a bold scheme to ship entire libraries from

England to the colonies for the benefit of the Anglican clergy, but Bray's effort cannot be considered a typical commercial venture of the time.

Who were the booksellers, book importers, and exporters during the seventeenth century, and how did they go about their business? Jack Sosin in *Agents and Merchants* points out that most businesses in the colonies were Anglo-American family concerns with brothers or other relations trading with one another across the waters of the North Atlantic. Were booksellers more independent than other merchants plying a trade that was dependent on shiping, and, if so, how was this freedom translated into their selection of reading material to be brought into the colonies? It is not clear if those who brought books to New England to sell were moved more by commercial than theological motives. Book importers might have served as important secularizing forces that unintentionally eroded the influence of the ministerial oligarchy, casting new light on booksellers' activities during this period, and enlarging their significance in the history of the political and cultural life of the colonies.

Regional and class developments and differences are other frameworks within which to place inquiries about this subject. In *The American Revolution Within*, Merrill Jensen quotes John Adams as writing that 'the principles of the American Revolution may be said to have been as various as the thirteen states that went through it, and in some sense almost as diversified as the individuals who acted in it. In some few principles, or perhaps in one single principle, they all united.' Although it may be difficult to sustain an argument that there were thirteen separate book cultures in the colonies, book historians' intercolony distinctions have been uncommonly crude, too often nothing more than pious glorifications of the Massachusetts reader or parochial attempts to skewer the southern mind on the barb of British Governor Berkeley's witticism that he was thankful that there was no press in Virginia to interfere with

English imperial policy. More sophisticated questions need to be posed in this area.

Book historians interested in such questions could find no better starting point than examining the model of pre-telegraphic communication advanced by Allan R. Pred, who uses newspapers, lines of commerce, and interurban travel as the basis for his conclusions in *Urban Growth and the Circulation of Information: The United States System of Cities, 1790–1840.* One of Pred's findings is that the country was divided among various spatial subsystems, each of which depended upon a dominant city within the region. In turn, these dominant cities were to one degree or another dependent upon New York, with the South being more reliant than the North. Equally interesting is his view that information traveled more quickly between the major cities of New York, Baltimore, Philadelphia, and Boston than it did between these metropolitan centers and outlying areas. Most importantly, Pred's evidence indicates that information circuits and economic dependence were aligned during this early period but that this interdependence broke down as the country moved into a period of increased manufacturing activity and electronic communication.

Increase Mather once boasted that little of significance was published that escaped his attention, yet there has been no comprehensive analysis since 1910 of the building of the formidable Mather family library. If one were undertaken it might reveal that the Mather correspondence is a guide to how the New England elite received information and formed opinions. In exploring the sociology of knowledge in early America through book distribution, historians need not restrict their investigations to the theological community. Theorists such as Jackson Turner Main and James Henretta construct models of social stratification based on wealth as measured by tax receipts. Since some towns may have as many book lists extant as tax rolls, social scientists may be able to compare the two types of records to begin to test Bernard Barber's proposition that knowledge, like wealth, is differentially distributed throughout any society and that 'this dimension of stratification produces effects independently of other dimensions [i.e. wealth, power, or religion]' (p. 293).

During the 1930s and 1940s a new cast of historians led by Lawrence Wroth begin to shift the emphasis in writing about the history of the American book from the seventeenth to the eighteenth century, particularly the period between 1700 and 1776. Wroth's *The Colonial Printer*, first issued by the Grolier Club in 1931 and then by the Southworth-Anthoensen Press in 1938 in a revised edition, was a revolutionary advance that moved the study of the book away from biographies of printers and towards a careful examination of books and how they were produced. Wroth's approach to colonial printing struck a responsive chord among various readers. The information Wroth provided bibliographers about American printing methods helped them to understand more fully the significance of some books and to establish the bibliographical details of others. Wroth's explanation of American colonial book production gave the many undistinguished-looking colonial books heightened significance to librarians and collectors who had been interested only in the literature about the early discovery and exploration of America. After Wroth's *The Colonial Printer*, scholars like Thomas Wright no longer needed to apologize for the unassuming Massachusetts almanacs and broadsides. As a guide to the literary taste of the common man, American imprints became a help to students in understanding how printing techniques shaped and sometimes transformed important texts. Wroth's *The Colonial Printer* contributed substance and detail to Littlefield's view of the American book as the product of a native press.

In his 1939 essay 'The Booktrade Organization in the Colonial Period,' published in Hellmut Lehmann-Haupt's *The Book in America*, Wroth extends the scope of his thinking about the colonial book from the history of production processes to that of distribution methods. In this ground-breaking piece, Wroth argues that the colonial trade was primitively organized, with one person serving the multiple roles of printer, publisher, and bookseller. Only the Boston trade, in Wroth's view, was sufficiently mature to allow specialization not only for production (between printer and binder) but also between the producer (printer) and the distributor (publisher). Wroth gives four outlets available to colonial printers and publishers for distributing books: bookstores, subscription publishing, traveling agents, and auctions. Together, these have served as the established definition of the colonial book distribution network since Wroth proposed this view in 1939. But several recent specialized studies modify and, in some instances, contradict Wroth's model. The role Wroth gives the bookstore in the book trade is directly challenged, and the accuracy of his description of the importance of subscription publishing and auctions in the colonial period is no longer certain. Some writers conclude that, in addition to Wroth's four outlets for distribution, private collectors and institutional libraries also played significant parts in the circulation of books in eighteenth-century American society.

Of Wroth's four distribution networks, the bookstore has been most thoroughly examined since *The Book in America.* Wroth's understanding of the function of the colonial bookstore is most clearly revealed in his *An American Bookshelf, 1755,* issued in 1934 between the publication of *The Colonial Printer* and 'The Booktrade Organization in the Colonial Period.' To convey in vivid terms the reading interests of urban Americans in *1755,* Wroth created in *An American Bookshelf, 1755* a fictitious but, in his view, a typical Philadelphia reader, Mr. Loveday. Loveday is a successful, well-traveled, and educated merchant who owns his own home and is interested in books. His business travels throughout the colonies allowed Loveday to buy books in bookstores in many cities.

Wroth writes, 'Wherever he [Loveday] went in the course of his journeys, he was notable even among well-informed associates for a persistent patronage of booksellers.' Considering Wroth's intensive research about printing practices for *The Colonial Printer*, it is not surprising that he concludes in *An American Bookshelf, 1755* that Loveday's reading consisted totally of American imprints such as Indian treaties, narratives of captivities, and sermons predicting that human corruption would result in earthquakes as a form of divine retribution. Wroth's description of Loveday's reading never reveals the American participation in British middle-class culture, a perspective found in Michael Kraus's *The Atlantic Civilization* and 'Literary Relations Between Europe and America in the Eighteenth Century,' in George S. Gordon's *Anglo-American Literary Relations*, and in the works of Louis Wright and Thomas Wertenbaker. If Wroth is right, Loveday settled into the library of his Rittenhouse Square townhouse with well-thumbed copies of books such as *Essays Upon Field Husbandry* and the *Faithful Narrative of the Many Dangers and Sufferings of Robert Eastburn*. It is more likely that Loveday's shelves were stocked with London and Dublin edition of Alexander Pope's poems, or the essays of Addison and Steele.

There has been no full-length study of the American colonial bookstore since 'The Booktrade Organization in the Colonial Period,' nor have there been any descriptions of bookstores in America before 1750; but several fine articles have focused on retail bookstores for the period between 1750 and 1776. The number of studies is small, yet these essays cover stores in the major colonial urban areas, with the exception of New York City. Elizabeth Carroll Reilly's 'The Wages of Piety: The Boston Book Trade of Jeremy Condy' and Worthington Chauncey Ford's 'Henry Knox and the London Book-Store, 1771–1774' give information about the activities of northern stores at the end of the colonial period. The shops of the middle colonies are represented in Robert Harlan's 'David Hall's

Bookshop and its British Sources of Supply' and 'A Colonial Printer as Bookseller in Eighteenth-Century Philadelphia.' Cynthia and Gregory Stiverson's 'The Colonial Retail Book Trade: Avalability and Affordability of Reading Material in Mid-Eighteenth-Century Virginia' and Calhoun Winton's 'The Colonial South Carolina Book Trade' present the activities of two southern establishments. Elizabeth Cometti's 'Some Early Bestsellers in Piedmont, North Carolina' is a fascinating account of a small, country bookstore in the South which, for its size and location, stocked an ambitious selection of books. Cometti's description of William Johnston's Little River Store stands alone to complement what scholars have learned about the urban stores located in Boston, Philadelphia, Williamsburg, and Charleston, South Carolina. Finally, the list of titles Henrick Onderock made available in his general store in Hempstead Harbor, New York, a list that is published in Herman Krooss and Charles Gilbert's *American Business History* (pp. 29–31), serves as a useful example of the types of books sold in stores that did not specialize in stocking books or book-related items such as stationery and ink.

In opposition to Wroth's view in 'The Booktrade Organization in the Colonial Period' and *An American Bookshelf, 1755* that the sale of American imprints formed the most important part of the colonial bookstore's business, the research by Reilly, Harlan, the Stiversons, and Winton shows that an American urban store's principal function was distributing English and not American books. Colonial readers expected their city stores to supply them with the latest popular books from London. The importance of English publications is highlighted by Benjamin Franklin's comment on colonial reading in his *Autobiography* that 'those who lov'd reading were oblig'd to send for their books from England.' Some booksellers even made occasional trips to England to renew their stock, as Jeremy Condy did.

The usual method for American booksellers to keep in contact with the British publishing scene was to establish a reliable relationship with a London factor who not only filled the bookseller's orders but also chose those British books that he thought would be salable in the colonies. Urban colonial bookstores succeeded to the extent that their owners maintained a channel to British publishing through an agent who was sensitive to American reading taste, possessed good contacts with British publishers, and was patient and sufficiently capitalized to extend the long credit and endure the many inconveniences that conducting business across the Atlantic Ocean necessarily entailed. Here is how the Stiversons described the bookseller-agent relationship: 'Every colonial bookseller was dependent on an English agent, and if that agent was not honest and informed the results might be disastrous' (p. 153). Harlan's description of James Rivington's attempt from London to capture a wider share of the colonial market illustrates some of the difficulties of conducting business at such great distances. The unscrupulous Rivington would offer to colonial booksellers a few popular titles at sharp discounts, causing many to break from their usual business associates in London. However, when filling the Americans' orders, Rivington sometimes supplied incomplete sets and completed shipments with books that the booksellers had not ordered and would find difficult to sell. The Americans experienced insurmountable problems trying to untangle their affairs with Rivington when communication between the colonies and Great Britain was only as timely as the ships crossing the Atlantic between major ports.

The number of studies is too small for one to be overly confident in sweeping summaries; but, with the thought that nothing so stimulates historians' enquiries as the opportunity to amend another historian's generalizations, it should be useful to draw an outline of colonial retail bookstore activity based on the research of Reilly, Harlan, the Stiversons, and Winton. Most importantly, the bond forged by Lawrence Wroth between the colonial printer and bookseller should be broken.

Although printers often sold books, most were sustained by selling copies of their newspapers. Many booksellers printed few or no books. In discussing the book trade in Charleston, South Carolina, Calhoun Winton writes, 'All students are familiar with Wroth's model of the typical colonial printing establishment as the center of village news . . . but the evidence suggests that with two or three important exceptions the various aspects of the book trade continued to go their separate ways in South Carolina until the end of the colonial era' (p. 75).

Bookstores depended on the sale of nonbook items for a substantial portion of their income. In urban areas the nonbook goods were stationery materials; in rural areas such goods were general store stock such as shovels, seeds, and dry goods. Urban bookstores, among them David Hall's in Philadelphia and Jeremy Condy's in Boston, stocked fewer American than British titles. Harlan observes that in David Hall's business 'the only American publications which added appreciably and consistently to the bookstore's stock were the very popular pamphlets entitled *A Pocket Almanack*, *A Primer*, *A Catechism*, and *Poor Richard's Almanack*' (p. 4). Harlan's conclusion is a reminder to investigators interested in early American literature that they should pay more attention to almanacs rather than limiting their study to early poetry and novels as guides to prevailing American literary taste and expression. Country stores offered a limited number of imported books and relied almost exclusively on a few popular native titles. Elizabeth Cometti's study of William Johnston's store in North Carolina indicates that in 1774 when Johnston offered the inhabitants of rural North Carolina a more urban selection —characterized by copies of books by Laurence Sterne, Oliver Goldsmith, and Henry Fielding—none sold even though his customers continued to buy Bibles, hornbooks, short religious tracts, and *The Pilgrim's Progress* in quantity. To some extent American urban stores served as secondary distribution points for the British trade by supplying some books to those outlets in smaller towns. The scanty records available for Williamsburg and Boston suggest that the clientele of urban stores in different geographic locations consisted of a similar mix of professional classes, although Massachusetts bookstores enjoyed more support from ministers. This finding supports Jackson Turner Main's undocumented thesis in *The Social Structure of Revolutionary America* that ownership of a significant number of books in the colonies correlated with a professional occupation, location near a city, and a high income level. However, Main's definition of the typical colonial book owner is more appropriate for the North than the South, because many southerners with significant collections of books did not live near densely populated areas.

In spite of the importance of British publishing to American readers, only two articles provide a general overview of the business of the Anglo-American book trade during this period, Giles Barber's 'Books from the Old World and for the New: the British International Trade in Books in the Eighteenth Century' and Stephen Botein's 'The Anglo-American Book Trade before 1776.' Barber's quantitative study of the ledgers recording British imports and exports kept in the Public Records Office in London demonstrates that the colonies were the most important overseas market for British publishers, commanding almost fifty percent of total British book exports and outstripping even Ireland as an importer. One of the most interesting statistical comparisons derived from Barber's work is that the southern colonies of Florida, Carolina, Georgia, Virginia, and Maryland easily outdistanced the New England colonies in the number of books imported from Great Britain. Botein's well-argued study affords students of the eighteenth-century book trade a glimpse at the dynamics between British suppliers and American consumers from the viewpoint of the English publishers. A few British publishers dominated the colonial market, according to Botein, and they had little interest in understanding or cultivating colonial readers; instead, they relegated North America as a convenient dumping ground for books whose sales had slowed in London, thus making them too expensive to keep in inventory. Botein's publishers had a nearby audience in London for popular British books, and there was little economic incentive to offer the long credit and endure the uncertainty of the transportation system to the colonies for these titles.

Views of the British publishing scene that differ from Botein's in some respects are Lyman Butterfield's 'The American Interests of the Firm of E. and C. Dilly, with the Letters to Benjamin Rush' and, to a lesser degree, Robert Harlan's 'William Strahan's American Book Trade, 1744–1776.' The involvements of the Dillys and Strahan in the Anglo-American book trade were rooted more in their many friendships with Americans like Benjamin Franklin than in any desire to manipulate the American market for disposing of unwanted stock.

The research by Botein, Butterfield, Harlan, and Barber makes the student of the American book eager for more information about transatlantic relationships in the book trade. Questions confront us on all sides. What part did the Irish and French pirate printers play? How did English writers view the American market? How did British export duties affect the trade? To what extent was English middle-class culture unavailable in America because some books were not imported to this country? What more can we learn about the agents in England who supplied Americans with books? It is astonishing that we have no full-length study of William Strahan or John Almon, who were both influential in the Anglo-American book trade. Contrasting American importers of books with those handling other commodities may offer new insights. Much of the colonial trade with Great Britain before the Revolutionary War relied on a bartering system using exports such as southern tobacco and New England timber. Colonial booksellers, on the other hand, may have depended on specie for buying British books since Great Britain had little interest in books printed in the colonies. Did the scarcity of specie affect what Americans could import or the British were willing to export? William Baxter's *The House of Hancock: Business in Boston, 1724–1775* has valuable information about domestic trading of credits used for payments by printers, data that certainly holds clues for international arrangements.

The lack of specialized research on the Anglo-American trade has disoriented cultural historians when using the book trade as evidence of general characteristics of American and British cultural relations before the Revolution. This is clearly shown in the disagreement between Merle Curti and Louis Wright about the speed of transmission of ideas between Great Britain and her North American dependencies. In *The Cultural Life of the American Colonies 1607–1763,* Louis Wright argues that the important aspects of English culture were immediately accessible to Americans. He writes, 'The advertisements of eighteenth-century colonial papers indicate a steady market for contemporary English publications and do not suggest that the cultural lag was longer than the time for books to reach the colonies after publication in England' (p. 53). In *The Growth of American Thought,* Merle Curti proposes that the colonies were insulated from current developments in English thinking. He points out that 'new ideas and new books reached America from England only at irregular and often long-delayed intervals; apparently one of the first copies of Newton's *Principia,* published in England in 1687, to arrive in the colonies was that which James Logan obtained in 1708. English intellectuals had sometimes qualified or even abandoned ideas before the colonists had received and assimilated them.' The speed of cultural transmission from England to the colonies may have varied from place to place, from time to time, and from idea to idea; further research is necessary to clarify the process.

Since the publication of 'The Organization of the American Booktrade,' the progress made in reformulating the role of the colonial bookstore in the distribution system has not been matched for Wroth's second distributor of books, the peddler. Victor Neuburg's *The Penny Histories*, R. K. Webb's *The British Working Class Reader, 1790–1848*, and Leslie Shepard's *The Broadside Ballad* are examples of studies of British imprints for which there are no counterparts in the United States. The fact that there are few extant records directly relating to American colonial book peddlers makes it difficult to recreate the lost world of these transient figures. The two best books about hawkers in America are Richardson Wright's *Hawkers and Walkers in Early America* and J. R. Dolan's *The Yankee Peddlers of Early America*, but neither contains much about those who sold books. Both Wright and Dolan find that peddlers specialized and associated with specific trades such as blacksmithing, clockmaking, or cordwaining; but it would be surprising if many could have lived solely by selling books on the road before the Revolution. Book peddlers sold books as one of many jobs to earn money and constituted what amounted to a temporary labor force for booksellers. Gerald McDonald describes one such relationship in 'William Bradford's Book Trade and John Browne, Long Island Quaker, as His Book Agent, 1686–1691.' The transient booksellers may differ from craft peddlers in other significant ways. The primary function of the peddlers, as described by Wright and Dolan, was to bring urban specialized services to rural areas that were unable to afford them on a continuing basis. In one sense, book hawkers brought books printed in urban areas to outlying regions, yet this method of bookselling was not limited to the countryside. In *The History of Printing in America*, Isaiah Thomas describes the means by which books were sold by peddlers in Boston. According to Thomas, 'It was the custom of the day to hawk about the streets every new publication.'

During the last generation, the chapbooks and broadside ballads of early America have become a lost literature. Victor Neuburg's *Chapbooks: A Guide to Reference Material on English,*

Scottish, and American Chapbook Literature of the Eighteenth and Nineteenth Centuries list no historical work done on American versions of this genre since Harry B. Weiss's articles during the late 1940s. I am not well-acquainted with a great number of these pamphlets and broadsheets, but those that I have seen are sensational, follow established formulas, and are regional in the sense that they almost always deal with local events such as the hanging of a town criminal. Although there were best sellers like *The Wonderful Hermit* that were often reprinted, the local nature of many stories suggests that individual chapbooks and broadsides had a geographically restricted distribution. The time is long past for someone to tackle this form of literature in a substantive way, as Marion Barber Stowell has done for almanacs in her fascinating *Early American Almanacs: The Colonial Weekday Bible.*

Lawrence Wroth's third and fourth networks of distribution, auctions and subscription publishing, are reserved for the section of this paper surveying the post-Revolutionary period. In the place of these two networks, researchers have elevated private and institutional collectors as significant factors in the circulation of books in colonial society. Two summaries of early collectors are Edwin Wolf 2nd's 'Great American Book Collectors to 1800' and Carl Cannon's sturdy *American Book Collectors and Collecting*. Often-cited analyses of individual libraries include the Library Company of Philadelphia's *The Library of James Logan of Philadelphia, 1674–1751*, William Peden's 'Thomas Jefferson: Book Collector,' Millicent Sowerby's *Catalogue of the Library of Thomas Jefferson*, and Julius Tuttle's 'The Libraries of the Mathers.' Some collectors' libraries have been the subject of much research. My 'Sowerby Revirescent and Revised' lists the many articles and parts of books about Jefferson's use of his library that have appeared since Millicent Sowerby completed her annotated catalogue of Jefferson's collecting in 1959.

Unlike those who habitually frequented American bookstores, the owners of large private libraries during the colonial period did not limit themselves to books currently fashionable in London but imported the most useful parts of Old World scholarship and tradition to serve as a base for learning in the New World. James Logan was overjoyed when after a long search he acquired a 1518 edition of Ptolemy's *The Almagest* and, as described in Howard Rice's *Thomas Jefferson's Paris*, Jefferson pressed his search throughout Europe for sixteenth- and seventeenth-century editions of Palladio's *Four Orders of Architecture*, among other titles. The major private collectors became large-scale importers of books and operated like bookstore owners by taking frequent book-buying trips abroad, staying in contact with those in Europe who could provide them with books, and by keeping close watch on foreign publishing through reviews in periodicals, as is shown in Norman Fiering's 'The Transatlantic Republic of Letters: A Note on the Circulation of Learned Periodicals.'

What makes these collectors important in colonial society is not only their political, social, or economic prominence but also the fact that the number of books they imported had a greater than normal impact on the reading public because of the scarcity of books in early America. Most had an international network of friends with whom they often exchanged books and ideas. Although occurring after the start of the Revolutionary War, there is no more dramatic example of how books imported by a private collector had an immediate effect on important events than the story of Thomas Jefferson's book buying in Europe for James Madison, a story told in Irving Brant's *James Madison the Nationalist, 1780–1787*. During Jefferson's stay in France as America's representative, he spent much time looking for books for himself and his friends. Brant wrote about one shipment Jefferson sent to Madison:

> By the time a shipping opportunity arrived the purchases were multipled—not only the books Madison asked for, but works of Burlamaqui, Wolfius, d'Albion, Mably, Voltaire, Mirabeau,

> Diderot, a dozen histories—the whole running to almost 200 volumes. . . . This literary cargo, as Madison called it, made an immediate impact upon his constitutional studies. Home from legislative duties in the late winter of 1785–86, he plunged at once into a study of ancient and modern confederacies. What were their elements of strength? Of weakness? Why did the old ones fall, why were the modern feeble? He took them up one at a time—the Lycian Confederacy, the Amphictyonic, the Achaean; the Helvetic, the Belgic, the Germanic. . . . Out of Madison's free hours in New York, while he was attending Congress in 1787, came his notable 'Vices of the Political System of the United States.' Finished in April, on the very eve of the meeting to revise the structure of American government, this brief article not only probed the weaknesses of the state and federal structures, but put into words the thoughts on government which its author had distilled out of the world's past and his own mind (pp. 410–11).

Institutional libraries, like personal libraries, have stimulated much research since Wroth's essay, but the role they played in circulating books is uncertain. The standard source for the early American college library is Louis Shores's *Origins of the American College Library, 1638–1800* and, for the non-academic library, Jesse Shera's *Foundations of the Public Library.* Bibliographies listing books and articles about early library history that have been published since Shera's and Shores's studies are Michael Harris and Donald Davis's *American Library History* and David Zubatsky's *The History of American Colleges and Their Libraries in the Seventeenth and Eighteenth Centuries: A Bibliographical Essay.* Of particular note is Joe Kraus's 'The Book Collections of Early American College Libraries,' which has the virtue of being the first study that systematically tries to examine the intellectual contents of early American college libraries; but it compromises its usefulness, in my view, by sorting the books into such broad categories of knowledge that only a superficial understanding of the collections is possible.

The exciting possibilities lying beneath the surface of such amorphous classifications as history, religion, and literature—employed by many writers about early libraries—can be seen in H. Trevor Colbourn's revealing study of Jefferson's history books in 'Thomas Jefferson's Use of the Past.' In this fine article, Colbourn draws upon his extensive research for *The Lamp of Experience* to show that Jefferson's selection of books for his library was not governed by an idle, pious reverence for history but was guided by his desire to systematically search the writings of Whig historians in order to find arguments about such things as individual rights that could prove useful to late eighteenth-century revolutionary America. It was this reading that informed Jefferson's attitude about the nature of individual rights and influenced his actions throughout his life.

The literature about early American institutional libraries with which I am acquainted offers little about the use of patrons of these collections. In speaking about the writing on college libraries in colonial America in *Education in the Forming of American Society* (1960), Bernard Bailyn observed that 'books and libraries are in themselves mute and unyielding sources for cultural history; for though it is obviously important to know what was available and desired in print, the critical question is what the reading material meant to its possessors and readers (p. 85).' David Robson's 'The Early American College and the Wider Culture: Scholarship in the 1970s' finds that this situation is changing for general histories of colleges, but he does not indicate if the college library participates in the evolution. Many eighteenth-century public and academic libraries were built by the donation of estates rather than by an aggressive book-purchasing program that sought to measure its clients' reading interests. In Samuel Eliot Morison's richly detailed view of early campus life, *Harvard College in the Seventeenth Century*, the school's library seems to be most noteworthy for its absence of involvement in academic life. Unless further research produces new evidence or insights, it may be that the irresistible conclusion in this matter is that colonial institutional libraries were unused warehouses of the discarded books of previous generations, rather than active agents in the promotion and circulation of ideas, at best reliquaries in those generations' reverence for the memory of their ancestors.

The exceptions to the passive role of institutional libraries are the many subscription and circulating libraries that were formed in the eighteenth century and continued to be an integral part of the American social and intellectual scene through the middle of the nineteenth century. David Kaser's *A Book for a Sixpence* is a survey of the subscription library. A description of a bookseller who developed a circulating library in his store can be found in George Raddin's *An Early New York Library of Fiction* and in LeRoy Kimball's 'An Account of Hocquet Caritat.' The Library Company of Philadelphia has received much deserved attention as a lightning rod for the intellectual activity in eighteenth-century Philadelphia. Margaret Korty's 'Benjamin Franklin and Eighteenth-Century American Libraries' and Edwin Wolf 2nd's two essays 'Franklin and Their Friends Choose their Books' and 'The Early Buying Policy of the Library Company of Philadelphia' show that this private Philadelphia library was a frequent importer of books and comprised an active group of influential subscribers who played prominent roles in national cultural life.

The fact that many of these circulating libraries, most prominently Caritat's, consisted of a high percentage of works of fiction suggests that Americans were interested in imaginative literature but did not think that it had enough permanent value to justify the purchase of these books for personal collections. Americans conceived of literature as a decorative commodity that periodically could be leased for a brief period and then returned to a vendor, much as one might rent a potted fern to ornament a room for a special occasion. The idea that the attitude of the national reading audience would be rooted in such a belief played no small role in the struggles of the American writer in the next century and perhaps it helps to illuminate the enormous success of American book clubs in the twentieth century that serve up a monthly menu of reading fare. In a revealing passage in *The Rise of Silas Lapham,* Colonel Lapham approvingly assesses his family's reading habits: '"Well, we do buy a good many books, first and last," said the Colonel, who probably has in mind the costly volumes which they presented to one another on birthdays and holidays. "But I get about all the reading I want in the newspapers. And when the girls want a novel, I tell 'em to get it out of the library. That's what the library's for"' (pp. 88–89).

The American book distribution system on the eve of the Revolution consisted of informal networks of friends, temporary laborers, independent agents, peddlers, bookstore owners whose income came only partially from books, and a few institutions and private individuals who imported European books that they thought would be most useful in the colonies. The system serving American printers was particularly rigid and unable to respond to demands for distribution beyond a small area. The most rapid method for circulating American books during the colonial period may have been reprinting. Richard Gimbel's *Thomas Paine: A Bibliographical Check List of Common Sense* depicts Thomas Paine's pamphlet as immediately creating both controversy and demand when it was issued in Philadelphia in 1776 by Robert Bell. One Philadelphia bookstore owner, Robert Aitken, immediately ordered several dozen copies. However, Bell could not quickly supply the demand outside of Philadelphia, and many printers, one as close as Lancaster, Pennsylvania, printed their own copies for local distribution. The roads, transportation system, labor conditions, and slow communications all conspired to hinder Bell's taking advantage of the popularity of *Common Sense* and served to limit the horizons of printers, readers, and booksellers alike. A full-scale analysis of the circulation of Paine's work would be beneficial because information on the pressure that such a rapidly selling book put on the distribution system would throw light on parts of the network that normally were dormant. Presumably such a study would catch printers at their most resourceful in getting books into the hands of an eager public in short order. A look at the distribution of a book like Harriet Beecher Stowe's *Uncle Tom's Cabin* could potentially perform a similarly useful function for the nineteenth-century trade.

Not only would a thorough study of the distribution of individual books prove useful but also new attention to the lives of key publishing figures would markedly improve our understanding. It is unfortunate that American scholarship has produced no biography of Benjamin Franklin since John Clyde Oswald's in 1917, which takes as its theme Franklin's close identification with the colonial book trade both as a printer and a bookseller. Franklin's enormous number of friends throughout the colonies and in Europe, his interest in developing a national postal service, and his sponsorship of printers throughout the colonies are among the crucial elements in a career that might help to demonstrate America's early struggles to break the tyranny of a distribution system that encouraged only local marketing of books.

An overview of the scattered secondary sources about the history of book distribution during the pre-Revolutionary War period shows that a rough consensus emerges about patterns of distribution and readership, but the agreement quickly dissolves when the question of the effects on society is brought up. These studies outline three groups of readers. The first rank consisted of an educated male elite of varying political and philosophical dispositions. These readers were aggressive buyers of books, receiving them from numerous international sources and aided by a network of correspondents and friends. They acquired books printed in many countries and secondhand volumes sometimes centuries old were among those most actively sought. This elite had a well-defined sense of America's place in history and definite views about their relationship with other Englishmen. In this catholic collecting activity, which knew no chronological or geographical restraints, this small, wealthy group was at times joined in some cities by middle-class artisans and professionals banding together, such as those who composed Benjamin Franklin's Library Company of Philadelphia, readers who held useful learning in high regard and who envisioned a society based on merit rather than class.

The second group was primarily urban, with more women than the first group. These readers patronized bookstores or subscription libraries in populous areas in search of the current fashionable productions of London publishers. They ignored out-of-print books and seldom enlisted the aid of agents in foreign countries; they seemed content to select passively what booksellers had available. They were also more interested in fiction than the first class of readers.

Rural inhabitants and literate working-class urban residents comprised a third group of readers. Small towns and even isolated farms did boast medium-size book collections, consisting principally of professional literature such as law or medical books and the works of a few classical or religious writers. But by and large these collections were not common. Rural readers relied heavily on traveling booksellers and occasional visits to cities to stock their shelves, and their interests were generally restricted to ephemeral productions such as chapbooks and broadsides. In contrast to the first group's enlarged sense of history, the third segment of American readers were those most isolated from European culture and removed from a sense of participating in a shared British heritage. Uniting all three groups were newspapers, practical works like almanacs, a very few popular religious texts such as *Pilgrim's Progress*, and the exceptional best seller like *Common Sense*.

The role assigned to books in influencing or shaping events depends to a large degree on one's opinion about the size and importance of the literate population, questions far from settled. Those interested in the history of books also will eventually confront the doubts and objections of historians who value the written word as nothing more than a subterfuge used to conceal decidedly nonintellectual motivations. To cite a noteworthy example, Charles Beard in *An Economic Interpretation of the Constitution* deals with the written expressions of his principal characters as an elaborate series of masks and blinds meant to shield their authors' venal aspirations and self-interests from the outside world. Such interpretations are at least in part influenced by an individual historian's view of human nature and as such are less the result of objective historical evidence and more a matter of personal interpretation. But such an argument should serve to remind those whose main interest is the history of books that they should not presume that all will uncritically accept any assertion of the importance of studying the use of books as an avenue for understanding society. Book historians will undoubtedly find much more congenial company among those interpreters of the past who believe that ideas play a verifiable role in culture. Three of these scholars are Bernard Bailyn, who argues in *Intellectual Origins of the American Revolution* that the colonists' historical reading produced their sense of identity as a wronged minority in British society, Arthur Schlesinger, whose *Prelude to Independence* depicts diverse groups as being motivated by what is printed in newspapers, and Rhys Isaac, whose study *The Transformation of Virginia, 1740–1790* shows an educated elite manipulating the channels of communications in society in order to work the levers of social, political, and economic power.

If the history of book distribution during the pre-Revolutionary period has been clouded by scholars' inability to deal simultaneously with imported books and American imprints, the picture is even murkier for the period immediately after the Revolution. The relationship between American booksellers and the English trade is unclear. Logic tells us that the book trade between the two countries during the Revolution was almost severed, but, to my knowledge, no research has verified this supposition. Indeed, it can be seen in Thomas Adams's *The American Controversy* and *American Independence* that there were exchanges of political books between America and England, because many pamphlets countered charges contained in a pamphlet printed in the other country. It is not difficult to imagine that some American exports to England increased during the war years because of the intense political discussions about the hostilities.

After the Treaty of Paris, some Englishmen continued to see their country's former colonies as an important book market. Lord John Sheffield anticipated this position during the Revolution in *Observations on the Commerce of the American States* and noted, 'This [a book] is a considerable article of exportation to America from Britain, and must continue so as long as the price of labour is high there, and the language the same. All school and common books can be sent cheaper from Britain than they can be printed in America, or sent from Ireland' (pp. 35–36). In his *Present State of Printing and Bookselling in America, 1796*, Lehman Thomas Rede described the situation in terms similar to Sheffield's: 'The people of North America manufacture their own paper, and in sufficient quantities for home consumption, but the price of labour is still so extremely high, that it seldom answers to print any work there: at least, they have hitherto seldom ventured beyond their own laws, temporary pamphlets, and newspapers, which every State now prints in abundance. . . . Of late, in the Northern States they print a few school-books, and occasionally, in New York, Philadelphia, and Baltimore, print any tract not remarkably large; translations from the French, and a few re-prints from English publication, are all that have hitherto been done there' (pp. 14–15). For the pre-Revolutionary period, the literature about the Stamp Act gives us some idea of how British regulatory actions affected American printers. Robert Harlan's 'David Hall and the Stamp Act' and 'David Hall and the Townsend Acts' discuss the effect of British legislation on one printer, but there are no counterparts for this work for booksellers after 1789. How did English publishers attempt to resume pre-war normal relations with America? Did they lobby their government for assistance?

After the Revolution, the new United States Congress acted immediately to protect native printers from English books, and Rollo Silver's exploratory essay 'The Book Trade and the Protective Tariff: 1800–1804' surveys some of the measures taken. Printers supported the increases in the tariff on books from five percent in 1792 to ten percent in 1794, and an increase to twelve and one-half percent in 1800. Silver's pioneer work has not been carried forward with the exception of Donald Marquant Dozer's 'The Tariff on Books.' Dozer's essay describes the American publishers' and authors' efforts to extend the high Civil War tax on books to the post–Civil War period as a brace to the republishing trade and as an attempt to diminish direct competition from British writers. It was one of the few areas of common ground that publishers and authors discovered. The history of the effect of tariffs on book importation is a subject long overdue for examination. Books were not singled out as an enumerated article before 1842, and there must have been some debate about keeping them part of the general schedule.

There was a persistent conflict between those who made the finished product—printers and publishers—and those who supplied the material and machines for producing the books—papermakers and type manufacturers. As early as 1793, Philadelphia printers and booksellers petitioned to lower the duty on imported paper so that the bookmakers could reduce their overhead and increase their margin of profit. In 1801 there was a massive lobbying effort on the part of mechanics and printers from Alexandria, Virginia, to Providence, Rhode Island, to increase the protective tariff on imported articles. At first Congress was adamant in turning down requests for cheaper paper and type on the grounds that such an action would adversely affect fledgling efforts at domestic manufacturing of paper and type. This protectionist sentiment was the central tenet of the country's trade legislation policy. By 1816 the *ad valorem* tax on imported paper was a prohibitive thirty percent, and on type, twenty-five percent. Some printers and publishers must have echoed the thinking of the trustees of Transylvania University, who pointed out to the Senate Committee on Finance in 1822 that the high duty on these items was not just a protection to native industries but was also a tax on domestic printers and readers. Such reasoning failed to impress the legislators who retreated from their hard-line position only to the extent that they allowed rags for making paper into the country without the onerous fees. Congress used the fact that the rags were duty-free to turn back a request from New Jersey, Pennsylvania, and Delaware papermakers for an even higher duty on paper.

During the first decades of the Republic, Congress repeatedly denied petitions that sought to exempt books from the import tax. In 1803 William McAuley and John McJimsey asked that the $2,365 worth of books held at the New York customs house be released without payment because they were meant for the study at the Associated Reformed Church of North America's new seminary, a worthy cause that would benefit society more than the revenues. The representatives turned a deaf ear to McAuley and McJimsey's pleas, charging the two petitioners to 'make an exertion to raise a little more money for this purpose.' In 1804, New Jersey College sought to avoid the duty on imported books as it endeavored to rebuild its library, which had been recently destroyed by fire. But the New Jersey school had no more success in this quest than did the representatives of the ministers and elders of the Reformed Church of North America. The Library Company of Philadelphia was also stymied in the same year in its effort to get books into the country from a donor in Kent County, England, who had bequeathed them to the institution.

To an extent, the revision of the tax schedule in 1816 did relieve the pressure on the situation by allowing books to be brought free into the United States if they were destined to be used by any society that was incorporated for literary or philosophical purposes. In spite of this change, there were some who felt that the arrangement still worked against the public good. In a letter to James Madison on September 16, 1821, Thomas Jefferson reported a plan by northern and western colleges to join forces with southern colleges to repeal the recently imposed duty on all imports including books. Arguing for Madison's support for the scheme, Jefferson wrote, 'Books constitute capital, a library lasts as long as a house, for hundreds of years. It [a book] is not then an article of consumption.' By 1822 the coalition was firm enough for Jefferson to approach Congress on the behalf of the University of Virginia. The American Philosophical Society and Transylvania University made simultaneous appeals. In his memorial to Congress, Jefferson protested that American printers were able to produce books only in English and cheap editions, leaving works in foreign, living languages, '(to serve) as vehicles of the important discoveries and improvements in science and the arts,' unpublished and not known in any copies throughout the entire United States. To the Congress's argument that it had already excepted literary and philosophical societies from the tax, Jefferson replied that books 'locked up in libraries can be of no avail to the practical man when he wishes a recurrence to them for the uses of life.' But the members of the Committee on Finance remained unpersuaded by Jefferson's logic and called these books 'extravagant expenditures' and 'foreign luxuries,' terms that recalled the debate a few years before about Congress's purchase of Jefferson's library to replace the one burnt by the British during their occupation of Washington in the War of 1812. In a remarkable summation of their resolve to indulge nationalism even at the expense of civilization, the legislators concluded that 'none, then, but the professional gentleman, who can afford to extend his library beyond the resources of American publishers, or the scholar of wealth and leisure, who could indulge his taste in selecting the most elegant and expensive editions of foreign authors' would benefit from a reduction in the tax. This opinion was so ingrained in the congressional attitude that when the revisions of the tax schedule were passed during the 1840s, the highest fees were always levied on foreign, living languages, even when increased competition between British and American schoolbook publishers was allowed.

The spectrum of opinion on this issue among the several segments of the book trade and the American public yet remains unclear. In his article on the protective tariff, Silver quotes Ebenezer Andrews as claiming that lower tariffs on books were necessary because American printers could not yet satisfy the needs of American readers. Andrews's position is diametrically opposed to that of most other printers at the time. Is it the case that opinion in the trade was sharply divided on the question of tariffs between its distribution segment (those who made a living primarily from selling English books to American readers) and its production segment (printers)? What roles did publishers, bookbinders, printers, papermakers, readers, and learned institutions play in the tax schedules during the Tyler administration? All parts of the book business were brought together at what they must have considered the dire prospect of Congress's accepting an international copyright agreement in 1842, which would have meant that English authors would be paid royalties on their works sold in America whether the book had been printed here or abroad. One of the arguments put forth most strenuously against such an agreement was that its enactment would mean that the country would be flooded by the works of English writers whose unacceptable attitudes towards the United States had not been weeded out by the diligent and patriotic American printer and publisher.

Turning from book imports to the distribution of American imprints, G. Thomas Tanselle's 'Some Statistics on American Printing, 1764–1783' shows that the number of books printed between 1794 and 1800 was four times that produced between 1764 and 1773. American printers increasingly produced editions of popular English books as well as printing works by Americans. There were a number of original American imprints that appeared: the first American mathematical work in 1788, the first book on milling in 1795, the first native anthology of fiction in 1797, the first book on dyeing in 1799, the first book on distilling in 1804, and the first book on engineering in 1805. The audiences for these books were probably small in comparison with those for British imports. The prefaces of numerous early America novels contain their authors' protests about the popularity of English fiction in America and its detrimental effect on American creativity. And indeed, the period after the Revolution was characterized by the hectic experimentations of American printers, publishers, and booksellers to discover ways to bypass the unresponsive distribution network of the colonial period and to appeal directly to readers to purchase books. These experiments included a new method of subscription publishing, and a marked increase in the use of auctions, newspaper advertisements, and catalogues.

The descriptions of colonial subscription publishing in F. E. Compton's *Subscription Books* and in Lawrence Wroth's 'The Colonial Booktrade Organization' portray it as a method for producing large, expensive books that otherwise would tie up printers' resources for a substantial amount of time. Those few books printed by subscription before 1776 used this publishing strategy primarily as a way to finance the printing of an expensive book, rather than as a way to distribute it. William Powell in 'Patrons of the Press: Subscription Book Purchasers in North Carolina, 1733–1850' writes about colonial subscription publishing, 'Subscribers to books undoubtedly considered themselves patrons of the press and were fully aware of the fact that only through their common support could the books be issued. . . . In some instances the announcement [of publication of the book] stated simply that the work would get underway as soon as the number of subscribers justified it financially' (p. 425). Richard J. Wolfe's *Jacob Bigelow's American Medical Botany, 1817–1821* and Waldemar Fries's *The Double Elephant Folio* demonstrate that prepayment through subscription sales continued to finance expensive books well into the nineteenth century. Madeleine Stern's 'A Salem Author and a Boston Publisher: James Tyler and Joseph Nancrede' presents an example of a subscription scheme for an ambitious geographical atlas that failed to gain enough support for the atlas to be published.

After the Revolution, a modified form of subscription publishing emerged that differed from that of the colonial period. Agents for publishers took subscription papers from town to town to secure orders for books, making the purpose of this part of the subscription trade more useful for distributing books than for financing their printing. The titles that Donald Farren finds published by subscription in 'Subscription: A Study of the Eighteenth-Century American Book Trade' and that Roger Stoddard compiles in 'Poet and Printer in Colonial Federal America: Some Bibliographical Perspectives' are inexpensive pamphlets rather than deluxe editions. In 'Mason Weems, Mathew Carey, and the Southern Book Trade, 1794–1810,' I try to show that the books that Mason Weems sold by subscription were already published and available in Carey's Philadelphia warehouse, and that it was therefore not necessary to underwrite them.

The explosion of catalogues and newspaper advertisements offering books for sale during the Federal period is additional evidence of the escalating efforts by booksellers, printers, and publishers to reach beyond the rigid structure of distribution offered by bookstores and to conquer the geographical obstacles confronting them. Robert Winans's *A Descriptive Checklist of Book Catalogues Separately Printed in America, 1693–1800* is the first installment of an extensive bibliographical treatment of American catalogues that offers a bright promise for valuable historical contributions in this area. Winans includes auction lists in his work, but the balance between bookseller auction catalogues and bookseller retail catalogues is far from even. Thus far, the figures in the published portion of Winans's work include only five separately published book auction catalogues for the pre-1776 period, a number that can scarcely be considered to represent a significant portion of the trade. Even from 1776 to 1800, there were few auctions and most of these were estate sales, an example of which Edwin Wolf 2nd describes in 'The Dispersal of the Library of William Byrd of Westover.' Robert Bell in Philadelphia was the sole bookseller who regularly included new books in his auctions. With the possible exception of the Boston market, the auction did not become a significant part of the commercial trade until the nineteenth century.

In contrast to the situation for auctions, many booksellers turned to catalogues as a way of selling books after the war, and there were almost as many catalogues issued from 1789 to 1800 as there were for the entire period before 1789. These catalogues consisted primarily of imported books, although the largest publishers like Isaiah Thomas and Mathew Carey also included a great number of their own imprints. The many imported books in the catalogues listed by Winans serve as companions to those that Charles Evans gave as guides to eighteenth-century American book culture in his *American Bibliography*. Sarah Pattee Stetson's 'American Garden Books Transplanted and Native, before 1807' and Helen Park's *A List of Architectural Books Available in America before the Revolution* suggest the possibilities that imported books open for researchers. Similarly, newspaper advertisements offering books for sale can also serve as a measure of American cultural activity. I know of no bibliographical description for newspaper advertisements that can compare to Winans's for catalogues, but John Edgar Molnar's 'Publication and Retail Book Advertisements in the "Virginia Gazette," 1736–1780' spots booksellers' increasing reliance on newspapers during the pre-1776 period. Molnar finds only one advertisement for books during the 1750s, five during the 1760s, but thirty-seven from 1770 through 1776. Howard Mumford Jones has made good use of newspaper advertising of books in two articles that attempt to gauge the influence of French culture in the United States, 'The Importation of French Books in Philadelphia, 1750–1800' and 'The Importation of French Literature in New York City, 1750–1800.' Those interested in Jones's approach should consult William Reitzel's 'The Purchasing of English Books in Philadelphia, 1790–1800,' which contains a caution about Jones's use of newspapers.

There is no greater obstacle to a fuller understanding of the history of American book distribution after the Revolution than the lack of adequate biographies of the two giant publishers of the period, Mathew Carey and Isaiah Thomas. Earl Bradsher's *Mathew Carey, Editor, Author, Publisher* and Clifford Shipton's *Isaiah Thomas, Printer, Patriot and Philanthropist, 1749–1831* are short books that offer yeoman service, but both are in desperate need of revision and expansion. Neither biographer is interested in his subject's distribution activities. The intent of Bradsher's work is to sketch the impetus Carey gave to early American literature. Shipton is primarily interested in Thomas's publishing during the War of Independence. The enormous number of books published by Thomas and by Carey, recently listed in William Clarkin's *Mathew Carey: A Bibliography of His Publications, 1785–1824* (1984), leads me to suspect that their careers hold much information about early efforts to expand the distribution networks of the American book trade from local to regional and national levels. Hints of Carey's activities can be gathered from Emily Ellsworth Skeel's *Mason Locke Weems, His Works and Ways*, which reprints so many of Carey's letters that it is one of the best published sources for primary documents relating to publishing history for the pre-1900 period.

Tantalizing clues contained in articles about Carey and Thomas show some of the diversity and extent of their efforts. Bradsher observes that Carey 'built up a trade that extended to all parts of the United States' but ventures no farther than this general observation. James Napier's 'Some Book Sales in Dumfries, Virginia' points out that Carey employed a postmaster in a rural area to sell books. In the countryside, local residents were forced to visit post offices, so the shipping of books to a postmaster was not only comparatively easy for Carey but also guaranteed that the books would be seen by prospective purchasers. Chester Hallenbeck's 'Book-Trade Publicity Before 1800' tells of Carey's use of newspapers and magazines throughout the United States as a means of selling books. My 'Mason Weems, Mathew Carey, and the Southern Book Trade, 1794–1810' tries to illustrate Carey's attempts to break into the southern market and Mason Weems's ambitious plan to establish a chain of bookstores with Carey from Virginia through South Carolina. They failed both because of the impracticability of the scheme in the face of a poor transportation system and slow communications and because of Carey's misunderstanding of southern literary taste.

Carey led the way in encouraging cooperation among publishers and booksellers throughout the northern and Middle Atlantic states. As did many in the trade at this time, he compiled book lists that were circulated to facilitate exchanging stock. The exchange partners chose from Carey's list the books that they thought appropriate for their area and returned to Philadelphia books from their own stock that were of equal value. This practice allowed Carey to increase the variety and amount of his stock in the Philadelphia store as well as to place his own publications before a wider and more diverse audience. The success of this informal system of book exchange prompted

Carey to establish a more elaborate network. Charles L. Nichols's 'The Literary Fair in the United States,' in George Parker Winship's *Bibliographical Essays: A Tribute to Wilberforce Eames*, takes a brief look at Carey's arrangement of an annual book fair modeled on the Frankfurt Book Fair in Germany. Its purpose was to gather together in one place publishers, booksellers, and printers in order to circulate information about the trade, to consolidate the industry's energies for promoting its general welfare, and to exchange books. The annual fairs lasted for only a few years and then succumbed, in Nichols's judgement, to poor economic conditions. Efforts other than the one that Nichols describes must have taken place. Shipton mentions that Isaiah Thomas attended a convention of the trade in 1788, but the purpose and the details of the event are not given.

In 1789 Isaiah Thomas's Boston plant alone was able to produce a 30,000-volume edition of a speller and still have reserve capacity for other titles. Such production capabilities must have made Thomas acutely aware of the need for efficient distribution methods. Although the picture of Thomas's career is not complete, what is known suggests that Thomas was more comfortable with formal business partnerships with other printers or publishers than with the informal exchange system developed by Carey. Thomas's many mergers include those with Henry Tinges in Newburyport in 1773, E. W. Weld in Springfield, Massachusetts, in 1788; E. T. Andrews and O. Pennington in Albany in 1796; and Alexander Thomas in Windsor, Vermont, in 1808. His business partnerships throughout New England forced him to form a private messenger service that may have had the additional benefit of serving as a book delivery service.

Carey's and Thomas's careers do not encompass all the experimentation during these formative years. Milton Hamilton's *The Country Printer, New York State, 1785–1830* tells of Elihu Phinney's fitting up a barge on the Erie Canal during the early nineteenth century to serve as a floating bookstore to bring literature to towns along the water. Mason Weems found county court and racing days to be among the best for selling books in the South because so much of the widely dispersed population could be found in one place. Even the first Federal Copyright Act of 1790 may have altered the existing networks of distribution. In 'Salesmanship of an Early American Best Seller,' Mrs. Roswell Skeel notes that Noah Webster sold the copyright of his *A Grammatical Institute of the English Language* to various regional publishers in order to limit the sale of his book to authorized agents in defined areas.

Despite the exhaustive bibliographical treatment of the output of the American press in the immediate post-Revolutionary period, no one has adequately explained the driving force behind the sudden new energy. Was it simply that there were more printers and people? Where did the printers come from? Certainly the presses, the roads, and the methods of transportation were no better after than before 1776. Aside from quelling the Bible trade and rebellious newspapers, there is no evidence that Great Britain actively suppressed American printers during the colonial years. The dominant political question for scholars of the Federal period has always turned on understanding the various efforts to forge a consensus on which to base a national government. Historians like Benjamin Spencer in *The Quest for Nationality* have transferred this issue from political to cultural studies by showing American writers and publishers energetically collaborating to forge modes of expression and themes that were distinguishable from English influence but still acceptable to their native readers. In this view, each pull of the printer's press bar inched America closer to fulfilling its vital literary mission; publishers and authors busily toiled to create a national literature that was worthy of their country's form of government and could serve equally well as a world model celebrating democracy and humbling the literary works produced by the subjects of the English monarchy, in much the same way Americans had humbled British soldiers at Yorktown. If some printers and publishers of this period envisioned a national audience or readership, then they were thinking in terms of a unified American cultural identity that had been unimaginable a few years earlier and that still eluded many political theorists.

One question that arises is whether or not the shock of the Revolution disrupted existing business arrangements in the trade and created a vacuum that produced economic opportunities, which in turn inspired much of the rhetoric about developing American literary products for a home market. Although there was probably a mix of self-interest and genuine national pride in this rhetoric, one could argue that this was not the first time that entrepreneurial greed stalked the land clothed in patriotic language. A historian of Charles Beard's temperament would undoubtedly have little difficulty finding evidence to support a thesis that publishers were mainly interested in grabbing for a larger market share as British exporters temporarily faltered. Was it not the case that American publishers deserted all but a few creative writers, making little effort to distribute their works? In a chapter in her work-in-progress entitled 'The Novel in the New Republic,' Cathy Davidson of Michigan State University deftly blends the sense of republican virtue and the instinct for profits that motivated many printers and publishers as she updates and fleshes out William Charvat's model of novelist-reader-publisher relations sketched in his 'Literary Economics and Literary History.' James Barnes has also caught the opportunism among publishers in 'Depressions and Innovation in the British and American Book Trade, 1819–1939.'

The trade restrictions during the War of 1812 excluded most foreign goods from entering American ports, forcing Americans to rely on native manufacturing more than at any time since the disruptions to commerce caused by the American Revolution. The jolt given the economy by the greater reliance on American resources, combined with both the larger urban markets and the surging population into western lands, signaled the beginning of a new era for book production and distribution in the nineteenth century. Enhanced production capabilities for books included the introduction of the stereotype process, steam power, the Fourdrinier machine, and mechanisms for mass producing case bindings that provided the industry with the means to print enough books to meet the new demands. The record for the years before the Civil War is less clear for distribution, and Carl Bode remarks, 'For the publishing industry, production turned out to be less of a problem than distribution. A publisher still had to sell his books. The market was there—indeed, it was growing all the time—but the question was how to reach it expeditiously.'

The brilliant first chapter of William Charvat's *Literary Publishing in America, 1790–1850* presents a thought-provoking thesis about the changes in book distribution caused by the new printing technologies and the expansion of publishers' markets in the nineteenth century, and the role these changes had in the shifting currents of influences on literary taste. Charvat was the first historian to link the transformation of the American book distribution network with that of the American transportation network. *Literary Publishing in America, 1790–1850* was enriched by the outstanding work in transportation history during the late forties and early fifties, notably Robert Albion's *The Rise of the Port of New York, 1815–1860*. Albion and his fellow transportation historians sense upheavals in the economic forces between the eastern and western parts of the country that were set in motion by the completion of the Erie Canal in 1817. Julius Rubin summarizes the canal's revolutionary impact: 'The Canal immediately took over from the turnpike a part of the westward trade and, when the immigrants it transported had built up the northern midwest, it carried their agricultural produce back to the east. For the first time, east and west were linked by a direct two-way trade' (p. 6). New York City's easy access to the canal, in these historians' view, allowed it to spurt ahead of its rivals—Baltimore, Boston, and Philadelphia—as the economic and manufacturing capital of America during the pre-Civil War years.

Charvat adopts the transportation historians' model of the flow of goods and services along the canal for cultural studies; the West provided the East with raw material and the East returned to the West manufactured products. Charvat proposed that books were among the manufactured products the East shipped and that as western consumers made New York City an industrial power so also western readers established New York City as the nation's publishing center. The most adventurous corollary of this thesis about the flow of culture was Charvat's conclusion that the West transmitted taste along the Erie Canal, controlling what the East published by buying some books and spurning others. He wrote, 'Up to 1850, the publishers of the axis [Philadelphia-New York axis] were the discoverers and interpreters of American literary taste and were the channel through which the taste of the South and West moved, to influence—for better or worse—the production of literature on the coast' (p. 37). Charvat's general western reader shaped the national literary sensibility, a reader he characterized as being 'somewhere between the avant garde and the consumers of mass fiction.'

The thesis presented in *Literary Publishing in America, 1790–1850* is fascinating but far from incontrovertible. I know of no one who has directly challenged Charvat's work, but many writers about the history of nineteenth-century publishing proceed from a different set of assumptions. Eugene Exman's description in *The House of Harper* of the founding of Harper's in 1817 makes New York City, not the West, the firm's primary market, stating that on 'these thirty-three booksellers [in New York City] the Harpers pinned their hopes for survival' (p. 7). Henry William Herbert's frustration at having to compete for eastern American readers with English authors is stressed by Luke White Jr. in *Henry William Her-*

bert & the American Publishing Scene, 1831–1858. Eastern publishers were under constant pressure to reprint popular English books quickly and to get them to New York City. White gives an example of how American publishers rushed English books into print: 'On the ship's arrival in New York, the copy would be rushed from the dock to the printers and divided among the speediest compositors. Presses would run night and day until the edition was on the market. Later, publishers even made arrangements to have the type set on shipboard during the voyage' (p. 11). The lapse of a few hours would not have been so crucial if the primary market were still weeks away by barge up the Erie Canal. David Kaser in *Messrs. Carey & Lea of Philadelphia* narrates another race to reprint an English book but adds that the competition was not only in getting the book printed but also in distributing it in New York City. Kaser gives Abraham Hart's account of the event, as recalled by James Derby in *Fifty Years Among American Authors, Books, and Publishers:*

> Mr. Hart says, that on the day it was received, they distributed the sheets of this advance copy [Edward Bulwer-Lytton's *Rienzi, the Last of the Tribunes*] among twelve different printers, in order to produce the book before Harpers put theirs on the market; and by nine o'clock the next morning, the sheets of the whole edition were delivered to the binders, who had the cases already made in shape for binding. That same afternoon 500 complete copies were forwarded to New York booksellers by the mail stage, the only conveyance by which they could reach New York by daylight the following morning, and this could only be accomplished by hiring all the passenger seats. Mr. Hart was the only passenger of the stage that morning, the remaining space in the coach being taken up with Bulwer's 'Rienzi.' The volume was for sale in all the New York bookstores, on the day earlier than Harpers' edition of the same work (p. 551).

Even if one accepts Charvat's conclusion in general, it is clear that some parts of the American publishing industry were intent on shaping the society of the West rather than bending to its whims. Many religious publishers during the pre–Civil War years were charged with bringing religious civilization to the moral wilderness east of the Alleghenies. One of the most remarkable travel accounts in American history, Samuel Mills and Daniel Smith's *Report of a Missionary Tour through that Part of the United States Which Lies West of the Allegany Mountains*, is a catalogue of westerners' moral lapses from community to community in Ohio, Tennessee, and Kentucky. The authors proposed that the salvation of the West was through Bibles and other religious reading matter, pointing out that only one in five westerners had a Bible and that some were forced to wait years to acquire one. Mills and Smith's conclusions sparked the formation of organizations such as the American Tract Society and the American Bible Society. Lawrence Thompson's 'The Printing and Publishing Activities of the American Tract Society from 1825 to 1850,' Creighton Lacy's *The Word-Carrying Giant: The Growth of the American Bible Society (1816–1966)*, and Edwin B. Bronner's 'Distributing the Printed Word: The Tract Association of Friends, 1816–1966' give some idea of the extensive publishing operations of such societies. According to the 1847 *Annual Report of the American Tract Society*, more than 150 million pages of religious tracts were printed during the year. In 1836 the American Bible Society employed thirty-six traveling agents to distribute books. In one year an American Bible Society agent claimed to have distributed almost seven thousand Bibles in Kentucky alone.

The best history of western publishing and distribution, Walter Sutton's *The Western Book Trade: Cincinnati as a Nineteenth-Century Publishing and Book-Trade Center*, arrives at a conclusion strikingly different from Charvat's about the relationship between the eastern and western sections of the country. Sutton argues that the West was insulated from eastern publishers until after the extension of the railroad lines into Ohio during the 1850s. This protective isolation from eastern book exports allowed Cincinnati publishers to establish themselves without competition as suppliers to Ohio and much of the rest of the western territory. Cincinnati's strength as a center for writers and publishers, according to Sutton, fed on a burgeoning sense of a western cultural identity that sought to distinguish itself from the East and on a system of internal improvements that welded the western states together into an economic unit. Cincinnati publishers issued the works of western writers like Daniel Drake that were then distributed by western jobbers and bookstores.

Other studies about the migration of books into newly formed western settlements present a confusing picture. Detroit's early settlers in Wallace Bonk's *Michigan's First Book Store* are interested in British authors, but it is not clear if they gathered books from New York, Philadelphia, or Cincinnati. In Howard Peckham's 'Books and Reading on the Ohio Valley Frontier,' early Ohioans augmented their reading material in new settlements by forming subscription libraries brought by wagons from Philadelphia. Peckham's emigrants tried to recreate the Pennsylvania culture they left behind by importing their former state's books. Louis Wright in *Culture on the Moving Frontier* saw Pittsburgh, at the confluence of the Monongahela and Allegheny rivers, as the staging area for pre-1815 culture in the Ohio Valley. Louis Wright's Ohioans attempted to establish 'a civilized way of life in the British tradition' by buying books from the Pittsburgh bookseller Zadok Cramer. Edward Stevens's methodologically inventive 'Relationships of Social Library Membership, Wealth, and Literary Culture in Early Ohio' garners evidence about the rapid diffusion of literary culture for middle and upper classes on the frontier through subscription libraries, but his study does not raise the question of book migration.

The disagreement about the direction and source of the flow of books, ideas, and culture in the early nineteenth century that is found in the works of Charvat, Sutton, Bonk, Peckham,

Louis Wright, and Stevens originates in part in the lack of scholarly attention given to specific book distribution systems. In spite of the many merits of the histories of nineteenth-century publishing houses, among them Ellen Ballou's *The Building of the House: Houghton Mifflin's Formative Years*, Eugene Exman's *The House of Harper* and *The Brothers Harper*, Warren S. Tryon's *Parnassus Corner: A Life of James T. Field, Publisher to the Victorians*, and David Kaser's *Messrs. Carey & Lea of Philadelphia*, only Walter Sutton's *The Western Book Trade* devotes a significant amount of space to distribution. The resulting difficulty in assigning the proper roles within the trade to retail bookstores, trade auctions, subscription publishers, the use of the mails, and new forms of transportation is inevitable.

The nineteenth-century trade auction is representative of the deficiency in knowledge about much of the system of book distribution in the United States. Held semiannually in Boston, Philadelphia, New York, and other cities, and often lasting for three or four days, the trade sale was a popular method of selling new and older books between 1825 and 1860. Alone among historians of East Coast publishing, John Tebbel includes this method of distribution in his study; but, because he took all of his evidence from the trade journals of publisher associations that were hostile to the practice, Tebbel thinks the trade sale undermined a stable price structure and hindered an effective distribution system. In his view, the trade sale flooded the market with unwanted books that discouraged publishers from issuing more. Looking at western bookselling, Sutton's *The Western Book Trade* takes a more positive view of early nineteenth-century commercial auctions. Sutton thinks that they served 'regional needs by providing Cincinnati publishers and booksellers with a means of distributing books through the Ohio and Mississippi Valley,' although there were abusive practices as time went on. Sutton's and Tebbel's brief discussions of this form of distribution leave many unanswered questions. Were booksellers or jobbers the major buyers at these auctions? What percentage of books in auctions was newly published material? Were schoolbooks or other types of books thought better candidates for these sales, or was the entire spectrum of published works auctioned?

Two dissenting voices are Fred Mitchell Jones's *Middlemen in the Domestic Trade of the United States, 1800–1860* and Warren S. Tryon's 'Book Distribution in Mid-Nineteenth Century America.' Jones's monograph is not restricted to books but addresses the distribution system for all goods in the American economy. Unlike Tebbel and Sutton, Jones does not find the trade sale an aberration but rather a normal and preferred form of dispersing goods for the time, offering the advantage of quick sales of large numbers of products to established customers, which in turn helped regulate credit between producers and retailers. Jones's view is that the trade auction moved the country's economic system further away from local markets dominated by craftsmen and towards a more efficient system for wider sections of the country. A study arriving at a conclusion similar to Jones's is Ira Cohen's 'The Auction System in The Port of New York, 1817–1837.' Using the records of the Boston publishing firm of Ticknor and Fields in 'Book Distribution in Mid-Nineteenth Century America,' Tryon considers the trade sale to have been an insignificant factor in mid-nineteenth-century book distribution but insists that the retail bookstore remained the most important part of the system. Tryon states that 'while many elements of the industrial revolution made up the needs and provided the means for a changing technique in book distribution, the process was channeled through the retail booksellers, which the rising urban movement in American life made effective' (p. 220). Highlighting the local New England market of Ticknor and Fields, Tryon points out that, in 1854, nine hundred of the three thousand copies of the first edition of Mrs. Eliza Otis's *The Barclays of Boston* were sold to Boston booksellers, a finding that confirms part of Charvat's thesis in *Literary Publishing in America, 1790–1850.* Giving a different interpretation of the impact of Boston's reliance on a Massachusetts market, Charvat believes that Boston fell behind New York City as a publishing center because of its dependence on local retail sales, in contrast to New York City's reliance on wholesale purchases. Tryon informs us that the Boston publishers usually shipped books to Cincinnati by first sending them to Philadelphia, where they were then shipped by canal or railroad to Pittsburgh before finally arriving in Cincinnati by steamboat. It was indeed a circuitous route to the interior.

Ticknor and Fields's direct relationship with retailers led the firm to manipulate pricing and aggressively to promote its books for increased distribution. William Charvat's 'James T. Fields and the Beginnings of Book Promotion, 1840–1855' explores the company's practice of inducing booksellers to buy books by offering copies on commission, establishing a policy to buy back unsold books, planning activities such as window displays, and distributing advertising circulars. Sometimes sending as much as ten percent of a book's first printing to newspapers and magazines, James T. Fields resorted to various strategies to influence editors to review his firm's books favorably. For Charvat, nineteenth-century book reviewing was venal and uninformed by any sense of propriety. He explained that 'reviews were, for the most part, short notices, laudatory if the publisher advertised or had influence, libelous if someone on the staff, or some favored outsider, disliked the author or publisher' (p. 79). Despite the fact that such practices were not restricted to Ticknor and Fields and that many publishers expected authors to promote their own books, Charvat's study is the only published one I have encountered for publishers' stakes in nineteenth-century book reviewing. Hazel Pfennig gathers some information about reviews for the works of major authors in her unpublished 'Periodical Literary Criticism (1800–65),' and Nina Baym has produced *Novels, Readers, and Reviewers,* which finds reviewers encouraging fiction.

Trade auctions are evidence that some publishers desired to shift the responsibility for distribution from their shoulders to those of the independent jobbers and retailers. Other publishers built their businesses on effective methods of mass distribution through subscription canvassing and mailing inexpensive paperbacks directly to the customers. Boston's Ticknor and Fields was committed to attracting writers highly regarded by the cultural establishments; but publishers of subscription books and cheap paperbacks found their greatest resource not in their authors' reputations but rather in their ability to reach readers quickly and inexpensively.

Because of the widespread reputation of Albert Johannsen's *The House of Beadle and Adams,* the misconception exists that Beadle and Adams's dime novels, the first of which appeared in 1860, were the first nineteenth-century paperbacks. However, Tebbel's *A History of Book Publishing in the United States* contains a short history of paperback publishing during the 1830s and 1840s (vol. 1, pp. 240–51). The growth of this kind of publishing was rooted in the popular education movement, according to Tebbel, who marks its beginning in 1829 with the establishment of the Boston Society for the Diffusion of Knowledge. The society's campaign to issue inexpensive educational books started in 1831 with the Library of Entertaining Knowledge. Also begun in 1831, Henry Carey's Library of Choice Literature was a venture similar to the Library of Entertaining Knowledge and came out weekly for ten cents in paperback. By 1839, paperback publishers were competing with traditional publishers through pirated reprints—in weekly newspaper formats—of the works of contemporary celebrated British authors such as Charles Dickens. These mammoth weeklies, as they were called, became so popular that the established publishers were forced to lobby the government to prohibit paperback books from being distributed through the mails.

Once this prohibition was in place, the paperbacks' distribution edge was eroded, and they faded in importance. Although Tebbel has provided a useful outline of the major events, the growth of the paperback publishing industry deserves more attention than it has received. The use of the mails to deliver books may have played a far larger role in history than has been realized. Wayne E. Fuller's *The American Mail* quotes the postmaster general's complaint, as early as 1814, that 'the mails were . . . overcrowded with novels and the lighter kind of books for amusement' (p. 119). If such a situation existed in 1814, then a new look at early nineteenth-century publishing and literary history is necessary. Charvat's Ohio River barges, Sutton's western auctions, and Tryon's New England bookstores may have supplied only a portion of the country's books. The flow of publications may be more properly traced along the post roads rather than along river and canal routes.

Researchers should be cautious about uncritically accepting the whole of Charvat's thesis in *Literary Publishing in America, 1790–1850*, as fascinating as it may be. The Erie Canal was only one among many novel methods of reaching out for markets during this time and was by no means the defining force Chavrat makes it out to be. The beginnings of deep cracks in the book distribution system begin to show during the pre–Civil War decades, cracks that would later splinter the industry. Publishers started to transform the book trade from an eighteenth-century version based on personal relations between bookseller-printers and readers to one established on more impersonal arrangements that groped towards defining larger groups spread out over wider geographical areas. Increasingly, higher investments in plants and equipment forced publishers towards regional distribution, although the local basis for distribution continued to exist in very rural areas, as Milton Hamilton points out. Before 1800, a printer looked toward his own city or town to sell books, and, if his imagination envisioned other audiences, special arrangements, such as the subscription form, were required. With the exception of country printers and small publishers in the South who retained their local orientation, this method of dissemination lost its position of importance during the nineteenth century, since publishers needed books that would sell well regionally or in several major markets. As the center of capital formation and manufacturing, with a plentiful supply of labor, blessed by a variety of transportation networks intersecting within its limits, and possessing widely read newspapers that could advertise on a primitively organized national level, New York quickly became the dominant publishing and distribution center for the country. That Boston could remain even remotely competitive was due in large part to the ability of its publishers to deal directly with the many retail outlets in the uniform culture of small towns throughout New England. Boston was to New England what New York was to the nation. Although books did make their way to the interior, their scarcity made them particularly prized, as booksellers' advertisements show. However, for all parts of the country, the magic formula matching books with readers, and both with a method of distribution and pricing, was seldom found before 1850, with the exception of reprints of popular British writers whose reputations created instant markets simultaneously in the largest American cities.

The sale of books by subscription canvassers in rural areas after the Civil War is a form of direct distribution that is outlined in general terms in Marjorie Stafford's 'Subscription Book Publishing in the United States, 1865–1930' and Beverly David's 'Selling the Subscription Book.' By the careful examination of annotations and sales information found in a salesman's sample book, Michael Hackenberg's 'Hawking Subscription Books in 1870: A Salesman's Prospectus from Western Pennsylvania' provides a useful glimpse into the canvassing activities of one agent in Pennsylvania. Walter Sutton's chapter 'Henry Howe: Twenty Thousand Agents Wanted!' in

The Western Book Trade shows Howe's frequent use of traveling agents in Cincinnati during the 1850s. Other publishers deserve the same attention Sutton has given Howe. There is no account of the Hartford subscription publishers for the pre-Civil War period, in spite of the fact that by 1868 they produced an average of 200,000 volumes per year. Although traditional trade publishers characteristically printed only about 2,500 copies of a book and kept a large number of titles in print, subscription book publishers concentrated on fewer titles but issued them in numbers far exceeding those published by the traditional trade. Both Albert Deane Richardson's *Beyond the Mississippi* and Joel Tyler Headley's *The Great Rebellion* sold approximately 150,000 copies by subscription. We have some information about the large numbers involved in soliciting book subscriptions, but this form of publishing and distributing books needs a comprehensive treatment presented in terms of American literary taste and intellectual history. The copies of salesmen's dummies that I have seen suggest that many subscription books were devotional works, travel accounts, self-improvement manuals, general historical works about the Civil War, or biographies of presidential campaigners.

What can be learned about the writers of subscription books? Neither Richardson nor Headley can be found in *The Oxford Companion to American Literature*, and Richardson rates only one sentence in *Literary History of the United States*, in spite of the impressive sales figures for his books. The philosophy of hard work, perseverance, and frugality, exemplified in this period by Horatio Alger's characters, finds additional champions among the most successful book canvassers of the time. In fact, *The Young Book Agent; or Frank Hardy's Road to Success* appeared under Alger's name in 1905. Mixing the gospel of success with a secular spirituality, egalitarianism, and their own company's best interests, managers of subscription book companies advertised that virtually anyone, no matter what his education, experience, or station in life, could achieve financial security through attention to the duties of a book agency. In a booklet sent out to his new agents, J. B. Smiley of Chicago wrote in *Instructions to Canvassers*: 'The basis of all success is *work*—steady, persistent work. The success is generally just in proportion to the amount of labor and thought given to the business. It is worse than folly to expect any success *without* work. With work, success can be attained. Anyone who resolves to canvass, as they would follow any other business, six or eight hours a day for one straight week, will succeed nineteen times out of twenty, if they can follow directions.'

Frank Compton's *Subscription Books* describes book agents as Civil War veterans, but this is not an encompassing description. Many of the memoirs of book agents were by women, such as the anonymously written *Facts, by a Woman*, *Annie Nelles; or, the Life of a Book Agent*, Mendell and Hosmer's *Notes of Travel and Life*, and Mrs. J. W. Likins's *Six Years Experience as a Book Agent*. These works are a particularly fascinating genre of nineteenth-century literature. Most books aimed at female audiences were light novels or fashionable romances in domestic settings. In the face of this frothy fare, the accounts of the female agents stand out in their depiction of earnest, hard-working women who acknowledge that their way of life causes them to be spurned by polite female society, understand that they do not have the access to society's modes of self-improvement enjoyed by men, but nevertheless press resolutely onward to take a defiant pride in their ultimate success. Their stories often begin with some devastating tragedy that deprives the author of house and home, forcing her to depend only upon her own exertions for support and consequently isolating her from the rest of society.

In *Annie Nelles; or, the Life of a Book Agent*, Nelles's mother, father, and siblings die, and the family plantation in Georgia is seized by a wicked stepfather. In Mrs. J.W. Likins's *Six Years Experience as a Book Agent*, Mrs. Likins opens her account with the forced sale of the family home. These traumatic events, which in each case symbolize the women's break with their traditional role in the community, cast them at the threshold of despair. At this crucial moment, an encounter with an advertisement recruiting agent proves to be the fortunate vehicle that leads them out of the dire straits in which they find themselves. Mrs. Likins remembers landing in San Francisco on August 11, 1868, as follows: 'Now begins the one great struggle of my life. I scarcely know where to turn or what to do. As I look around the room, I see nothing but want and poverty on every hand. Bidding my dear ones keep up courage . . . , I started for the Post-office. Not being able to pay car hire, I went on foot. On my way I passed the book-store of H. H. Bancroft, then on the corner of Montgomery and Merchant street. In the window I noticed a card with the words "Agents Wanted" on it' (p. 52).

The anonymous author of *Facts, by a Woman* offers a strikingly similar scenario:

> Debating the question of ways and means, I hopelessly sat till my blood became chilled. Coldly shivering, I arose at last to wrap me away into deeper covering of my blanketed bed. I clad myself in my sleeping-gown and was woefully engaged in extinguishing the gas which gave a delicate light, through the dignified fixture of a tallow candle, and where, by its persistent obstinacy and repeated refusal to cease its bluish and sickening flame of existence, through a coinciding spirit with my own. I was prompted instinctively to pick up a city newspaper . . . , [and] I was instantly thrown into complete respiration and retroaction. It was a simple announcement, an advertisement only, of A. Roman & Co., who wanted agents to canvass 'Tom Sawyer, Mark Twain's new book' (pp. 34–35).

Although it is difficult not to suppress a smile at the tone of these passages, which almost seem to recall a divine visitation, it is important not to let their symbolic importance elude us. Unlike the typical Alger story in which a stroke of luck elevates a sincere, ambitious boy to a world of better things, or the similar tale aimed at girls in which a young lady in impoverished circumstances marries the shopowner's son, the female book agents arrive at their good fortune solely by their own ability and industry. These autobiographies serve as effective counters to the fantasy world of the American 'strive-and-succeed' novel, and they remind their readers in vivid terms that achievement can be a bruising experience.

The market for subscription books is also not yet fully defined. Recounting his legal battles with the subscription house of Pollard and Moss in *Memoirs of a Publisher, 1865–1915*, George Haven Putnam gives his opinion about the composition of the market for subscription books. After the copyright for many of Washington Irving's works held by Putnam's firm expired, Pollard and Moss brought out an abridged version of Irving's writing. Putnam was not successful in legally preventing the sale of the Pollard and Moss edition and in his memoir argues that the distribution of the abridged edition substantially hurt the sales of his firm's authorized publication. Putnam assumed that the markets for his books and the Pollard and Moss subscription books were the same. However, a view different from and more credible than Putnam's is available in Hamlin Hill's *Mark Twain's Letters to His Publisher, 1867–1894*. Clemens thought the markets did not overlap. Hill quotes Clemens about his decision to publish travel books with subscription houses rather than with traditional publishing firms. In Clemens's view, 'Harper publishes very high-class books and they go to people who are accustomed to read. That class are surfeited with travel-books. But there is a vast class that isn't—the factory hands and the farmers. *They* never go to a bookstore; they have to be hunted down by the canvasser. When a subscription book of mine sells 60,000, I always think I know whither 50,000 of them went. They went to people who don't visit bookstores' (p. 7).

Hamlin Hill's *Mark Twain and Elisha Bliss* and *Mark Twain's Letters to His Publishers*, Arthur Vogelbeck's 'The

Literary Reputation of Mark Twain in America, 1869–1885,' Samuel Webster's *Mark Twain, Business Man*, and Leon Dickinson's 'Marketing a Best Seller: Mark Twain's "Innocents Abroad"' establish Samuel Clemens's reputation as the best-known subscription book writer. Among Clemens's books sold by subscription agents were *The Adventures of Tom Sawyer* (1876), *Following the Equator* (1897), *The Gilded Age* (1874), *The Innocents Abroad* (1869), *Roughing It* (1872), *The Adventures of Huckleberry Finn* (1885), *The American Claimant* (1892), and *A Connecticut Yankee in King Arthur's Court* (1889). Clemens was an anomaly because most novelists who wanted critics and reviewers to take their work seriously avoided subscription houses, thinking they were held in low repute and would taint their books' reception. Bryant Morey French in *Mark Twain and the Gilded Age* quotes a Boston *Literary World* editor's remark in 1874 that 'subscription books are in bad odor and cannot possibly circulate among the best classes of readers, owing to the general and not unfounded prejudice against them as a class' (pp. 10–11).

The fascinating thesis of Arthur Vogelbeck's 'The Literary Reputation of Mark Twain in America, 1869–1875' is that the sale of Clemens's books by subscription adversely affected his literary reputation among his contemporaries. Since subscription publishing houses did not usually send advance copies of books to newspapers and magazines for review, many of Clemens's books got little attention from the press. Vogelbeck also proposes that some critics dismissed Clemens's novels because of prejudice against books sold by subscription. Citing the case of *The Stolen White Elephant*, Vogelbeck argues that this comparatively minor work received more reviews than the popular and critically acclaimed *The Adventures of Huckleberry Finn* only because *The Stolen White Elephant* was published by the established firm of J. R. Osgood, whereas *The Adventures of Huckleberry Finn* was sold by subscription. A *Chicago Tribune* critic remarked about the publication of *The Stolen White Ele-*

phant that 'this time he has done as other authors do, and placed his work in the hands of a respectable publisher.' Not only Clemens's reputation but also his writing was altered by the decision to distribute his books by subscription. Hamlin Hill's 'The People's Author,' in *Mark Twain and Elisha Bliss*, shows how Clemens employed anecdotes to lengthen his books so that they would be well received by typical subscription book purchasers.

Those interested in the stratification and the dispersal of ideas and culture in the last half of the nineteenth-century may discover that study of the forms of book distribution methods are the best evidence of the readership and circulation of books. Because books were scarce during the eighteenth century and their ownership better documented, there are more points of access available and a higher degree of precision possible for this early period than for the nineteenth century. David Lundberg and Henry May's 'The Enlightened Reader in America' and Mel Gorman's 'Gassendi in America' are two studies on the eighteenth-century based on evidence that historians who deal with the mountains of literature and people in the nineteenth century must envy. The Lundberg and May work analyzes 261 personal collections, library catalogues, and booksellers' list in order to count the appearances of British and European writers associated with the Enlightenment. Lundberg and May acknowledge that in the strictest statistical sense their analysis is flawed, because it gives equal weight to a title remaining unsold on a bookseller's shelf and one in a circulating library that was read by a score of people. Nevertheless, the fact that Charles Rollin's and Hugh Blair's books occur far more frequently than those of Montesquieu and Joseph Priestley should give American intellectual historians of the period some pause. Mel Gorman's 'Gassendi in America' examines extant copies of Pierre Gassendi's books on astronomy for ownership marks, the appearance of titles in library catalogues, and adaptations of his theories in textbooks and almanacs as guides to this seventeenth-century scientist's reputation in America.

The enormous increases in readers and publishers in the nineteenth century makes the use of Gorman's and May and Lundberg's research strategies unlikely if not impossible. Books were too common to be listed by title in wills after 1800, and personal and institutional library catalogues are not useful measures for many of the cheap books published. A book's method of distribution may be the only evidence for a guess about its readership and the approximate number of copies printed. It is seldom possible to know exactly who read many books; but further research about distribution practice will allow intelligent speculation about the characteristics of typical readers and the role of books in sociointellectual history.

If the use of the mails to deliver paperbacks, subscription publications, and materials in trade auctions has not yet received its due from historians of the book, the formation of an orderly wholesale network has gone virtually unnoticed. 'The Machinery of Wholesale Distribution,' in Donald Sheehan's *This Was Publishing*, is a rare attempt to understand the role of independent jobbers and commercial travelers in nineteenth-century book distribution. Sheehan notes that wholesale independent jobbers like the American News Company distributed some books, among them *Mark Twain's Sketches*, but the companies devoted more time to magazine distribution. The American News Company's role during the nineteenth century is not certain, but it is a powerful force in the twentieth century. The firm's *Serving the Reading Public* claims that its book department was responsible for the sale of twenty to thirty-five percent of most popular books, including more than one million copies of Margaret Mitchell's *Gone With the Wind.*

Unlike subscription agents, who operated on a retail level, commercial travelers sold books wholesale to retail outlets. They helped distribute books by ensuring smooth relations between publishers and bookstores concerning ordering instructions, transportation, prices, and credit. By hiring commercial travelers, the traditional trade publishers became more aggressive about book distribution and ceased shifting the burden to others. As early as 1869 there existed a Society of Commercial Travellers with the purpose of advancing the common interest of commercial travelers from several New York City publishing houses. In *The System of Commercial Travelling in Europe and the United States*, members of this society argue that they are not subscription canvassers and should be exempt from the many state and municipal laws prohibiting drummers or peddlers. More needs to be known about these commercial travelers, how they operated, the books they sold, the markets they served, and the influence they exerted on the editors of the firms that employed them. Although the Society of Commercial Travellers was short-lived, a similar organization, the Brotherhood of Commercial Travellers, was organized in 1884. The status of commercial travelers quickly increased in publishing companies during the nineteenth century and by the early twentieth century they were among the most powerful figures in the industry.

A closer look at the wholesale network gives the clue to the direction taken by the machinery of distribution during the last half of the nineteenth century. During the eighteenth and early nineteenth centuries, geography had always been the publishers' enemy in distributing their books. Publishers and printers continually strived to conquer the problem of distance, fretting about getting books from Boston to small New England towns, or from Philadelphia to New York, or from New York to Ohio. Scholarship on the period after the mid-nineteenth century has always followed Charvat in assuming that geography remained the central worry of publishers and distributors. However, to proceed along these lines is to miss the most important trend in the distribution network, a development that in the end would shape the world of twentieth-century publishing. As the nineteenth century moved on, large-scale publishers shifted their attention from overcoming geography to identifying common consumer groups in diverse areas. These consumer groups, which Daniel Boorstin calls 'statistical communities' in *The Americans: The Democratic Experience*, had similar interests to which publishers could tailor their products. Here was the answer to the search for the widest possible distribution of books: tightly-bunched markets replicated in city after city, with many local retail distribution points that were easily accessible by the expanding mechanized transportation network being built after the Civil War. In a sense, newspaper publishers had discovered this strategy long before book publishers happened upon it. Even early in the nineteenth century, newspapers associated with political parties or religious or reform movements circulated well in multiple cities or even regional areas because they spoke to captive, well-defined audiences.

One of the first classes of readers to be identified as a consumer market for books were women, whose role as portents of the publishing revolution has not been fully appreciated. Fred Lewis Pattee in *The Feminine Fifties* was a pioneer in recognizing the cultural phenomena of women writers and readers at midcentury. For many years Pattee's was the last word on this subject, but the recent rise in interest in women's studies has produced questions about Pattee's conclusions without diminishing the importance of his observation that women readers were a potent audience for a large segment of the publishing industry. Mary Kelley's *Private Women, Public Stage* is an adept account of Hawthorne's 'scribbling women' that neatly ties the influence of the publishers with the careers of the writers. Leaving aside the current debate about whether these women writers were revolting against the imposed constraints on their lives, or whether they were simply blindly following a blatantly sentimental stereotype, the fact remains that as a group they contributed a formulaic literature that deliberately aimed at a specific national strata of the population. Before this time, even New York publishers had not thought routinely on a national scale. In 'The Domestic Novel as a Commercial Commodity: Making a Best Seller in the 1850s,' Susan Geary highlights the use of advertising schemes by publishers to produce large sales. Geary astutely observes that the publishing industry adjusted its marketing, advertising, and distribution budgets to fit best sellers, leaving other books to fend for themselves. For example, publishers offered bigger discounts to retailers if they purchased in large quantities. Since such a plan increased booksellers' profits for books that were ordered in bulk, these few titles drew a disproportionate amount of attention. The result was, according to Geary, 'an ever narrowing channel because of the self-limiting mechanism of the best seller syndrome, first because the few books achieved popularity at the expense of the many, then because those few books set the pattern for others' (p. 392).

The most important and vigorous elements in the post–Civil War period, story papers and dime novels, followed the lead of the publishers of feminine fiction of the 1850s. Story papers were novels, in most cases romantic fiction, that were printed in newspaper format and achieved a circulation in many instances of more than 100,000, dwarfing most other forms of book publishing. Occasionally, works long out of print, such as *Charlotte Hall* or *Emma*, would be issued as a story paper and would compile sale statistics far in excess of their original hardbound editions. It was as if the format and the access to the distribution mechanisms alone were able to transform any unknown commodity to a best seller. Dime novels, small cheaply printed paperbacks that contained sensational western stories, were equally successful in selling large numbers of copies.

Raymond Shove's *Cheap Book Production in the United States, 1870 to 1891* and Albert Johannsen's excellent *The House of Beadle and Adams* hint at the energy of the paperback industry after the Civil War but cannot cover the vast amount of literature and the dispersed and diverse audiences. Johannsen's book has enhanced the reputation of paperbacks related to the American West, but other types of books were printed. Who were the readers of the reprinted classics in the Munro Library or the Seaside Library, to mention only two examples? J. S. Ogilvie, John Lovell, and George Munro, the titans of the paperback trade, do not yet have adequate biographies. Little about the distribution of paperbacks is known. Johannsen writes that dime novels were read by 'bankers, and bootblacks, clergymen and clerks, lawyers and lawbreakers, workmen and tramps, work girls and girls of leisure, soldiers and sailors, President Lincoln and President Wilson, Soapy Sam and Slippery Frank, men and boys, drummers and other train travelers, Henry Ward Beecher, Chief Justice Fuller, and a host of others' (vol. 1, p. 9). To claim that these books were read by everyone leaves unanswered the question of their primary audience and method of distribution.

Despite the difference between their typical subjects, the story papers and the dime novels were united in their strategy for capturing large audiences. In *Villains Galore,* Mary Noel reveals the basic strategy employed for producing popular fiction. Noel writes, 'Story-paper world, like the real world of the nineteenth century America, was governed by conventions. . . . Again and again the helpless authors of story-paper plots used the accepted, time-worn devices to accomplish their devious ends. The forged letter, the birthmark, the drug that would give the semblance of death, the accidental meeting, the two unrelated characters who looked exactly alike, all these aids were not only indispensable, they were desirable in themselves. A story without them was hardly acceptable' (p. 144). Readers of dime novels also demanded consistency of narrative structure and familiarity of characterization. The hero of the dime novel literature seems to transcend the genre by sheer force of repetition to enter an almost mythic plateau that expresses an important strain of the American spirit. In *The Dime Novel Western,* Daryl Jones finds that the plot requirements of the dime novel were different from popular romances but that the necessity of following unstated rules and formulas was just as essential for success.

Although much remains to be learned about the distribution of these two forms of literature, there are some indications that they took advantage of the existing newspaper outlets that used national periodical distribution services such as the American News Service or Dexter & Brother. The more books became like newspapers or magazines, the wider was their distribution and the greater the profits they chalked up for their publishers. Once publishers discovered the easy access to this large audience, the more they relied on it, encouraging works that would satisfy its readers. Formula plots once established were endlessly repeated in order to fulfill the expectations of the readers who had previously purchased dime novels. The desire to encourage innovative literature was subordinated to the need to produce books with which the mass market audience felt comfortable. Advertising was diverted to trying to establish a brand-name loyalty to certain series and authors. Publishers endeavored to keep alive some authors' names such as those of Bertha Clay, Nick Carter, and Ned Buntline long after the stories offered under them were written in-house by many hands. Packaging became more and more important as publishers used dramatic and colorful graphics in their advertisements and on the covers of their books to spark customers' interest. Series were invented that would enable buyers to quickly identify the type of story that they might find. Examples are Beadle's Dime Baseball Players, DeWitt's Stories of the Sea, Factory Life Library, Munro's New York Boys' Library, Ogilvie's Railroad Edition, Soldiers' and Sailors' Dime Library, Young Athletes' Weekly, and the Vatican Library. All efforts were geared to allow a reader to make an instantaneous decision to buy on the basis of a quick glance at a book's cover rather than on the basis of a review, knowledge of the quality of a book's contents, or on the literary reputation of an author.

In a work-in-progress, Jean Masteller of Whitman College analyzes one category of story paper and dime novel fiction, the working-girl story. At the end of the nineteenth century, young women flocked to cities to find jobs, and publishers soon identified them as a potential new market. Masteller finds that there was a separate band of writers who devised novels with a new pattern of conventions in plot and characterization for this growing audience. These writers, who sometimes worked for several companies but seldom varied their story lines, produced books that at once appealed to these women's romantic dreams of escape from the drudgery of their lives and also their anger at the conditions in which they found themselves. The result was a long series of books like Laura Jean Libbey's *Leonie Locke; or, The Romance of a Beautiful New York Working Girl*, Francis Smith's *Bertha, the Sewing Machine Girl*, and *Maggie, the Factory Girl*. Masteller's work helps document how story paper and dime novel publishers created a new formula to fit an emerging class of urban readers.

In *Books: the Culture and Commerce of Publishing*, Coser, Kadushin, and Powell show convincing evidence that today's American publishing scene is increasingly dominated by chains of large, discount bookstores, impersonal multinational corporations, and nonliterary public relations agents. As this study points out, the result of this domination is a generic literature of books shaped by the tyranny of easy distribution channels. In a remarkable chapter, 'Books Without Authors,' they describe publishing factories that first try to identify a large, predictable, and easily accessible audience and then commission a book from a sometimes anonymous writer for these readers. Calling the product of these writing factories 'non-books,' they write, 'Non-books are to real books what frozen TV dinners are to home-cooked meals. They are not the creations of individual authors; they are much more like products manufactured on an assembly line. Non-books have assumed such an importance in the publishing industry that to ignore them would seriously distort a picture of its workings' (p. 260). One need look no further than the story papers and dime novels for the roots of this contemporary publishing phenomena as outlined by Coser, Kadushin, and Powell. During the last half of the nineteenth century, the publishing industry began to turn in a new direction through the driving momentum of George and Norman Munro, Irwin and Erastus Beadle, and Robert Bonner. Ironically, publishers' accomplishments in establishing a distribution system increasingly held them captives of their own successes. In order to maintain profit margins, dime novel and story paper publishers sought or commissioned books that they knew would be well received by the mass market reader that they so efficiently reached. In many ways, distribution began to shape the types of books being produced in a large segment of the publishing world.

Individuals such as Henry Holt, William Appleton, James Harper, Charles Scribner, and George Putnam stood apart from this trend and self-consciously styled themselves as gatekeepers of the country's culture. They scorned the commercialism in their business and mourned the death of the gentlemanly agreements on which many of their publishing decisions had been based. They saw the established retail bookstore as their primary outlet and prided themselves on producing quality books. They lamented other publishers' efforts to take over bookstores across the country in order to create a virtual vertical monopoly in the book trade. But it was clear even to them that their efforts to turn the tide of mass market publishing were futile, and they settled into a resigned coexistence with many of their colleagues. The memoirs they produced at the end of their lives are full of remorse and disparaging remarks about the state of the trade. In *Sixty Years as a Publisher*, Henry Holt effectively expresses this sentiment for the group: 'I see little in the present [1910] conditions of the trade that gives me much satisfaction or hope—little but exaggerated competition in royalties, advances, discounts, drumming and advertising, all of which has brought the trade to a point where it takes many times as much effort and many times as much capital to make a dollar, as it did when I began business. . . . But, take it all in all, my main hope for the future is that things must move—and as they cannot get very much lower than they are at present, possibly there may be a return, if even a forced one, toward the old spirit of co-operation, self-restraint, and self-respect' (p. 212).

In summary, the book industry splintered at the end of the nineteenth century with many of the fragments regrouping according to modes of distribution. Publishing houses based their choice of books and their method of operations on their adopted form of distribution and, consequently, the type of reader to which each wanted to appeal.

The literature of the history of book distribution in America has been astonishingly ahistorical in character. Many researchers have mined narrow, albeit rich, veins seemingly without a sense that they followed any tradition of scholarship or without rising to a level of generalizationthat would enable them to distinguish the fundamental difference between their conclusions and those expressed by others in the field. The purposes of this essay are several: to assemble the scattered secondary sources about book distribution in America; to begin to sharpen some of the differences in the literature; to give a general coherent outline of the main trends of book distribution that later writers can expand, challenge, or amend; to highlight a few of the areas needing further investigation as they have occurred to me; and to clarify several of the themes available to prospective researchers. A short catalogue of themes includes: speed of cultural transmission; relationship of types of literature, classes of readers, and forms of distribution; the importance of crucial individuals such as the London factors in the eighteenth century; the effects of general economic conditions; the impact of government legislation and the activities of organizations like the American Bible Society;

the effects of general economic conditions on the distribution of specific forms of books; how distribution affects authors' and books' reputations or even genres of literature; portals or spheres of geographical influence; the relationship between printing technologies and distribution networks; and the influence of the landscape and transportation systems on distribution. In this essay, each theme is associated with a specific period of American history, but all are not restricted to this chronology. There are examples of seamless webs of readers for nineteenth-century studies as well as those that I have discussed for the seventeenth century. I have used Samuel Clemens's publishing practices as one instance of how distribution can affect a book's content and an author's literary standing; others could have been chosen. Books that are circulated clandestinely may come to symbolize change in a community. Ronald Story's 'Class and Culture in Boston: The Athenaeum, 1807–1860' and Agnes Cleaveland's *No Life for a Lady*, a narrative of a woman's experience on the late nineteenth-century frontier, both illustrate how the acquisition of books represents tradition, authority, or power in radically different circumstances.

Some topics are omitted in this discussion because so little has been accomplished relating to them. Among these are the distribution of books in the Confederate States and in the far West. A recent work on colportage in the South is Gorrell Prim's 'Born Again in the Trenches: Revivalism in the Confederate Army.' Frank Freidel's 'The Loyal Publication Society: A Pro-Union Propaganda Agency' is a rare effort to cast some light on the circulation of pamphlets during the Civil War. Freidel adds some new information about this subject in the introduction to his *Union Pamphlets of the Civil War, 1861–1865*. There exists no detailed discussion of the relationship between price and distribution for American books. I have not strayed far into the thickets of the controversy of whether the act of reading and the book itself are associated only with an elite class, although those interested can discover a survey of this literature in Jennifer Tebbe's 'Print and American Culture' and David Hall's 'The World of Print and Collective Mentality in Seventeenth-Century New England,' in John Higham and Paul Conkin's *New Directions in American Intellectual History*. So much remains to explore in all areas that it is perhaps sanguine to expect a balanced and complete history of book distribution before 1876 in the foreseeable future. However, the lack of such an encapsulation is of little consequence, as long as we have the stimulus of informed differences of opinion as expressed by imaginative writers like Sutton and Charvat who investigate book distribution with a sensitivity to the economics of the trade but with full attention to the book's place in all levels of American intellectual society.

List of Secondary References

Adams, Thomas. *The American Controversy: A Bibliographical Study of the British Pamphlets about the American Disputes, 1764–1783*. Providence and New York: Brown University and the Bibliographical Society of America, 1980.

———. *American Independence: The Growth of an Idea*. Providence: Brown University Press, 1965.

Albion, Robert. *The Rise of the Port of New York, 1815–1860*. New York: Charles Scribner's Sons, 1939.

American News Company. *Serving the Reading Public: America's Leading Distributor of Books, Magazines, and Newspapers Celebrates 80 Years of Growth*. New York: American News Company, 1944.

Bailyn, Bernard. *Education in the Forming of American Society: Needs and Opportunities for Study*. Chapel Hill: University of North Carolina Press, 1960.

———. *The Ideological Origins of the American Revolution*. Cambridge: Harvard University, Belknap Press, 1967.

Ballou, Ellen. *The Building of the House: Houghton Mifflin's Formative Years*. Boston: Houghton Mifflin Co., 1970.

Barber, Bernard. 'Social Stratification.' *International Encyclopedia of the Social Sciences* 15 (1967):288–95.

Barber, Giles. 'Books from the Old World and for the New: The British International Trade in Books in the Eighteenth Century.' *Studies on Voltaire and the Eighteenth Century* 151 (1976):185–224.

Barnes, James. J. 'Depression and Innovation in the British and American Book Trade, 1819–1939.' In *Books and Society in History*, ed. Kenneth E. Carpenter. New York: R. R. Bowker Co., 1983.

Baxter, William T. *The House of Hancock: Business in Boston, 1724–1775.* Cambridge: Harvard University Press, 1945.

Baym, Nina. *Novels, Readers, and Reviewers: Responses to Fiction in Antebellum America.* Ithaca: Cornell University Press, 1984.

Beard, Charles. *An Economic Interpretation of the Constitution of the United States.* New York: Macmillan Co., 1913.

Blumenthal, Joseph. *The Printed Book in America.* Boston: David R. Godine Publisher, Inc., 1977.

Bode, Carl. *The Anatomy of American Popular Culture, 1840–1861.* Berkeley: University of California Press, 1959.

Bonk, Wallace. *Michigan's First Book Store: A Study of the Books Sold in the Detroit Book Store, 1817–1828.* Ann Arbor: Department of Library Science, University of Michigan, 1957.

Boorstin, Daniel. *The Americans: The Democratic Experience.* New York: Random House, Inc. 1973.

Botein, Stephen. 'The Anglo-American Book Trade before 1776: Personnel and Strategies.' In *Printing and Society in Early America*, eds. William L. Joyce et al. Worcester, Mass.: American Antiquarian Society, 1983.

Boynton, Henry. *Annals of American Bookselling, 1638–1850.* New York: John Wiley and Sons Inc., 1932.

Bradsher, Earl. *Mathew Carey, Editor, Author and Publisher.* New York: Columbia University Press, 1912.

Brant, Irving. *James Madison the Nationalist, 1780–1787.* Indianapolis: The Bobbs-Merrill Co. Inc., 1948.

Bronner, Edwin. 'Distributing the Printed Word: The Association of Friends, 1816–1966.' *Pennsylvania Magazine of History and Biography* 91(1967):342–54.

Butterfield, Lyman. 'The American Interests of the Firm of E. and C. Dilly, with the Letters to Benjamin Rush.' *Papers of the Bibliographical Society of America* 45(1951):283–332.

Cannon, Carl. *American Book Collectors and Collecting from Colonial Times to the Present.* New York: H. W. Wilson Co., 1941.

Charvat, William. 'James T. Fields and the Beginning of Book Promotion, 1840–1855.' *Huntington Library Quarterly* 8 (1944):75–94.

———. Literary Economics and Literary History. In *English Institute Essays,* ed. Alan S. Downer. New York: Columbia University Press, 1950.

———. *Literary Publishing in America, 1790–1850.* Philadelphia: University of Pennsylvania Press, 1959.

Cleaveland, Agnes. *No Life for a Lady.* Boston: Houghton Mifflin Co., 1941.

Cohen, Ira. 'The Auction System in the Port of New York, 1817–1838.' *Business History Review* 45(1971):488–510.

Colbourn, H. Trevor. 'Jefferson's Use of the Past.' *William and Mary Quarterly* 15(1958):56–70.

———. *The Lamp of Experience: Whig History and the Intellectual Origins of the American Revolution.* Chapel Hill: University of North Carolina Press, 1965.

Cometti, Elizabeth. 'Some Early Bestsellers in Piedmont, North Carolina.' *North Carolina Historical Review* 16(1950):324–37.

Compton, Frank E. *Subscription Books.* New York: New York Public Library, 1939.

Coser, Lewis A., Charles Kadushin, and Walter W. Powell. *Books: The Culture & Commerce of Publishing.* New York: Basic Books, Inc., Publishers, 1982.

Curti, Merle. *The Growth of American Thought.* New York: Harper and Row Publishers Inc., 1964.

David, Beverly. 'Selling the Subscription Book.' *Hayes Historical Journal* 1(1977):192–200.

Davis, Richard Beale. *Intellectual Life in the Colonial South, 1585–1763*. Knoxville: University of Tennessee Press, 1978.

Derby, James. *Fifty Years Among American Authors, Books, and Publishers*. New York: G. W. Carleton and Co., 1884.

Dickinson, Leon T. 'Marketing a Bestseller: Mark Twain's "Innocents Abroad." ' *Papers of the Bibliographical Society of America* 41(1947):107–22.

Dolan, J. R. *The Yankee Peddlers of Early America*. New York: Clarkson N. Potter Inc., 1964.

Dozer, Donald Marquant. 'The Tariff on Books.' *Mississippi Valley Historical Review* 36(1949):73–96.

Essays Honoring Lawrence Wroth. Portland, Me.: Printed by Southworth-Anthoensen Press, 1951.

Exman, Eugene, *The Brothers Harper: A Unique Publishing Partnership and Its Impact on the Cultural Life of America from 1817 to 1853*. New York: Harper and Row Publishers Inc., 1965.

———. *The House of Harper; One Hundred and Fifty Years of Publishing*. New York: Harper and Row Publishers Inc., 1967.

Facts, by a Woman. Oakland, Calif.: Pacific Press Publishing House, 1881.

Farren, Donald. 'Subscription: A Study of the Eighteenth-Century American Book Trade.' Ph.D. diss., Columbia University, 1982.

Fiering, Norman. 'The Transatlantic Republic of Letters: A Note on the Circulation of Learned Periodicals.' *William and Mary Quarterly*, 3d ser. 33(1976):642–60.

Ford, Worthington Chauncey. *The Boston Book Market, 1679–1700*. Boston: The Club of Odd Volumes, 1917.

———. 'Henry Knox and the London Book-Store, 1771–1774.' *Proceedings of the Massachusetts Historical Society* 61(1927–28):225–303.

Franklin, Benjamin. *The Autobiography*. Boston: Houghton Mifflin Co., 1923.

Freidel, Frank. 'The Loyal Publication Society: A Pro-Union Propaganda Agency.' *Mississippi Valley Historical Review* 26 (1939):359–76.

———. *Union Pamphlets of the Civil War, 1861–1865.* Cambridge: Harvard University Press, 1967.

French, Bryant Morey. *Mark Twain and The Gilded Age, the Book That Named an Era.* Dallas: Southern Methodist University Press, 1965.

Fries, Waldemar. *The Double Elephant Folio: The Story of Audubon's Birds of America.* Chicago: American Library Association, 1973.

Fuller, Wayne E. *The American Mail: Enlarger of the Common Life.* Chicago: University of Chicago Press, 1972.

Geary, Susan. 'The Domestic Novel as a Commercial Commodity: Making a Best Seller in the 1850s.' *Papers of the Bibliographical Society of America* 70(1976):365–93.

Gilreath, James. 'Mason Weems, Mathew Carey, and the Southern Booktrade, 1794–1810.' *Publishing History* 10(1981):27–49.

———. 'Sowerby Revirescent and Revised.' *Papers of the Bibliographical Society of America* 78(1984):219–32.

Gimbel, Richard. *Thomas Paine: A Bibliographical Check List of Common Sense.* New Haven: Yale University Press, 1956.

Gordon, George. *Anglo-American Literary Relations.* London: Oxford University Press, 1942.

Gorman, Mel. 'Gassendi in America.' *Isis* 55(1964):409–17.

Hackenberg, Michael. 'Hawking Subscription Books in 1870: A Salesman's Prospectus from Western Pennsylvania.' *Papers of the Bibliographical Society of America* 78(1984):137–53.

Hallenbeck, Chester. 'Book-Trade Publicity before 1800.' *Papers of the Bibliographical Society of America* 32(1938):47–56.

Hamilton, Milton. *The Country Printer, New York State, 1785–1830.* New York: Columbia University Press, 1936.

Harlan, Robert. A Colonial Printer as Bookseller in Eighteenth-Century Philadelphia: The Case of David Hall. In *Studies in Eighteenth-Century Culture*, ed. Ronald C. Rosbottom, vol. 5. Madison: University of Wisconsin Press, 1976.

———. 'David Hall and the Stamp Act.' *Papers of the Bibliographical Society of America* 61(1967):13–37.

———. 'David Hall and the Townsend Acts.' *Papers of the Bibliographical Society of America* 68(1974):19–37.

———. 'David Hall's Bookshop and Its British Sources of Supply.' In *Books in America's Past: Essays Honoring Rudolph H. Gjelsness*, ed. David Kaser. Charlottesville: University Press of Virginia, 1966.

———. 'William Strahan's American Book Trade, 1744–76.' *Library Quarterly* 21(1961):235–44.

Harris, Michael, and Donald G. Davis. *American Library History: A Bibliography*. Austin: University of Texas Press, 1978.

Hart, James. *The Oxford Companion to American Literature*. New York: Oxford University Press, 1965.

Henretta, James A. 'Economic Development and Social Structure in Colonial Boston.' *William and Mary Quarterly*, 3d ser. 22(1965):75–92.

Higham, John, ed. *New Directions in American Intellectual History*. Baltimore: Johns Hopkins University Press, 1979.

Hill, Hamlin. *Mark Twain and Elisha Bliss*. Columbia: University of Missouri Press, 1964.

———, ed. *Mark Twain's Letters to His Publishers, 1867–1894*. Berkeley: University of California Press, 1967.

Hindle, Brooke. *The Pursuit of Science in Revolutionary America, 1735–1789*. Chapel Hill: University of North Carolina Press, 1956.

Holt, Henry. *Sixty Years as a Publisher*. London: Allen and Unwin, Ltd., [1934].

Howells, William Dean. *The Rise of Silas Lapham*. New York: Limited Editions Club, 1961.

Isaac, Rhys. *The Transformation of Virginia, 1740–1790*. Chapel Hill: University of North Carolina Press, 1982.

Jensen, Merrill. *The American Revolution Within*. New York: New York University Press, 1974.

Johannsen, Albert. *The House of Beadle and Adams and Its Dime and Nickel Novels.* Norman: University of Oklahoma Press, 1950–62.

Jones, Daryl. *The Dime Novel Western.* Bowling Green, Ohio: Popular Press, Bowling Green State University, 1978.

Jones, Fred Mitchell. *Middlemen in the Domestic Trade of the United States, 1800–1860.* Urbana: University of Illinois Press, 1937.

Jones, Howard Mumford. 'The Importation of French Books in Philadelphia.' *Modern Philology* 32(1934):157–77.

———. 'The Importation of French Literature in New York City, 1750–1800.' *Studies in Philology* 38(1931):237–51.

Kaser, David. *A Book for a Sixpence: The Circulating Library in America.* Pittsburgh: Beta Phi Mu, 1980.

———. *Messrs. Carey and Lea of Philadelphia: A Study in the History of the Booktrade.* Philadelphia: University of Pennsylvania Press, 1957.

Kelley, Mary. *Private Women, Public Stage: Literary Domesticity in Nineteenth-Century America.* New York: Oxford University Press, 1984.

Kimball, LeRoy. 'An Account of Hocquet Caritat, XVIII Century New York Circulating Librarian, Bookseller, and Publisher.' *Colophon* 18(1934): n.p.

Korty, Margaret. *Benjamin Franklin and Eighteenth-Century American Libraries.* Transactions of the American Philosophical Society, n.s., vol. 55, pt. 9. Philadelphia, 1965.

Kraus, Joe W. 'The Book Collections of Early American College Libraries.' *Library Quarterly* 43(1973):142–59.

Kraus, Michael. *The Atlantic Civilization: Eighteenth-Century Origins.* Ithaca, N.Y.: Cornell University Press, 1949.

———. 'Literary Relations Between Europe and America in the Eighteenth Century.' *William and Mary Quarterly*, 3d ser. 1(1944):210–34.

Krooss, Herman, and Charles Gilbert. *American Business History.* Englewood Cliffs, N.J.: Prentice-Hall Inc., 1972.

Lacy, Creighton. *The Word-Carrying Giant: The Growth of the American Bible Society* (1816–1966). South Pasadena, Calif.: William Carey Library, 1977.

Laugher, Charles. *Thomas Bray's Grand Design: Libraries of the Church of England in America, 1695–1785*. Chicago: American Library Association, 1973.

Lehmann-Haupt, Hellmut. *The Book in America: A History of the Making, the Selling, and the Collecting of Books in the United States*. New York: R. R. Bowker Co., 1939.

Lewis, Peirce F. 'Common Houses, Cultural Spoor.' *Landscape* 19(1975):1–22.

The Library Company of Philadelphia. *The Library of James Logan of Philadelphia, 1674–1751*. Philadelphia: Library Company of Philadelphia, 1974.

Likins, Mrs. J. W. *Six Years Experience as a Book Agent in California, Including My Trip from New York to San Francisco Via Nicaragua*. San Francisco: Women's Union Printing Office, 1874.

Literary History of the United States. New York: Macmillan Co., 1948.

Littlefield, George. *Early Boston Booksellers, 1642–1711*. Boston: The Club of Odd Volumes, 1900.

Lundberg, David, and Henry May. 'The Enlightened Reader in America.' *American Quarterly* 28(1976):262–93.

McDonald, Gerald. 'William Bradford's Book Trade and John Browne, Long Island Quaker, as His Book Agent, 1686–1691.' In *Essays Honoring Lawrence Wroth*. Portland, Me.: Printed by Southworth-Anthoensen Press, 1951.

Main, Jackson Turner. *The Social Structure of Revolutionary America*. Princeton, N. J.: Princeton University Press, 1956.

Mendell and Hosmer. *Notes of Travel and Life*. New York: For the authors, 1854.

Mills, Samuel, and Daniel Smith. *Report of a Missionary Tour through That Part of the United States Which Lies West of the Allegany Mountains*. Andover, Mass.: Flagg and Gould, 1815.

Molnar, John Edgar. 'Publication and Retail Book Advertisements in the "Virginia Gazette," 1736–1780.' Ph.D. diss., University of Michigan, 1978.

Morison, Samuel Eliot. *Harvard College in the Seventeenth Century*. Cambridge: Harvard University Press, 1936.

Napier, James. 'Some Book Sales in Dumfries, Virginia.' *William and Mary Quarterly*, 3d ser. 10(1953):441–45.

Nelles, Annie. *Annie Nelles; or, The Life of a Book Agent*. Cincinnati: The author, 1868.

Neuburg, Victor. *Chapbooks: A Guide to Reference Material on English, Scottish, and American Chapbook Literature of the Eighteenth and Nineteenth Centuries*. London: Woburn Press, 1971.

———. *The Penny Histories: A Study of Chapbooks for Young Readers over Two Centuries*. New York: Harcourt, Brace & World, 1969.

Nichols, Charles L. 'The Literary Fair in the United States.' In *Bibliographical Essays: A Tribute to Wilberforce Eames*. Cambridge: Harvard University Press, 1924.

Noel, Mary. *Villains Galore: The Heyday of the Popular Story Weekly*. New York: Macmillan Co., 1954.

Oswald, John Clyde. *Benjamin Franklin, Printer*. Garden City, N.Y.: Doubleday, Page and Co., 1917.

Park, Helen. *A List of Architectural Books Available in America before the Revolution*. Los Angeles: Hennessey and Ingalls, 1973.

Pattee, Fred Lewis. *The Feminine Fifties*. New York: D. Appleton-Century Co., Inc., 1940.

Peckham, Howard H. 'Books and Reading on the Ohio Valley Frontier.' *Mississippi Valley Historical Review* 44(1958): 649–63.

Peden, William. 'Thomas Jefferson: Book Collector.' Ph.D. diss., University of Virginia, 1942.

Pfenning, Hazel. 'Periodical Literary Criticism (1800–65): A Study of the Successive Works of Irving, Cooper, Poe, Hawthorne, Bryant, and Thoreau Which Appeared in American Publications within the Lifetime of the Individual Authors.' Ph.D. diss., New York University, 1932.

Powell, William S. 'Patrons of the Press: Subscription Book Purchasers in North Carolina, 1733–1850.' *North Carolina Historical Review* 39(1962):423–99.

Pred, Allan R. *Urban Growth and the Circulation of Information: The United States System of Cities, 1790–1840.* Cambridge: Harvard University Press, 1973.

Prim, Gorrell Clinton, Jr. 'Born Again in the Trenches: Revivalism in the Confederate Army.' Ph.D. diss., Florida State University, 1983.

Purcell, James. 'A Book Peddler's Progress in North Carolina.' *North Carolina Historical Review* 29(1952):8–23.

Putnam, George Haven. *Memoirs of a Publisher*, 1865–1915. New York and London: G. P. Putnam's Sons, 1915.

Raddin, George Gates. *An Early New York Library of Fiction; With a Checklist of the Fiction in H. Caritat's Circulating Library.* New York: H. W. Wilson Co., 1940.

Rede, Lehman Thomas. *Present State of Printing and Bookselling in America, 1796.* Chicago: Private printing, 1929.

Reilly, Elizabeth Carroll. 'The Wages of Piety: The Boston Book Trade of Jeremy Condy.' In *Printing and Society in Early America*, eds. William L. Joyce et al. Worcester, Mass.: American Antiquarian Society, 1983.

Reitzel, William. 'The Purchasing of English Books in Philadelphia, 1790–1800.' *Modern Philology* 35(1937):159–71.

Rice, Howard. *Thomas Jefferson's Paris.* Princeton, N.J.: Princeton University Press, 1976.

Robson, David. 'The Early American College and the Wider Culture: Scholarship in the 1970's.' *American Quarterly* 32(1980): 559–76.

Rubin, Julius. *Canal or Railroad? Imitation and Innovation in the Response to the Erie Canal in Philadelphia, Baltimore, and Boston.* Transactions of the American Philosophical Society, n.s., 51, pt. 7. Philadelphia, 1961.

Samson, Peter. 'The Department Store, Its Past and Its Future: A Review Article.' *Business History Review* 55(1981):26–34.

Schlesinger, Arthur M. *Prelude to Independence: The Newspaper War on Britain, 1764–1776.* New York: Alfred A. Knopf Inc., 1958.

Sheehan, Donald. *This Was Publishing: A Chronicle of the Book Trade in the Gilded Age*. Bloomington: Indiana University Press, 1952.

Sheffield, John. *Observations on the Commerce of the American States.* London: Printed for J. Stockdale, 1784.

Shepard, Leslie. *The Broadside Ballad: A Study in Origins and Meaning*. London: H. Jenkins, 1962.

Shera, Jesse Hauk. *Foundations of the Public Library: The Origins of the Public Library Movement in New England, 1629–1855.* Chicago: University of Chicago Press, 1949.

Shipton, Clifford K. *Isaiah Thomas, Printer, Patriot and Philanthropist, 1749–1831*. New York: Printing House of Leo Hart, 1948.

Shores, Louis. *Origins of the American College Library, 1638–1800.* Nashville, Tenn.: George Peabody College, 1934.

Shove, Raymond Howard. *Cheap Book Production in the United States, 1870 to 1891*. Urbana: University of Illinois Library, 1937.

Silver, Rollo G. 'The Book Trade and the Protective Tariff.' *Papers of the Bibliographical Society of America* 46(1952):33–44.

Skeel, Emily Ellsworth. *Mason Locke Weems, His Works and Ways.* New York: Privately published, 1929.

Skeel, Mrs. Roswell. 'Salesmanship of an Early Bestseller.' *Papers of the Bibliographical Society of America* 32(1938):38–46.

Skotheim, Robert. *American Intellectual Histories and Historians.* Princeton, N.J.: Princeton University Press, 1966.

Smiley, James Bethuel. *Instructions to Canvassers* [Chicago: J. B. Smiley, ca. 1884].

Society of Commercial Travellers. *The System of Commercial Travelling in Europe and the United States: Its History, Custom, and Laws.* Cambridge Mass.: Riverside Press, 1869.

Sosin, Jack M. *Agents and Merchants: British Colonial Policy and the Origins of the American Revolution, 1763–1775.* Lincoln: University of Nebraska Press, 1965.

Sowerby, Millicent. *Catalogue of the Library of Thomas Jefferson.* Washington: Government Printing Office, 1952–59.

Spencer, Benjamin. *The Quest for Nationality: An American Literary Campaign*. Syracuse: Syracuse University Press, 1957.

Stafford, Marjorie. 'Subscription Book Publishing in the United States, 1865–1930.' Master's thesis, Graduate School of Library Science, University of Illinois, 1943.

Stern, Madeleine. 'A Salem Author and a Boston Publisher: James Tyler and Joseph Nancrede.' *New England Quarterly* 47 (1974):290–301.

Stetson, Sarah Pattee. 'American Garden Books Transplanted and Native, before 1807.' *William and Mary Quarterly*, n.s., 3 (1946):343–69.

Stevens, Edwards. 'Relationships of Social Library Membership, Wealth, and Literary Culture in Early Ohio.' *Journal of Library History* 16(1981):574–94.

Stiverson, Cynthia A. and Gregory A. 'The Colonial Retail Book Trade: Availability and Affordability of Reading Material in Mid-Eighteenth Century Virginia.' In *Printing and Society in Early America*, eds. William L. Joyce et al. Worcester, Mass.: American Antiquarian Society, 1983.

Stoddard, Roger. 'Poet and Printer in Colonial and Federal America: Some Bibliographical Perspectives.' *Proceedings of the American Antiquarian Society* 92(1982):265–361.

Story, Ronald. 'Class and Culture in Boston: The Athenaeum, 1807–1860.' *American Quarterly* 27(1975):178–99.

Stowell, Marion Barber. *Early American Almanacs: The Colonial Weekday Bible*. New York: B. Franklin, 1977.

Sutton, Walter. *The Western Book Trade: Cincinnati as a Nineteenth-Century Publishing and Book-Trade Center*. Columbus: Ohio State University Press, 1961.

Tanselle, G. Thomas. 'Some Statistics on American Printing, 1764–1783.' In *The Press and the American Revolution*, eds. Bernard Bailyn and John B. Hench. Worcester, Mass.: American Antiquarian Society, 1980.

Tebbe, Jennifer. 'Print and American Culture.' *American Quarterly* 32(1980):259–79.

Tebbel, John. *A History of Book Publishing in the United States*. New York: R. R. Bowker Co., 1972–78.

Thomas, Isaiah. *The History of Printing in America.* Barre, Mass.: Imprint Society, 1970.

Thompson, Lawrence. 'The Printing and Publishing Activities of the American Tract Society from 1825 to 1850.' *Papers of the Bibliographical Society of America* 35(1941):81–144.

Tryon, Warren S. *Parnassus Corner: A Life of James T. Fields, Publisher to the Victorians.* Boston: Houghton Mifflin Co., 1963.

———. 'Book Distribution in Mid-Nineteenth Century America.' *Papers of the Bibliographical Society of America* 41(1947): 210–30.

Tuttle, Julius. 'The Libraries of the Mathers.' *Proceedings of the American Antiquarian Society* 20(1910):269–356.

Vogelback, Arthur. 'The Literary Reputation of Mark Twain in America, 1869–1885.' Ph.D. diss., University of Chicago, 1939.

Webb, Robert Kiefer. *The British Working Class Reader, 1790–1848: Literacy and Social Tension.* London: Allen & Unwin, 1955.

Webster, Samuel, ed. *Mark Twain, Business Man.* Boston: Little, Brown and Co., 1946.

Weiss, Harry. 'American Chapbooks, 1722–1842.' *Bulletin of the New York Public Library* 49(1945):587–96.

White, Luke Jr. *Henry William Herbert and the American Publishing Scene, 1831–1858.* Newark, N.J.: The Carteret Book Club, 1943.

Winans, Robert. *A Descriptive Checklist of Book Catalogues Separately Printed in America, 1693–1800.* Worcester, Mass.: American Antiquarian Society, 1981.

Winterich, John. *Early American Books and Printing.* Boston and New York: Houghton Mifflin Co., 1935.

Winton, Calhoun. 'The Colonial South Carolina Book Trade.' *Proof* 2(1972):71–87.

Wise, Gene. *American Historical Explanations.* Homewood, Ill.: Dorsey Press, 1973.

Wolf, Edwin, 2nd. 'The Dispersal of the Library of William Byrd of Westover.' *Proceedings of the American Antiquarian Society* 68(1958):19–106.

———. 'The Early Buying Policy of the Library Company of Philadelphia.' *Wilson Library Bulletin* 30(1955):316–18.

———. 'Franklin and Their Friends Choose Their Books.' *Pennsylvania Magazine of History and Biography* 80(1956):1–36.

———. 'Great American Book Collectors to 1800.' *The Gazette of the Grolier Club*, n.s., 12(1971):3–25.

Wolfe, Richard J. *Jacob Bigelow's American Medical Botany, 1817–1821: An Examination of the Origin, Printing, Binding, and Distribution of America's First Color Plate Book*. North Hills, Pa.: Bird & Bull Press, 1979.

Wright, Louis. *The Cultural Life of the American Colonies, 1607–1763*. New York: Harper, 1957.

———. *Culture on the Moving Frontier*. Bloomington: Indiana University Press, 1955.

———. *The First Gentlemen of Virginia: Intellectual Qualities of the Early Ruling Class*. San Marino, Calif.: Huntington Library, 1940.

Wright, Richardson. *Hawkers and Walkers in Early America*. Philadelphia: J. B. Lippincott Co., 1927.

Wright, Thomas Goddard. *Literary Culture in Early New England, 1620–1730*. New Haven: Yale University Press, 1920.

Wroth, Lawrence. *An American Bookshelf*, 1755. Philadelphia: University of Pennsylvania Press, 1934.

———. *The Colonial Printer*. New York: Grolier Club, 1931.

———. *The Colonial Printer*. Portland, Me.: Southworth-Anthoensen Press, 1938.

Zubatsky, David. *The History of American Colleges and Their Libraries in the Seventeenth and Eighteenth Centuries: A Bibliographical Essay*. Champaign, Ill.: Graduate School of Education, University of Illinois, 1979.

Books and Culture: Canned, Canonized, and Neglected

DAVID GRIMSTED

Woody Allen's modern everyman, Zelig, in the film of that name, dies with but one regret: having just begun *Moby Dick*, he'll never know precisely how it turns out. Sitting in a movie house reading this printed quip that ends the film, one ponders some of the questions that plague all considerations of the role of both popular culture and books in people's and society's life. Is *Zelig* popular culture and *Moby Dick* not? Has Melville's classic become a part of popular culture, so much so that Allen can count on a certain reaction to its mention, with part of the joke being that everyone knows how it comes out even if they, unlike Zelig, never begin it? And may Allen's movie soon become an artifact for the erudite, known to a handful of scholars and of interest to few of them? Why are the final words of the film put in print instead of given to the voice-over narrator who has told us most of the story? Does the printed word have some peculiar power, or does the very process of reading dictate some more intense or complicated involvement with the jokes or information or myths conveyed? And what do I learn from seeing *Zelig*—or Zelig from reading *Moby Dick*—if we think about it? What is learned if, as is more common, we don't particularly care to think about it? Is my watching and his reading a mark of our being mass men, representing the commonplace means through which we are made identical to every-

This paper, in a slightly different form, was prepared for a needs and opportunities conference on the history of the book in American culture, held at the American Antiquarian Society, November 1–3, 1984.

one else, something that Zelig's earlier peculiar propensities—when with the Chinese, he becomes Chinese—illustrated in more dramatic form? Or does his reading and my viewing entail a broadening of our freedom by suggesting some aspects of human possibility and experience more clearly or poignantly than we might otherwise have known?

In thinking about the relation of books and popular culture, I was reminded of a distant undergraduate argument about Puritanism when a young sceptic told me that two terms I'd used, 'sins' and 'God,' had no empirical meaning. 'My sins,' I assured him, 'are empirical enough.' We know what books, like sins, are, though there may be some gray areas of doubt, especially about including the more ephemeral or venial varieties, such as pamphlets, periodicals, newspapers, broadsides, or scholarly journals. As I understand the doctrines of this latitudinarian society for the study of the book, there is little that is printed that falls outside the scope of its proper moral consideration.

If we know what books are, empirically or by definition, 'popular culture' retains something of divine or satanic elusiveness. One need only read in the many accounts of the field to become convinced that we still view this entity, despite its very rich and varied self-conscious contributions in the last two decades, through a glass darkly, if not a fun house mirror distortedly. In fact, the religious analogy seems especially appropriate for a field in which theory tends to veer wildly between visions of apocalypse and what might be called zingy paeans to Pop-a-lisp. This paper will suggest some of the benefits that may grow from an emphasis on the solid, hand-bound book in a field that often seems flighty, going wherever the wind blows, listing zanily without ballast. I'll suggest some particular areas and topics where books and popular culture might be—and have been—drawn together, but this I do incidentally in arguing the benefits of closer ties between respectable books, representing the canonized lineage of humane scholarship, and the burgeoning if somewhat declassé field of popular or canned culture.[1] I'll argue that, since much designationally unsanctioned intercourse—some of it wonderfully productive—has been going on for a long time, a formal marriage of convenience is in order. With the hopefulness of all matchmakers, I think this union might give a valuable sense of care and responsibility to a field often too happy-go-lucky, and contribute some added vitality to the noble house of historical-literary scholarship, always in danger of suffocating under the weight of traditional pedantry.

I'll call the banns in the traditional three stages: (1) pondering the problems of definition and teleological moralism in the theories of popular culture; (2) considering some of the limiting aspects of major methodologies applied in the field, and difficulties commonly seen in some of the relevant work on the pre–1860 period; and (3) suggesting a few of the many directions that might be taken in what is in fact a respectably ancient intellectual pursuit.

Vagaries in the definitions of the field of popular culture complicate its elusiveness. Despite frequent hazy evocations of numbers, no scholar has suggested that popular culture be defined in contrast to unpopular culture by establishing some numerical threshold of readers, viewers, or practitioners in different areas. Most critics agree only about what popular culture is *not*: it is certainly not 'high' culture, or related to the art and thought of the elite; and (most agree) it is not folk culture, the art and myths and music and traditions of preliterate or at any rate 'precommercial' common people.

[1] Throughout the paper there are some problematic distinctions that should be explicitly listed: (A) Much writing on popular culture dates back to the 1920s and 1930s of this century and development of the *field* to the 1960s, which for convenience might be symbolized in the founding of the *Journal of Popular Culture* in 1967. (B) I use the term 'popular culture' with some breadth (as it is commonly employed), and with no rigorous determination to distinguish it sharply from elite or folk culture studies, something I find impossible to do. (C) Some historical fields retain some clarity by insisting on a focus on one topic: politics diplomacy, economics, music, religion. But fields that stress integration—i.e., intellectual, cultural, and social—are by their nature not capable of sharp definiton or precise segmentation.

This is clear enough until one begins to try to establish the precise lines of demarcation. The primary distinguishing criteria seem to involve money and class. Folk art is allegedly done for free, and high art for reasons of personal creativity, while canned art is made for money. Yet enslaved Solomon Northup played his fiddle, not only because he liked to, but because it bought him opportunities for better food and longer holidays from his chores. And surely this concern about reward was in the tradition of medieval troubadors and tribal storytellers and Navaho weavers, as well as their modern followers such as Woody Guthrie or the young woman playing a mandolin behind a hat on the subway. Sarah Parton, as 'Fanny Fern,' drove hard bargains for her immensely popular sketches, but she couldn't hold a candle to Ludwig von Beethoven for single-minded rapaciousness. Some great artists wrote for years with slight or no emoluments, but so did writers who were neither great nor popular. Nathaniel Hawthorne and Harriet Beecher Stowe served about equally long, underpaid magazine and annual apprenticeships before success came. When his poems didn't sell, Whitman took on a government clerkship. When his novels ceased to pay, Melville joined the customs house crew that Hawthorne had escaped. Margaret Fuller turned to conversations and journalism to earn a living, and wrote the better for it. Ralph Waldo Emerson spent as much time lecturing as writing because it was more profitable. It was Samuel Woodworth who remained faithful to writing popular plays and songs while living in near-destitution. If the *Dial* and 'Swing Low, Sweet Chariot' were labors of love, so were 'The Hunters of Kentucky' and 'The Old Oaken Bucket.'[2]

[2] Solomon Northup, *Twelve Years a Slave* [1841–53] (Baton Rouge, 1968), pp. 163–66; on Parton's financial demands, see Mary Kelley, *Private Woman, Public Stage: Literary Domesticity in Nineteenth-Century America* (New York, 1984), pp. 152–58; Margaret V. Allen, *The Achievement of Margaret Fuller* (University Park, Pa., 1979). The introduction to Samuel Woodworth's first published book of verse offers a picture of his destitution, a situation that changed little in his later years. See *The Poems, Odes, Songs, and Metrical Effusions of Samuel Woodworth* (New York, 1818).

Such random evidence suggests a very simple psychological truth: that a desire to create, and a need to live, and a yen for money or recognition are not warring but joined elements in human beings. Such a gross truism would hardly be worth making did it not relate to one of the most popular of explanatory put-downs of popular culture. To decry popular culture because it's involved with profit motives is to disparage all levels of culture, all similarly tinged with personal adulterated motives. Few human conceptions are immaculate, and nothing helps less in understanding or evaluating popular culture than the pretense that something profoundly telling is revealed when a profit motive is discovered. Most prophets are willing to take their profits, too, and, as far as is known, no early American refused royalties, salaries, or other rewards for being too high, any more than has any recent scholar who points with disgust at the money others make. The truth seems to be that people create as their needs and taste and abilities allow, whatever the mixed underside of their motivation. Successful popular culture radiates the same honesty as does effective high or folk culture, despite the trammels of conventionality on all levels of aesthetic tradition. There is much more often a crossover of taste—the popularity of Emerson as lecturer, for example—than there is of efforts by popular writers to turn out, against all financial considerations, the Great American Novel or Epic, or of efforts by 'high' writers to slum for profit. There were some competent playwrights in the late nineteenth century and some good screenwriters in the 1930s, but these did not include the profit-seeking Henry James or William Faulkner or F. Scott Fitzgerald. A reading of Walt Whitman's temperance novel is the best way to appreciate the literary merits of Timothy Shay Arthur.

The class and literacy distinctions between popular and other cultures also are dubious, especially in American society, Here, as studies increasingly suggest, illiteracy was never great, even in those groups with whom folk culture is especially associated: blacks, and Appalachian and frontier whites.[3] Illiteracy was predominant among slaves, of course, but efforts by blacks changed that quickly, once freed from enforced separation from printed matter. The emphasis on Bible reading in the evangelical Protestantism of Appalachian and black social-cultural life underlined the commitment toward literacy in these groups. Seemingly, literacy does less to undercut folk culture within groups than does prosperity, the ability to buy the creativity and entertainment that otherwise needs to be produced at home. In the Corcoran Gallery's recent beautiful exhibit of black American noncommerical art of the twentieth century there was conspicuous emphasis on words in a great many of the richest folk paintings, sculptures, and constructions. And the country's leading folklorist, Richard Dorson, has always recognized, somewhat reluctantly, the impossibility of separating out the mutual influences between oral and commercial or printed (or, after Edison, recorded) formulations of folk tradition. Davy Crockett became a folk hero on the printed page before the folk talked of him and long before Tin Pan Alley 'Fess-Parkered' him for intellectual toddlers. Estes Kefauver, donning the coonskin cap in his 1950s campaigns, was simply restoring folk and commercial borrowings to their calculatedly political sources. And the 'slave music' that Solomon Northup played for Southern black and white folk doubtlessly was drawn from the popular songs of New York where he grew to manhood.[4]

[3] Lee Soltow and Edward Stevens, *The Rise of Literacy and the Common School in the United States: A Socioeconomic Analysis to 1870* (Chicago, 1981), esp. pp. 28–57, 148–92. The work uses Kenneth Lockridge's earlier study entitled *Literacy in Colonial New England* (New York, 1974). In European societies, boundaries between popular and elite culture, and between literate and illiterate peoples, were often sharper, owing to more divisive class and educational lines. Peter Burke argues interestingly that such divisions came to European cultures only in the early modern era, and that scholars like Montaigne and Herder began elite appreciation of the culture of the people, once the divisions were clearly drawn. See *Popular Culture in Early Modern Europe* (New York, 1978), esp. pp. 244–86.

[4] Northup was thirty-three when kidnapped and enslaved. Born in New York State, he played his violin for dances, shows, and circuses there (*Twelve Years*, pp. 8–14).

Class lines are even less easy to connect with particular levels of culture. It is not, of course, that classes didn't exist in the United States, although they did lack important elements of permanency and clarity that defined the traditional vision of what class means. But there seems little question that class essentially rested on money, and there is no indication that taste followed whatever broad financial divisions might be traced. The intellectual center of canonized American culture in the mid-nineteenth century was Concord, Massachusetts, a political and economic backwater. There was some travel into Boston, of course (similar to the sneak forays of Henry David Thoreau and his laundry from Walden to Concord), but Emerson at least claimed that the only knowledge of transcendentalism on State Street, the hub of New England power, was that it seemed to threaten the sanctity of contracts.[5] When opera and minstrelsy developed simultaneously toward separate theatrical forms in the 1840s, their initial appeal seems to have been cross-class and parallel, with the expected elite-lower sorts differentiation developing eventually less from taste than from prices, which skyrocketed for opera.[6] The genteel embodiment of elite culture, the poetry of Sigourney, Longfellow, and Lowell, was immensely popular. Does this make Walt Whitman an elitist because his audience was small? Or does Emily Dickinson become a folk poet because her work

---

James Atkins Shackford, *David Crockett, the Man and the Legend* (Chapel Hill, N.C. 1956), offers the best resume of the many 'sources' of this legend. Richard Dorson coined the term 'fakelore' to attack ersatz literary creations of folk material, but his own studies have tended to rely on written sources for most things, such as frontier humor. Presumably, there is some background in oral tradition, but one could argue that Dorson's American folklore is very much old fakelore. Perhaps this accounts for his recent admission that the relation between folk and popular culture may be one of 'interpenetration instead of confrontation.' See Dorson's 'Folklore and Fakelore,' *American Mercury* 70 (March, 1950): 335–43; *American Folklore* (Chicago, 1959), pp. 19–63; *Folklore and Folklife: An Introduction* (Chicago, 1972), p. 41.

[5] William Gilman and J. E. Parsons, eds. *The Journals and Miscellaneous Notebooks of Ralph Waldo Emerson*, 16 vols. (New York, 1974), 8:108.

[6] David Grimsted, *Melodrama Unveiled: American Theater and Culture, 1800–1850* (Chicago, 1968), pp. 107–10, 190–91, 238–39; Deane L. Root, *American Popular Stage Music, 1860–1880* (Ann Arbor, 1981).

earned her nothing, and because that genial representative of elite cultural arbiters, Thomas Wentworth Higginson, discouraged her from printing her poems unless she smoothed out the meter and didn't rhyme 'day' and 'eternity'? Two American writers who have remained in the elite canon, Washington Irving and James Fenimore Cooper, were the most popular American authors in the early decades of the nineteenth century. Does Cooper change from a popular writer to a representative of elite culture when his bile rises and his sales plummet in the late 1830s? It does not seem likely, since the *North American Review*, the elite intellectual journal, liked his popular tales and scorned his bad-tempered snarls at democracy, just as the masses did.[7]

If one looks at the most popular early 'imported' literature, probably more widely read than the native product, the difficulty of separating popular taste from elite or high standards is clear. Surely Samuel Richardson, Lord Byron, Sir Walter Scott, and Charles Dickens remain within scholars' holy canon, and these were the most popular writers in the United States. Even writers like Jane Austen and George Eliot are prominent on Mott's problematical bestseller lists. The list of favorites included some minor figures like Hannah More or Thomas Hood, and certainly they excluded some greats like William Blake and John Keats. Still, the distinctions one looks for between good and popular taste are wholly hazy, and those between classes are almost always the product of unsubstantiated assertions and assumptions. In fact, the whole presumed divisionary structure of popular culture may represent a twentieth-century perspective, which closer eighteenth- and nineteenth-century work may puncture. Certainly this century's rejection of traditionalism, and the development of a variety of mass media as well as mass production of art on all levels,

[7] Robert Spiller, *James Fenimore Cooper, Critic of His Times* (New York, 1973), chronicles the largely hostile assessments of the unpopular 'domestic' novels in journals like *Knickerbocker*, *New York Review*, and *North American Review*.

has created disgust with others' taste and a desperate desire to assert the superiority of one's own. Hence, Ezra Pound's friendly 'Salutation' to the bourgeois shows the tripartite division of cultural styles that has infiltrated popular culture studies:

O generation of the thoroughly smug
  and thoroughly uncomfortable,
I have seen fishermen picnicking in the sun,
I have seen them with untidy families,
I have seen their smiles full of teeth
  and heard ungainly laughter.
And I am happier than you are,
And they were happier than I am;
And the fish swim in the lake
  and do not even own clothing.

The unbuttoned folk are happy as fish, Pound insists, but he is happier (and wiser) than we, the aesthetically jacketed and emotionally tied bourgeois. Yet Pound clearly shows that he, too, is uncomfortable because it's difficult to be thoroughly smug, amidst the clamoring competition for smug superiority. Hence we have Dwight MacDonald's charming phrase 'mid-cult' to prove that he—and his readers, of course—look down on the taste of those who look down on the taste of 'mass-cult.' Doubtless these concepts could be intellectually refined: upper mass-cult, middle mid-cult, perhaps lower high-cult for MacDonald (or should that be upper mid-cult?).[8] This lust for badges of superiority accounts partly for Pound's own steady parade of cultural allusions to prove—perfectly convincingly—that he knows many things that we don't, a concern even surpassing that of Cotton Mather, who seemingly trotted out and pushed in infinite random knowledge to show how effulgently culture grew in wilderness. Of course, much of the breathless enthusiasm for popular culture grows from a similar need to prove superiority by being securely high enough to enjoy

[8] Ezra Pound, 'Salutation,' in *The Collected Shorter Poems* (London, 1968), p. 94; Dwight MacDonald, *Against the American Grain* (New York, 1966).

slumming, say, in Susan Sontag's camp. When so many appreciate Verdi and Van Gogh, a major cultural imperative of our 'with it' society, one-up-personship, demands obeisance to Campbell soup cans and Captain Marvel and being 'Caged' in silent symphonies.

I don't mean to disparage the process much; it's kind of fun, if semidesperate fun at times. And obviously one can't think or write or laugh about the process without fully participating in it. Yet there's some need to question broad cultural theories born so clearly of intellectual status seeking.

A recognized grounding of popular cultural studies in pretwentieth century books and periodicals should also cut through some of the distorting elements related to the teleological dimensions often given the field. Much of the difficulty with theories of popular culture involves their concentration on moralistic negativism on the one hand and uncritical enthusiasm on the other. The first wide-scale scholarly attention to popular culture came in the revolution that infiltrated all intellectual and artistic fields in the years between 1885 and 1914. Thinkers besieged the Victorian or genteel notions of a moral, providential, or natural law with which the post-medieval world had asserted moral harmony and fended off the idea that life might be guided merely by chance or by power.[9] In this creative and volatile environment, each art form and intellectual discipline underwent a transformation (if not a formation) that gave shape to the modern world by calling into question the values and the assumptions that had gone before. Out of this came a divided reaction to popular culture. On the one hand, some scholars discovered and praised the vitality of vaudeville, or Yiddish theater, or black spirituals—a movement that had its most lasting American scholarly offshoots in

[9] Morton White, *The Revolt Against Formalism: Social Thought in America* (New York, 1949); Thomas Haskell, *The Emergence of Professional Social Science . . . and the Crisis of Nineteenth-Century Authority* (Urbana, 1977); Burton Bledstein, *The Culture of Professionalism: The Middle Class and the Development of Higher Education in America* (New York, 1976).

the rediscovery and encapsulation of folk art, music, and literature.[10] The second negative strand had stronger roots in Europe, where there was more fear about the rise of the influence of the masses. Ortega Y Gasset's *Revolt of the Masses* was the classic—and very popular—elite alarm bell, but the ideas were a part of a much larger lament for a passing old order that runs, in differing forms, from the novels of Galsworthy through the plays of Chekhov and the histories of Spengler. The new technological media, especially films, records, and radio, were young in the United States when World War I ended, and American study of popular culture turned into diatribe against its bourgeois emptiness. Writers like H. L. Mencken, Sinclair Lewis, Van Wyck Brooks and Paul Elmer More made careers out of scorn for mass-American traditions, though the more robust of them did so with some mixed feelings.[11]

The 1930s joined the European voice to the American perception in a situation where the fear and distaste of modern mass or popular culture seemed justified by the twin totalitarian viciousness of fascism and communism. The move of the 'Frankfort school' to the United States gave a theoretical grounding to the study of mass culture for the first time, but one that strongly stressed the negative. As fugitives from fascist Germany, their fears of mass society were reasonable enough, but they hardly deepened critical understanding by seeing only 'decadence' in mass culture.[12] Their judgments—

[10] Some of this interest grew from William Graham Sumner's richly suggestive *Folkways* (New York, 1906).

[11] Sinclair Lewis presented an amusing sketch of the conflict between the intellectuals and the 'booboisie' in 'Main Street's Been Paved,' *Nation* 119 (Sept. 10, 1924): 255–60. The fascist propaganda of Ezra Pound shows a strange combination of insanely virulent anti-Semitism with an exultation in American slang and colloquialisms. See Leonard W. Doob, ed., '*Ezra Pound Speaking*': *Radio Speeches of World War II* (Westport, Conn., 1973).

[12] The best introduction to the Frankfort school's views on popular culture is the 1944 study by Max Hockheimer and Theodor Adorno, *The Dialect of Enlightenment* (New York, 1972). Martin Jay stresses the group's Marxist commitment in *The Dialectical Imagination: A History of the Frankfort School and the Institute of Social Research, 1923–1950* (Boston, 1975), while George Friedman discusses the group's roots in the theories of Oswald Spengler and Ortega Y Gassett in *The Political Philosophy of the*

and their depth of analysis—of popular culture were almost perfectly parallel to those of Bible-belt revivalists and Legion of Decency censors. They also broadened the politics of this theology of popular decadence from the elitist, sometimes crypto-fascist leanings of Ortega, Pound, and Eliot to the liberalism of Theodor Adorno, the home-grown radicalism of Dwight MacDonald, and the Marxism of Herbert Marcuse. Marcuse probably did most to develop the idea of mass culture as the opiate of the masses and to suggest capitalist manipulation of it in semiconspiratorial terms.[13] Certainly there are odd political bedfellows among those who decried the destructiveness of popular culture: elite traditionalists, radical Marxists, and religious conservatives (the populist wing of the coalition), intellectually represented by those pop psychologists who periodically declared that comic books or horror films or rock music were sapping the nation's moral fiber.[14] In all three positions the dislike for mass culture was tied to disgust with the United States' development. For elitists, mass culture was a product of American democracy; for Marxists, it was the result of American capitalism; and for the religious, most popular culture was the fruit of an American humanist plot to ensure a society where anything goes by making sure the eternal verities went first.

Such glib predictions of apocalypse have generated reasonable if sometimes equally glib assurances that things aren't so bad. Pop culture wasn't all or always bad, people suggested—

Frankfort School (Ithaca, 1981). Also valuable is Phil Slater, 'The Aesthetic Theory of the Frankfort School,' in Peter Davison *et al*, eds., *Culture and Mass Culture*, 1 vol. (Cambridge, Eng., 1978), 1:307–48.

[13] Marcuse developed the most specifically Marxist formulation, especially in *One-Dimensional Man* (Boston, 1964) and *The Aesthetic Dimension* (Boston, 1978). The stress on a return to the people and to American traditions during the New Deal also encouraged much rich, if untheoretical, work in earlier popular culture. For examples, see footnote 19.

[14] Patrick Brantlinger covers various theories that tie popular culture to social collapse, present or predicted, in *Bread and Circuses: Theories of Mass Culture as Social Decay* (Ithaca, 1983).

or, more amusingly, had always been awful. Remember bear-baiting, suggested David Manning White, and comic book horrors come to seem tame. They also insisted that the funeral for all things of value was, like Tom Sawyer's, somewhat premature.[15] Such correctives were in order but, like much academic revisionism, they had their own disappointing aspects. Herbert Marcuse's one-dimensional argument, overturned or tipped on its head, remains one-dimensional. And in the 1960s, when America was greening and charring, some students of popular culture took the offensive in the name of the nameless masses of consumers. Rock music had a politically revolutionary beat; Superman comics were primal myths; *Star Wars* and *The Man Who Fell to Earth* were religious allegories that hailed a second coming; *The Godfather* films presaged and promoted the fall of capitalism. Zap! Bang! Wow![16]

Such works were often insightful about dimensions of popular culture and how it might be interpreted. Indeed, much of the myth finding (and making) paralleled what scholarly critics regularly did to canonized culture. Yet analysis often seemed paralyzed by the discovery of a pretentious connection. When a traditional myth was found in Lil' Abner, or when John Kennedy was proclaimed a pop prince of a campy Camelot, the quest was often over.[17] And the suggestion usually was

[15] David Manning White, 'Mass Culture in America,' in Bernard Rosenberg and David M. White, eds., *Mass Culture: The Popular Arts in America* (Glencoe, Ill., 1957), p. 14. This collection, which in many ways marked the initiation of popular culture as a field, offered a rich array of perspectives and types of study. The two editors took opposite views in their introductions, with Rosenberg blaming popular culture for everything from Madame Bovary's fall to the trivialization of modern life and the projected demise of highbrow cultures. In another study, Fred E. H. Schroeder suggests the ways that definitions of popular culture are amended to suit different materials in his edited collection *5000 Years of Popular Culture: Popular Culture Before Printing* (Bowling Green, Ohio, 1980).

[16] John Hess, 'Godfather II,' in Bill Nichols, ed., *Movies and Methods* (Berkeley, 1976), pp. 81–90; Gary Herman and Ian Hoare, 'The Struggle for Song,' in Carl Gardner, ed., *Media, Politics, and Culture* (London, 1979), pp. 51–60.

[17] Marshall Fishwick's amusing, wide-ranging, once-over-lightly volumes perhaps represent this approach most clearly. See *Parameters: Man-Media Mosaic* (Bowling Green, Ohio, 1978), and *Common Culture and the Great Tradition: The case for Renewal* (Westport, Conn., 1982). He turns gloomy predictions on their head by asserting that

that all this showed that the things the negative viewers found dangerous were just pure delight: technology, mass society, American society, modern society, kitsch, lack of taste, inert watching, rapidly changing values, determined commercialism.[18] In essence, rejection of the standards by which critics tried to distinguish high from vulgar art—vague as those were—led to a celebration of tastelessness and an insistence that worrying about those forces with which popular culture critics were concerned marked a nail-biting fuddy-duddy. The puffing enthusiasts of popular culture often gave analyses, for all their desperate cheerfulness, little richer than opponents' whines about decadence. Reading much recent popular culture theory creates a longing for something in between Oswald Spengler and Dr. Pangloss, a craving for considered judgment of things related to popular culture unshadowed by a conviction of the four horsemen or the Millenium riding in their immediate wake. In short, one wants the attitude one has in reading a book: hope of finding something of value—or at least of being jogged to connect it with something of interest—and sufficient skepticism to ensure that that value not be too easily produced.

Barbara Pym, in her novel *A Few Green Leaves*, amusingly sketches the extremes of the fastidious opponents of popular culture and its all-accepting proponents. In a scene where a gourmet complains to his village doctor of his depressed irritability at canned culture, at 'being offered vinegary bottled mayonnaise instead of home-made, or sliced bread, or processed cheese, or there being no dijon mustard . . . , or freshly ground

---

twentieth-century popular arts are restoring a 'common culture,' one not divided by class, to all, and are renewing the 'great tradition' that will help end corrosive social divisions. See Fishwick, *Common Culture*, pp. 19–41.

[18] Marshall McLuhan's theories lie behind much of the more utopian thinking about mass culture, though he himself presents his hopes with tart irony. See *Understanding Media: The Extensions of Man* (New York, 1964), and *The Mechanical Bride: Folklore of Industrial Man* (New York, 1951). The latter, McLuhan's richest handling of popular culture, treats the marriage as a delight, while the reiterated central image conjures up Mary Shelley's—and Elsa Lancaster's—chilling vision.

coffee, and finally, the use of tea-bags—that seemed to upset him quite unreasonably.'

The doctor, who pushes platitudes more than pills, has ready advice: 'Try not to be quite so critical—learn to like processed cheese and tea-bags and instant coffee, and beef burgers and fish fingers, too. Most of the people in the village live on such things, and they're none the worse for it.' Well, possibly none the worse, but does one have to choose between waxing depressed over fish sticks and Big Macs and waxing lyrical over them? Pym asks with uninsistent reasonableness, a tone one yearns for in popular culture studies.

If, as I believe, the price of liberty is some mixture of eternal hope and eternal fretting, theories that permit only half the equation are not only flattening but dangerous. Texas may have nothing to say to Maine, as Thoreau tartly suggested to those who predicted a better world was to be strung on telegraph lines, but the world seems hardly threatened by their chance to talk. On the other hand, need we laugh along with a leader who finds (off the air, of course) nuclear annihilation a big joke, the humor obviously embodying the wish fulfillment over which conscious knowledge and inhibitions hold loose rein. Apocalypse is possible, and need only happen once to be statistically significant, humanistically speaking. If it seems excessive to see the end in the unending *Search for Tomorrow* or even *The Texas Chainsaw Massacre*, all democrats should be concerned about how their society channels its passions and technological chainsaws, and about what *The Young and The Restless* as well as the middle-aged and disillusioned, the old and embittered, the poor and oppressed and the rich and supercilious are up to. At its best, the study of popular culture can make people not only aware of telling clues to society, but also make them thoughtfully appreciative *and* wary of them.

One advantage of grounding popular culture in earlier periods is that this almost automatically destroys much emphasis on teleological determinism. Quite clearly, minstrelsy and the dime novel led neither to Eden nor the End. Chronological perspective also underlines that, while popular culture may be a new field, studying aspects of popular culture is a long-established reality. There are numerous early books on the subject: Frank Luther Mott's surveys of newspapers, magazines, and best-selling books, the latter a field also covered in James Hart's *The Popular Book*; Douglas Branch's genial handling of fads, fashions and mores in *The Sentimental Years*; Harry Jaffa's unsurpassed evaluation of the Lincoln-Douglas debates; George Pullen Jackson's account of Southern white spirituals, and Sigmund Spaeth's survey of popular songs; Charles Johnson's descriptions of the rituals of camp meetings; Constance Rourke's handling of American humor; Carl Wittke's sketch of minstrelsy or David Brion Davis's study of detective fiction.[19] These books range from profound and exciting to useful, but they clearly illustrate that there was a wide array of histories of nineteenth-century popular culture before there developed a 'field' in the 1960s. Often in academic work, the stress on revising what came immediately before creates a degree of amnesia about earlier works, at least equally interesting in terms of data and idea. John Bach McMaster's old history is still one of the best accounts of the antbellum years that integrates materials from popular culture into a general history of the era.[20]

[19] See Frank Luther Mott, *American Journalism: A History of Newspapers in the United States* (New York, 1941), as well as his studies *A History of American Magazines* (Cambridge, 1938), and *Golden Multitudes: The Story of Best Sellers in the United States* (New York, 1947). See also James Hart, *The Popular Books: A History of America's Literary Taste* (New York, 1950); E. Douglas Branch, *The Sentimental Years, 1836–1860* (New York, 1934); Harry Jaffa, *Crisis of the House Divided: An Interpretation of the Issues in the Lincoln-Douglas Debates* (Garden City, N.J., 1959); Sigmund Spaeth, *Read 'em and Weep: The Songs You Forgot to Remember* (Garden City, N. J., 1926); George Pullen Jackson, *White Spirituals in the Southern Uplands: The Story of the Fasola, Their Songs, Singing, and 'Buckwheat Notes'* (Chapel Hill, N. C., 1933); Constance M. Rourke, *American Humor: A Study of National Character* (New York, 1931); David Brion Davis, *Homicide in American Fiction, 1790–1860: A Study in Social Values* (Ithaca, 1957); Carl Wittke, *Tambo and Bones: A History of the American Minstrel Stage* (New York, 1930).

[20] John Bach McMaster, *A History of the People of the United States: From the Revolution to the Civil War*, 8 vols. (New York, 1883–1913). The quality of McMaster's comment and interpretation is also generally impressive.

If one goes back to the seventeenth and eighteenth centuries, one finds interesting evidence about the way in which divisions between high and popular culture tend to reflect scholarly convenience rather than clear separations dictated by level or quality of audience. For these periods of American history, cultural scholars read mostly sermons, diaries, journals and political essays; they look mostly at portraits; they listen to hymns or marches. This is basically true not because the tastes of elites or the quality of popular culture changed, but because after 1800 America began producing rather than importing its eventually canonized culture. Hence scholars concentrate on a fairly fixed body of aesthetically ambitious material large enough to exclude from general anthologies—and often general consideration—equally valuable and vital materials.[21] What writing tells as much of Puritan and American values as John Winthrop's sermon 'Model of Christian Charity'? Yet one suspects it would have few readers were the literary competition keener, just as do Charles Grandison Finney's better-written sermons, which are equally crucial to the understanding of American religion's democratic transformation.

American scholars should be glad to have even passing acquaintance with the diaries of Samuel Sewall or William Byrd II. We should all lament that so few read the extraordinary diaries of George Templeton Strong or Mary Boykin Chesnut, both of whom, in my judgment, wrote more dependably controlled and vigorously original prose than Emerson, Hawthorne, or Melville. Historically, both Strong and Chesnut exist largely as conservative caricatures instead of the complicated and superb social observers they were. Chesnut has fared a bit better because there's less canonized Southern culture, although perhaps the chief image of her remains Martin

[21] The interest during the 1920s in the question of elite and other tastes lay behind the academy's finally beginning a serious incorporation of the major American literary texts into courses. Until that time, colleges viewed these texts with the same disdain now often expressed toward still-unsanctified texts of popular culture.

Duberman's caricature of a palpitatingly snobbish racist. For poor Strong, the 'conservative' label remains so pervasive that no one seems to read him, except in search of passages to illustrate this 'self-evident' truth.[22]

Or consider ballads, the center of thriving scholarly study until the nineteenth century but neglected thereafter. Yet I know of no tragic ballad more powerful than one written and published (presumably for profit) as a broadside in Albany, New York, in 1843 as 'Verses on Mariah Hocrij':

> As her folks were at Work in the dairy, one day,
> At scalding the curd, for the cheese, in the *Whey*,
> They let down the *Kettle* by a *Windless* or crank,
> Below the first floor, into a Caldron or tank.
>
> The caldron was boiling, with Water, half full;
> They used it, sometimes, for their hogs and the fowl,
> To boil up their food and to fatten them well,
> 'Twas adjoining the place where those animals dwell.
> The kettle being rais'd, she was steadying the same,
> When she slip'd, and into the caldron she came.
> Her father let go of the *Windless* and *Crain*,
> To save his dear child from the scalding and pain.
>
> Being in haste, he was careless, did not make them fast,
> And the kettle went down on this dear creature's breast
> Where it held her so fast, that two minutes, or more,
> Elaps'd, before he his child could restore.
> In that liquid flame, what tortor she felt;
> Her cries would have made e'en an adamant melt.
> Submerged in the boiling hot Water, she lay,
> Held down by the *Kettle* of hot scalding *Whey*
>
> Her face and her hands, they only escap'd
> This hot bath of fire, that she had to take;
> And she was so scalded that her flesh it gave way,
> In taking her out of the place where she lay.

[22] Martin Duberman, *In White America: A Documentary Play* (New York, 1965); George M. Frederickson, *The Inner Civil War: Northern Intellectuals and the Crisis of the Union* (New York, 1965), pp. 55, 101. The recent republication of Chesnut's work and of her original diary suggest correction of this neglect. See C. Vann Woodward, ed., *Mary Chesnut's Civil War* (New Haven, 1981), and C. Vann Woodwood and Elizabeth Muhlenberg, eds., *The Private Mary Chesnut* (New York, 1984).

As they took off her clothes, the skin and the flesh
Came off in large masses, *we* here do confess.
Her blood turned inward, and so freely did flow,
Out of the cavities made, it forced its way through.

. . .

Yet she liv'd for some hours, though greatly distress'd
And her God and her friends alternately address'd.
She said she felt peace, thro' the blood of the Lamb,
And for her redemption, could trust in his name.

The tendency to fit forms of cultural expression into hierarchical categories—so close to the heart of the field of popular culture—distorts careful reading and understanding fairly dependably. Culture is treated with trinitarian absolutism—awesome, all right or awful—in ways that impede thought about it on all levels. Thomas Hooker was a superb prose stylist; until Henry David Thoreau, no writer did so much to bridge the abstract and the everyday with metaphor. But, in Hooker's phrase, 'that wind shakes no corn,' because scholars are not told to look for anything except ideas in his sermons, despite some insightful suggestions from Perry Miller. Hooker is all right but not awesome, so readers don't think much about how he writes, any more than they generally notice the centrality of puns, English, Latin, and Greek, in the writings of Cotton Mather, who developed this form of American humor, again to reach perhaps its literary apex in Thoreau.

My plaints here essentially center on the fact that, when one thinks of 'popular culture,' the 'popular'—to contrast it with elite and folk—gets emphasized rather than the 'culture.' And this encourages a quest for categories and divisions that tend to be, in practice, empty fabrications and obfuscations that distract attention from the true grail, understanding more clearly and more richly how human beings lived and thought and felt. If one emphasizes, instead, 'culture' in the old-fashioned anthropological sense of those ideas or beliefs that give unity to the various aspects of society, attitudes that tie together child-rearing practices and economic customs, myths and political structure, and sexual patterns and totems and taboos, it becomes clear that the antitheses that are made so much of in theories of popular culture are empty. What matters is coming to understand a bit more what the styles of greeting and parting, or what the tales and talismans of the high priests suggest about an aspect of culture and its relation to the whole. This is vague and more generalized than some of the recent anthropological theories that have had some impact on historical and especially popular culture studies, such as semiology, or the structuralism associated especially with Levi-Strauss, or the ritual analysis of Clifford Geertz, and the theorizing of Victor Turner.[23] Yet such intellectual approaches are often limited by the theoretical abstraction that is part of their virtue and appeal. They encourage abstracting a single entity—a cock fight, or a poem, or a style of etiquette—to analyze its parts more closely, but in a way that often cuts it from the broader culture of which it's a part. Semiology and structuralism define their subjects as alienated from outside connections, in a way that makes the approach an excellent starting point for cultural analysis but often a sterile ending point.[24] And users of the anthropological theories too frequently finish rather than begin with the announcement that dime novels embody primal

[23] Clifford Geertz, *The Interpretation of Cultures: Selected Essays* (New York, 1973), and *Local Knowledge: Further Essays in Interpretive Anthropology* (New York, 1983); Victor Turner, *The Ritual Process: Structure and Anti-Structure* (Chicago, 1969), and *Drama, Fields, and Metaphors: Symbollic Action in Human Society* (Ithaca, 1974); Roland Barthes, *Mythologies* (New York, 1972); Claude Levi-Strauss, *Triste Tropiques* (New York, 1973), and *Structural Anthropology* (New York, 1963). A useful brief statement of his position is Levi-Strauss, 'The Structural Study of Myth,' *Journal of American Folklore* 78 (1955): 428-44. Thomas H. Ohlgren and Lynn M. Berk apply structuralist approaches to the mass media in a way that suggests the tendency to lose sight of meaning in the organization of types of 'rhetoric.' See their study *The New Languages: A Rhetorical Approach to the Mass Media and Popular Culture* (New York, 1977).

[24] Good critiques of these positions are found in Gregory Baum, ed. *Sociology and Human Destiny* (New York, 1980), and especially in the essays by G. R. Kress and Robert Hodge in C.W.E. Bigsby, ed., *Approaches to Popular Culture* (Bowling Green, Ohio, 1976), pp. 85–128. Stuart Clark offers somewhat parallel criticisms of constrictive theories in 'French Historians and Early Modern Culture,' *Past and Present* 100 (1983): 62–99.

myths and militia musters are complex social rituals, so that preordained truths are illustrated, rather than the cultural context to which the myths partially gave meaning.

To the self-enclosed limitations of recent anthropological or structuralist myths, rituals, and synagyms, Marxist theories offer a valuable corrective by insisting on the connections between cultural artifacts (that is, the intellectual-aesthetic manifestations of a society) and their socioeconomic setting. Surely no scholar recently has done more to consider culture thoughtfully than Raymond Williams.[25] Yet, despite the contribution of the Marxist approach to the field, this analysis of popular culture commonly contains two debilitating ideas in relation to the actual handling of artifacts, both of them derived fairly directly from the master. One is that economy broadly dictates cultural artifact rather than interacts with it, in a way that abstracts the complex cross-traffic of cultural networks into a predetermined one-way street. Whatever the element of truth in the Marxist belief that people must eat before they think, the notion does suggest a group of scholars who have seldom had to prepare meals. And this certainty about basic cause and purpose in culture often inhibits close search for meaning in the artifact itself, which contributes to the second flaw, the tendency to deride all bourgeois manifestations of culture, often in semiconspiratorial terms, and to pretend that the eventual classless culture will be wholly freeing, just as that of bourgeois society is wholly enfeebling.[26] In the field of popular

[25] Raymond Williams's contribution to the field centers on two points. He has, more than anyone else, suggested both the need for a theoretical (or at least broadly thoughtful) approach, while doing good close cultural analysis. Second, he has stressed the socio-economic ties of cultural manifestations, without implying economic dictation. Even in his later, more avowedly Marxist work, Williams insists on 'interactions' of a complex sort between thought, artifact, and economy. See *Culture and Society, 1780–1950* (New York, 1958); *The Long Revolution* (New York, 1960); *Keywords: A Vocabulary of Culture and Society* (New York, 1976), and *Marxism and Literature* (Oxford, 1977).

[26] The Gardner collection, *Media, Politics, and Culture,* cited in footnote 16, is valuable in part because the essay by Williams contrasts so strongly with the more doctrinaire Marxist approaches in the rest of the book. Tony Bennett et al., eds., *Culture, Ideology, and Social Process: A Reader* (London, 1981), has a good section on

culture, Marxist scholars have a lot of company in posing some vague total evil against a utopian total good, but the crowd appeal of such ideas to scholars makes them no less destructive of thoughtful consideration of what might be seen if the objects at hand were looked at microscopically rather than through a teleological telescope.

The advantage of the older anthropological theories of culture—basically, those that Caroline Ware presented to historians in the 1930s—is that their humanistic and platitudinous quality, that is, looking at things closely and connectedly, without undue prescription about how that must be done, avoids what seems to me the disabling precept that some more or less strict methodology will provide a path to truths that will finally be cumulative and complete.[27] The richest answers that scholars give are not those that pretend to prove conclusively, but those that suggest realities, connections, and possibilities not fully realized previously.

If one is going to add an adjective to 'culture' to distinguish the areas usually conjured up by popular culture, I'd suggest that 'neglected' might be better. At least it avoids the stress on numbers as the antithesis of quality, the stupidities of which are so apparent if one thinks of Sophocles and Shakespeare, but an argument that is equally untenable if seriously applied to

---

structuralism, but is most interesting in the presentation of Antonio Gramsci's ideas, with an analysis of them by Chantal Mouffe. Many Marxists have found in Gramsci's concept of 'hegemony' what they consider a 'nonreductionist' approach to ideology and cultural artifacts, although I have trouble seeing how hegemony does much more than admit the obvious in Marxist theory, namely, that the economic direction of ideas and culture is often subtle, unconscious, and unforced. See esp. pp. 191–234.

[27] Caroline Ware, *The Cultural Approach to History* (New York, 1940). Ware's book was obviously a product of the ideas and popularity of Ruth Benedict's *Patterns of Culture* (New York, 1934). The problem in this theory is open-endedness and the elusive use of key terms. See Alfred L. Kroeber and Clyde Kluckhohn, *Culture, A Critical Review of Concepts and Definitions* (Cambridge, Mass., 1952). This looseness is what Levi-Strauss refers to as 'a lawless humanism' in *The Savage Mind* (Chicago, 1966), p. ix. The question involves determining if there are 'laws' that permit as rich a handling of materials as does a flexible carefulness that encourages openness in exploring connections. The study by Ray Browne, Sam Grogg, and Larry Landrum, eds., *Theories and Methodologies in Popular Culture* (Bowling Green, Ohio, 1978), presents several theories suggesting a very casual and eclectic approach.

more recent culture. And the term suggests precisely what popular culture study does at its best: looking closely at what other scholars have neglected in their attempts at establishing, intentionally or willy-nilly, a canon about what is significant. It also suggests that aesthetic or intellectual evaluation is not a matter of absolute criteria, but of understanding the elements of depth and sincerity and complexity that enter into many kinds and levels of creativity. To scoff at *Simple Gifts* because it's not Beethoven's *Ninth* is ridiculous. To neglect Samuel Woodworth's rollicking treatment of the American con man in his popular song 'Dr. Stramonium' because it's not like Melville's weighty *The Confidence-Man* is equally mistaken. And not to read Sarah Parton's essays in *Little Ferns for Fanny's Little Friends* because they are not like Emerson's is about as intelligent as rejecting Emerson's because they are not like Addison's or Carlyle's. It's also to miss how tartly observant and how richly suggestive about society the sentimental mode of the very popular 'scribbling women' of the mid-nineteenth century could be.[28]

If one thinks about some of the major contributions to American history in these years, it becomes clear that the argument that the study of popular culture through books is valuable is less a plea for a new tack than an appreciation for much of the most significant work that has been done. Vernon Parrington's literary histories were path-breaking surely not because of the categorization of everything around a democratic-aristocratic axis, but because he included in his study political, theological, economic, and folk thinkers, along with the canonized literary greats. Basically, he joined many neglected sidestreams to the main currents of American thought, in supply sufficient to irri-

[28] On topics like popular magazines, novels, and songs, a method of 'content analysis,' tied to sociology, might be useful. The precategorization of the material hinders subtlety of interpretation, but some general sense of pattern would obviously be a helpful beginning. For examples, see Patrick Johns-Heine and Hans H. Gerth, 'Values in Mass Periodical Fiction, 1921–40,' in Rosenberg and Manning, *Mass Culture*, pp. 226–34, and Donald L. Shaw, 'At the Crossroads: Change and Continuity in American Press News, 1820–1860,' *Journalism History* 8 (1981):38-53.

gate several scholarly fields for generations. And could there be a stronger argument for the historical study of books representing neglected culture than the precedent of what seems to me the greatest work of American history in this century, Perry Miller's study of Puritanism? What Miller did might be done in any number of directions: he read thousands of overlooked documents, mostly books, that other scholars had neglected because they were supposedly uninteresting. And, because Miller read them both appreciatively *and* critically, a major section of American history was salvaged from the twin evils of antiquarian pietism and modernist denigration. He made us see the Puritans as people whose very special struggles both separated them from us and tied us to them in an intellectual tradition very different from the earlier moralistic pattern, which Parrington so completely accepted in its negative form.

Because Miller did his work so profoundly, most subsequent study on colonial New England has been minor, if often quite sophisticated, embroidery on his tapestry. Once Miller drew vital attention to what had been neglected materials, others began to worry productively about what he neglected. One of several valuable results of such ponderings has been the debate over the relation of ministerial beliefs to the 'popular religion' of common people in seventeenth-century New England. Had Miller not suggested so richly the structure of thought of the Rev. Thomas Shepard, there could have been little probing consideration of how Shepard's congregant's faith paralleled or diverged from the ministerial pattern.[29] The best of works

[29] Perry Miller's *The New England Mind: The Seventeenth Century* (Cambridge, Mass., 1938), and *From Colony to Province* (Cambridge, Mass., 1953), offer the richest suggestion of the perfect compatibility of intellectual history with popular sources integrated into a social context. The publication of *Thomas Shepard's Confessions* (Boston, 1981) by the Colonial Society of Massachusetts under the editorship of George Selement and Bruce C. Woolley made generally available an unusual source relative to popular religion: the spiritual testimonies of common men and women as they applied for church membership. Selement and David D. Hall, in separate essays in the January 1984 issue of the *William and Mary Quarterly,* define some of the interpretations suggested by this document about the relationship between ministerial and congregant faith. (*William and Mary Quarterly,* 3d. ser. 41 (1984): 32–55). Since the 1960s

obviously don't end debates, but generate, inform, and enrich new ones.

Much of the most exciting new work in Revolutionary historiography has grown from close inspection of neglected aspects of more popular culture rather than the canonized political theories of John Locke and the philosophes. Bernard Bailyn collected American political pamphlets and essays and suggested their ties to Caroline Robbins's Commonwealth polemicists, to give a different and richer sense of the American Revolution's ideological origins. And in somewhat related efforts, Henry May looked especially at people's libraries to suggest the several 'enlightenments' from which Americans drew. May emphasized strongly Scottish roots, a perception developed insistently and interestingly in Gary Wills's gesture toward *Inventing America.* In somewhat different directions, Alfred Young and others have sought in the rituals of riot, parade, and pageant the sources of a radically democratic tradition.[30] The contribution of these studies grew from overlooking the previously accepted sources for the American Revolutionary political and cultural tradition, and looking at probably more popular and certainly more neglected artifacts.

While one could trace many of the major studies in American history to the scholarly pursuit of popular or neglected culture, the explicit interest and theorizing about it as a field grew up in the 1960s, as a corollary to the interest in those groups that were deemed outside the elite political-economic-diplomatic-intellectual structure. For the pre-twentieth century period at least, the most notable products of this interest were the works in quantitative history that used numbers to try to give clearer

demographic-quantitative studies have added new data related to understanding colonial New England, often drawn from issues Miller broached.

[30] Bernard Bailyn, *Pamphlets of the American Revolution, 1750–1776* (Cambridge, 1965), and *The Ideological Origins of the American Revolution* (Cambridge, 1967); Alfred F. Young, *The Democratic Republicans of New York: The Origins, 1763–97* (Chapel Hill, N. C., 1967); Henry F. May, *the Enlightenment in America* (New York, 1976); Garry Wills, *Inventing America: Jefferson's Declaration of Independence* (Garden City, N.J., 1978).

shape to the demographic, economic, and legal lives of ordinary men and women, whom we know only as names on birth and death certificates, or in wills, court cases, and census tabulations.

Much of this interest in the 'inarticulate' or 'historically voiceless' (perhaps a better adjective again would be 'neglected') grew out of dislike for or disinterest in the 'establishment,' which came in a variety of political hues.[31] There was, especially in those works tied to the field of popular culture, a strong sense of Americanism, of pride in those things—radio, film, tv, pulp magazines, canned food, Wonder bread, graffiti—seen as the great neglected representatives of truly American sensibilities. Read any early issue of the *Journal of Popular Culture*, begun in 1967, if you doubt this propatria impulse. This stress was certainly understandable in a field where scorn for popular culture was commonly intertwined with mistrust of democracy, technology, mass enthusiasms, and other essential aspects of the American way of life. Perhaps the most important recent study to deal with varieties of popular culture in the early nineteenth century was Daniel Boorstin's second volume of *The Americans*, the volume subtitled *The National Experience*. If Boorstin's Americanism had different political roots than Marshall Fishwick's twentieth-century studies, that simply shows how this field, more than most, draws people of opposite political persuasion toward the same conclusion. Boorstin's work was, in a sense, both a culmination and a departure from his earlier works. In perhaps his best and certainly his most intellectually interesting work, *The Lost World of Thomas*

[31] Tamara Hareven, ed., *Anonymous Americans: Explorations in Nineteenth-Century Social History* (Englewood Cliffs, N. J., 1971), offers a good introduction to the ties between popular culture materials and the new social history. Perhaps the two most influential early quantitative studies both listed below, suggest especially well how broad conclusions rest less on the data than on cultural assumptions and implications that need to be explored through other kinds of sources as well. See Lee Benson, *The Concept of Jacksonian Democracy: New York as a Test Case* (Princeton, 1961), and Stephan Thernstrom, *Poverty and Progress: Social Mobility in a Nineteenth-Century City* (Cambridge, Mass., 1964). Mary Ryan's recent study illustrates the growing integration of popular culture to quantitative data in reaching answers. See *Cradle of the Middle Class: The Family in Oneida County, New York, 1790–1865* (New York, 1981).

Jefferson, Boorstin detailed the limitations of the vision of Jefferson and his 'circle' by suggesting the many areas in which they simply assumed rather than explored basic positions. Boorstin developed this idea, more abstractly and much less critically, in his *Genius of American Politics* where, in line with his own transformation toward assertive patriot, he now treated a rather simplistic pragmatism—no one cares about ideas, so we Americans all get on right friendly and effectively —as the source of unparalled national virtue and success.[32] These ideas were pasted onto *The Colonial Experience*, most oddly in the section on the Puritans, who surely cared about right ideas as strongly as any social group could. By the time Boorstin wrote *The National Experience*, however, his book came to illustrate rather than argue his thesis. What ideas popped up were handled so casually that the material equally illustrated the opposite argument. Given the threadbare quality of repeated paeans to anti-intellectualism, the intellectual loss was slight, and many of the topics he spilled out—place names, community boosterism, the balloon-frame house, claims clubs—were stimulating. Like twentieth-century studies of popular culture, it drew attention to many areas that could be investigated, but it also suggested that such topics were there to be enjoyed more than pondered. The book intimated that American scholarship, like American life, was, at its best, characterized by genial thoughtlessness.

In the meantime scholarship, serious enough for any taste, was going forth regarding the 'neglected'—perhaps most notably women, workers, and blacks. Quite soon it became clear that quantitative study, valuable and necessary as it was, pro-

[32] Daniel Boorstin, *The Lost World of Thomas Jefferson* (New York, 1948); *The Genius of American Politics* (Chicago, 1953); *The Americans: The Colonial Experience* (New York, 1958); *The Americans: The National Experience* (New York, 1965). In this last book, for example, Boorstin insists that community precedes government, in a discussion where the evidence suggests the opposite (pp. 65–72). Russell B. Nye offers rather similar treatment in his useful survey of the more common topics of popular culture. See his work *The Unembarrassed Muse: The Popular Arts in America* (New York, 1970).

vided not answers but data that had to be worried into meaning, much like personal letters, or newspaper opinions, or folk tales. Sometimes the figures might contradict an assumption or conclusion; often they might suggest answers or probabilities. But never was their meaning self-evident. In addition to the uncertainties in the data, there also lurked questions that the most perfect figures would scarcely answer. Did workers move a lot from place to place because they were desperate, or because they were ambitious, or because, like much of the middle class, they were restless? Was the fact that the poorest laborers in a community seldom advanced in job category, but tended to buy homes and have bank savings and see a substantial portion of their children move up a notch, proof of the falsity or the truth of the promise of American life? Did the separation of middle class women from the world of paid work and formal politics isolate them or open to them involvement in certain areas of society from which they formed beachheads of female power? How often need slaves be whipped to make that form of action a central aspect of their control? What yearly rate of family separation need occur to make that a 'significant' aspect of slavery? What do wages, or amount of land ownership, or divisions of wealth in a community tell about the elusive realities of power and prestige there? If many new people became wealthy but many old rich families stayed wealthy, does this support or deny the notion of America as a land of opportunity?

To many of these questions, the confusions lay in ambiguities of definition of the kind William James suggested in the problem his philosophical friends debated after they walked around a tree to better see a squirrel, which foiled them by circling behind the trunk from them as they circled it. And had they gone around the squirrel? But it also became clear that the questions involved not simply the data and definitions but the consciousness of those experiencing the situation. And how could one get at that, except by looking, not at canonized culture, but at those remnants of popular culture that might tell how people responded to and structured their experiences: letters, diaries, reminiscences, newspapers, books, theater, social practices, dress, home furnishings, recipes, place names, popular songs, hymns, public meetings and communal lynchings, sports, sewing circles, parades. The list could, and should, be extended indefinitely. Zelig might have finished *Moby Dick*; people, even undergraduates, have been known to. But historians may live, and die, happily knowing that they won't ever exhaust popular or neglected culture. People and societies have too much variety and inventiveness to require that scholars try to understand them only by interpreting *Moby Dick* or the causes of the Civil War, for the two hundred-sixty-fourth time—unless they prefer to, of course. But let's hope that some scholars, like Melville's Bartleby regarding the canonized conventionalities, 'prefer not'—without starving.

What's needed in popular or neglected culture is some of the intensity and rigor and complexity that scholarship at best brings to its study of canonized political or intellectual or aesthetic culture, a determination to figure out what's going on in the minds that create, or practice, or absorb it. Good things are being done, such as Lawrence Levine's study of slave songs and tales, Eugene Genovese's fascinating exploration of slave religious experiences, and aspects of Herbert Gutman's handling of worker culture. Yet even in valuable works on popular culture, there tend to be disappointments that fall broadly into two compartments, both connected with the joint tendency of deplorers and enthusiasts to take the content of neglected culture lightly.

First is the tendency, especially strong in liberal historiography, to deplore earlier prejudices, instead of trying to understand more fully their roots and their limitations. Let me illustrate with three examples, all books that I respect, drawn from the Jacksonian period, which should make clear these difficulties. These illustrations also show how old, varied, and essential are historical contributions to the study of popular culture.

The first is Ray Allen Billington's *The Protestant Crusade*, the classic study of nativist books of the era, surely an excellent example of properly uncanonized culture. No one could argue with Billington's basic description of much of nativist feeling as 'bigotry' (with an occasional aside that sometimes Catholics may have triggered hostility). Yet there is loss, I think, in the fact that readers are encouraged to come away from the material comfortably concluding that nativists were paranoid nasties instead of pondering how hard it is to preserve freedom in a complicated context: in a society where opposing groups have many legitimate interests that aren't fully reconcilable; in a world where hate, paranoia, and scapegoating always skirt the edges of issues that deeply divide; in a situation where relativism threatens all commitment, and pretensions to peculiar guardianship of universal truth challenge serious dissent. One cannot object to Billington's horror at Philadelphia nativists' burning Catholic churches and Irish homes. One should object, I think, to his glib acceptance of the reasonableness of the Irish attack on a nativist political rally in a public square in an Irish section of town. And if one thinks about the issues involved here, specifically those of freedom of speech and political assembly, and of the people killed—all of whom were nativists shot to death before there was any suggestion of violence on their part—the story becomes not a moral melodrama of simple villains and even simpler victims, but a complicated morality play involving issues at the heart of democracy. Surely the lesson of the dangers of bigotry is deepened not denigrated if one is led to see the tragedies of these events less in terms of their perpetrators' vileness than in relation to a democratic society's inevitable dilemmas and potential for viciousness.

In the books as well as the events related to his story, Billington seeks out the excess rather than the limitations. Why, despite the popularity of the respectable pornography of Maria Monk, and the twisted excesses of the picture of Catholic practices, did no nativists ever suggest banning convents or cathedrals, or urge legal suppression of priests and nuns? Convent visitations were a nasty joke (at which few failed to laugh when the chief Massachusetts investigator took along his mistress at public expense), while some ludicrousness adhered to the nativists' primary proposal, requiring twenty-one-years' residence here prior to citizenship—on the grounds that, if it took American males twenty-one years to prepare to vote, it should take the Irish *at least* equally long. Yet this is hardly a pogrom, and there is need to consider not only the sources of mean-spirited attacks on particular groups, but the causes that often limited and blunted them.[33]

Ruth Miller Elson's survey of textbooks, *Guardians of Tradition*, a good work on a major subject, also fits the data too readily into expectations of what should exist. Elson's handling of children's textbooks, probably the best indicators of a nineteenth-century American common culture, ties everything to the capitalist ethic—honesty, promptness, hard work, thrift—or to national, religious, and racial narrowness.[34] In my reading of one of Elson's central texts, I catch glimpses of some of these things, and reiterated emphasis on a few, especially honesty. But several other stresses contradict or complicate Elson's portrayal. The patriotism of McGuffey's Readers seems always tied to the best actions and writings in the American tradition, and never argues and seldom intimates national superiority. It is also modified by respect for writings and peoples of other countries. Elements of the 'Protestant ethic,' such as thrift, are seldom mentioned, and never at the expense of

[33] Ray Allen Billington, *The Protestant Crusade, 1800–1860: A Study in The Origins of Nativism* (New York, 1938).

[34] Ruth Miller Elson, *Guardians of Tradition: American Textbooks in the Nineteenth Century* (Lincoln, Neb., 1964). Elson wholly neglects humor and specifically denies any expressions of sympathy about poverty. I've looked only at McGuffey's Readers, perhaps a skewed sample, although they sold about 107 million copies between 1836 and 1890. See John A Neitz, *Old Textbooks* (Pittsburgh, 1961), pp. 72–73. My selections come from the *Fifth Reader* (Cincinnati, 1844), the only one edited by Alexander (rather than William) McGuffey, but there are similar passages in the other readers.

that trait given cardinal emphasis, generosity. While there are few pictures of Catholics or blacks—despite some passages from writers like Cardinal Newman and Father Matthew—there were no derogatory portrayals either. And the bestowal of material rewards, of a modest kind anyway, at a story's end suggests, not the complacent equation that 'well-off equals worthy,' but rather the insistence that there was moral meaning in the universe. This stress is made clear as many of these heroes and heroines suffer a near lifetime of privation—all the time remaining wholly virtuous—before providence rewards not their hard work but their moral integrity and generosity. And although never suggesting much practical reform, the stories repeatedly present social suffering that has nothing to do with personal flaws. One selection, 'It Snows,' presents several stanzas showing how pleasant snow is for the well-off but then concludes:

> 'It snows!' cries the Widow, 'O God!' and her sighs
> Have stifled the voice of her prayer;
> Its burden ye'll read in her tear-swollen eyes,
> On her cheek sunk with fasting and care.
> 'Tis night, and her fatherless ask her for bread,
> But 'He gives the young ravens their food,'
> And she trusts till her dark hearth adds horror to dread,
> And she lays on her last chip of wood.
> Poor sufferer! that sorrow thy God only knows;
> 'Tis a most bitter lot to be poor, when it snows!

Such dark hearths are overlooked in studies of both nineteenth-century texts and of the poem's author, Sarah Hale. The problem is that students of popular culture, unlike those who work with elite artifacts, neglect what is surprising or strangely deepening because they expect their material to wear its meaning on its sleeve. Yet, the suggestive nuances require as subtle handling as those in high culture, perhaps even more so because the deepest implications are more subconsciously than consciously expressed.

Elson neglects the puzzling comic selections in McGuffey's Readers, a substantial portion of the whole, which often mock the very values upheld in the serious sections. What would an eleven-year-old make of patriotism, heroism, faithfulness, love, and even life, when taught to read partly on 'Faithless Nelly Gray':

> Ben Battle was a soldier bold,
> And used to war's alarms;
> But a cannon-ball took off his legs,
> So he laid down his arms!
>
> . . .
>
> Now Ben, he loved a pretty maid,
> Her name was Nelly Gray;
> So he went to pay her his devoirs,
> When he'd devoured his pay.
>
> But when he called on Nelly Gray,
> She made him quite a scoff;
> And when she saw his wooden legs,
> Began to take them off!
>
> 'O Nelly Gray! O Nelly Gray!
> Is this your love so warm?
> The love that loves a scarlet coat
> Should be more uniform!'
>
> Said she, 'I loved a soldier once,
> For he was blithe and brave;
> But I will never have a man
> With both feet in the grave!
>
> 'Before you had these timber toes,
> Your love I did allow,
> But then, you know, you stand upon
> Another footing now!'

Convinced that, although he has no feet, someone else was standing in his shoes, the former soldier got a rope, again 'enlisted in the Line,' and hanged himself by removing his wooden legs. The poem concludes:

And there he hung, till he was dead
  As any nail in town:
For, though distress had cut him up,
  It could not cut him down!

Just what traditions were the people who accepted such passages guardians of? Certainly something more interesting, I think, than comes from our treasured cliches about Victorianism.

Robert Toll's study of ministrelsy, *Blacking Up*, much more self-consciously a part of the 'new' popular culture field, shows similar limitations. For Toll, the key to minstrelsy is racism, an argument (like Billington's) convincing enough. It's easy to see in these stage skits and songs the seeds and sometimes the husks of subsequent racial stereotypes. Yet, one also sees in them sentimental pictures of romantic blacks, sharp folk wisdom, the wit of wise fools, and many not very covert attacks on slavery and racism. Faithless Nelly Gray is very different from the faithful love of her darker namesake:

One night I went to see her, but 'she's gone,' the neighbors say
  The white man bound her with his chain.
They have taken her to Georgia for to wear her life away,
  As she toils in the cotton and the cane.

chorus:

Oh my poor Nelly Gray, They have taken you away.
  And I'll never see my darling anymore.
I'm sitting on the river and I'm weeping all the day
  For you've gone from the Old Kentucky shore.

How are the thesis-jarring elements of sentimental sympathy and covert antislavery protest in these lines tied to the more negative tone of racism? Certainly Toll's assertion that minstrelsy offers no favorable portraits of blacks and black traits, save that of 'the asexual Old Darkey,' is contradicted by much of the material he includes and more that he doesn't.[35]

[35] Robert Toll, *Blacking Up: The Minstrel Show in Nineteenth-Century America* (New York, 1974). I develop these problems more fully in an article written with William Stowe, 'White-Black Humor,' *Journal of Ethnic Studies* 3 (1975):78–96.

Another flaw accompanies the tendency to see only a simple version of what we already know in popular culture. Meaning often becomes truncated because there is so little contextual or comparative understanding, so little sense of what preceded, followed, paralleled, or contributed to the main show. In Billington, the Catholics are, for the most part, passive victims and not active participants in the battle. Nor does Billington explore how Protestant leaders who were not nativists responded either to Catholicism or to the anti-Catholic crusade. Catholic views about Luther, or Methodists, or religious toleration are not handled, even though they are obviously germane to any consideration of bigotry. With Elson there is almost no consideration of textbooks in other countries, or in later periods, or in parochial schools that might give a sharper sense of what was peculiar in the public school texts of that era. And Toll makes few probing references to the parallel low comedy stereotyping of Irish, Frenchmen, Jews, sailors, or Yankees—types that often became especially popular with the groups they caricatured—in ways that might clarify the influences of racism in changing such characterizations.

Because the understanding of popular culture is always complex, the common notion that one study of various subjects is enough (or more than enough) is mistaken. Understanding will grow, as it does in other fields, with competing interpretations, and will not always come quickly. Perhaps no area has so been so richly explored recently as women's culture: Among the writers addressing the subject are Linda Kerber and Mary Beth Norton on Revolutionary women; Julie Jeffries on frontier women; Nancy Cott on the bonds of womanhood, Carroll Smith-Rosenberg on female friendships; as well as Daniel Scott Smith, Barbara Berg, and Barbara Epstein on domestic feminism and its social adjuncts. The list could be easily much extended. From this perspective has come attention to a group of mid-nineteenth-century women writers who were all immensely popular. Ann Douglas has continued the tradition of earlier male scholars in disparaging the conventionality and moralism of these authors, which she sees at the heart of a trivializing feminization of American culture in the nineteenth century.[36] Other scholars of the period have tended to react to such easy put-downs by stressing the opposite argument, namely, that a covert protest at women's limited role was shown by their heroines' triumph over hostile circumstances, although these victories were presented in conventional rather than questioning terms. Some have even claimed a radical unconventionality in these novels.[37] Mary Kelley has most recently surveyed these best selling women authors with strong admission of 'ambiguities,' but her concern has been with collective biography more than with an analysis of the books themselves.[38] Despite this variety of able scholarship, these books and articles give little sense of why this fiction was so attractive. None of them consider very much the less successful female fiction that might offer some key to peculiar sources of popularity. None of them strongly differentiate between the various works in the genre. And there are few clues about how to evaluate this literary form. None offer me much explanation about why *Ruth Hall* and the Fanny Fern sketches strike me as so vital, while I could finish Mrs. E. D. E. N. Southworth's *Ishmeal* only through true grit and Maria Cummins's *The Lamplighter* not even with that. I sense that the historical suggestiveness of this fiction is just beginning to be touched, and its aesthetic qualities scarcely at all.

[36] Ann Douglas, *The Feminization of American Culture* (New York, 1977). Her ideas largely repeat those in Leslie Fiedler, *Love and Death in the American Novel* (New York, 1960) and Henry Nash Smith, *Democracy and the Novel: Popular Resistance to Classic American Writers* (New York, 1978). All represent variants on Dwight MacDonald's notion of a 'Gresham's law of culture,' namely, that bad art drives out good.

[37] Much more enthusiastic arguments about the critical and radical views in this literature appear in Dee Garrison, 'Immoral Fiction in the Late Victorian Library,' *American Quarterly* 28 (1976):71–89; Nina Baym, *Women's Fiction: A Guide to Novels By and About Women in America, 1820–1970* (Ithaca, 1978); and, most richly, in Helen Papashvily, *All the Happy Endings: A Study of the Domestic Novel in America* (New York, 1956).

[38] Mary Kelley, *Private Women, Public Stage: Literary Domesticity in Nineteenth-Century America* (New York, 1984).

In the area of worker culture, scholarly efforts have been even more a product of assertion that analysis, partly because it's less easy to find obvious sources. Paul Faler has best suggested the kind of literary source that might be used—letters, diaries, newspapers, but their sparsity and their questionable ties to worker sensibilities gave some thinness to even his account. For Faler's 'radical' group, for example, the proof rests on a short-lived worker paper, edited not by a Lynn laborer but by a transient advocate-newspaperman. In this field we need to discover more telling books or documents, and perhaps interpret more closely things like public celebrations, worker festivities, parades, and 'turnout' rhetoric and practices.[39] It would be highly telling if we could learn a bit about what books workers owned or borrowed, what songs they sang, what family rituals they practiced. The very question of whether there is anything that could be meaningfully segregated as working class culture (or middle class or elite) depends on exploring more closely the similarities, differences, and, most important, the shadings of difference in emphasis within general assumptions and traditions.

The list of what might be done with books is so broad that one can do little more than list some of one's favorite things—if other people would only do them. Get a decent, careful index of *Niles' Register*, and maybe a few other major periodicals, so that one could use magazines more readily for what they tell about response to many topics. Decently index at least one major newspaper for the same purpose. Explore more seriously the good penny press that grew up in the 1830s, without glib assurance that it represents primarily sensationalist journalism. My cursory reading in the *Baltimore Sun* and the *Philadelphia Public Ledger* suggests that they represented major

[39] Paul G. Faler, *Mechanics and Manufacturers in the Early Industrial Revolution: Lynn, Massachusetts, 1780–1860* (Albany, 1981); John F. Kasson, *Civilizing the Machine: Technology and Republican Values in American 1776–1790* (New York, 1976); Sean Wilentz, *Chants Democratic: New York City and the Rise of the American Working Class, 1790–1865* (New York, 1984).

gains in journalistic as well as marketing competence, though the attempts to apply 'objectivity,' that twentieth-century talisman, obscure the real issues.

My wish list goes on. Study hymns. Explore the social convictions of mainline Protestant and Catholic journals. Analyze the toasts at political, cultural, and occupational banquets. Examine the questions and answers that engaged debating societies. Give a close reading to frontier, political, and urban humor. Examine the agricultural press, since by far the largest group of American worker-entrepreneurs in this period, farmers, have been most neglected. Ditto for farm women. Consider nuns, the most neglected large group of working women and communitarian experimenters. Read the subterranean literature of large cities: brothel directories, fireboy songs, and protest literature like *The Almighty Dollar*. Analyze police dockets and the police columns—and lists of sermon topics—in various newspapers. Read vigilante publications, without taking their obviously self-justifying myths at face value. Consider communal promotional and historical literature, to see when and how towns and cities and neighborhoods gave a semblance of permanence to themselves when all quantification seems to suggest perpetual flux. Ponder cookbooks and the menus of oyster houses and Delmonico's. If possible, figure out who checked out what books from merchants', mechanics', church, and public libraries. Think about what children were taught in Sabbath schools and confirmation classes. Study more closely and variously political culture in the age, and, until that's done, avoid plugging materials into Democrat-Whig pigeonholes on the basis of cliches drawn from Progressive historiography, one of the commonest techniques for explaining away instead of exploring this material.[40]

[40] The assumptions of simplistic political ideology, drawn from progressive cliches, is clear, I think, in much of the cultural treatment of James Fenimore Cooper and in works like Kenneth Lynn's *Mark Twain and Southwestern Humor* (New York, 1959), where the Whig label is put on a group of writers, mostly Democrats, and broad patterns extrapolated from works by Augustus Longstreet, most of which are not found in

And do all this—and much more, of course—with the caring and carefulness that one would give to another analysis of the words of Abraham Lincoln or *Moby Dick*. Do such things, and surely we will have a more interesting scholarly world through this formal wedding between books and neglected culture, as we do now through their casual intercourse.

'I (y)am what I (y)am,' saith Yahweh and Popeye. But scholarship, lacking omniscience and always in need of spinach, is what, and how richly, scholars learn to see and connect. We are what we do. And exploring widely varied aspects of neglected culture will remain, as it always has been, part of the unfinished work. Despite the claims of new departures from all sides, a field can hardly be new or faddish when it was the speciality of that 'father of history,' Herodotus, who explored comparative popular culture with such geniality. Now, had that been tied to Thucydides' analytic bent . . . . Ah, well. The work continues, stumblingly, imperfectly, glibly, apocalyptically, tellingly—humanly, you might say.

---

the writings of other members of the school. Collections of historical sources for this period suggest many potential topics related to popular culture. See John Demos, *Remarkable Providences, 1600–1760* (New York, 1972); Gordon S. Wood, *The Rising Glory, 1760–1820* (New York, 1972); Carl Bode, *Antebellum Culture* (Carbondale, Ill., 1970); David Brion Davis, *Antebellum American Culture: An Interpretive Anthology* (Lexington, Mass., 1979); David Grimsted, *Notions of the Americans, 1820–1860* (New York, 1970); Alan Trachtenberg, *Democratic Vistas, 1860–1880* (New York, 1970).

A Comment on Mr. Grimsted's Paper

It is not an easy task for me to comment on a paper so deeply rooted in a culture that is not my own—and all of Mr, Grimsted's allusions are not as clear to me, as for example. the first reference to *Zelig*. I want to say also that the expression 'popular culture' surely has not the same immediate meaning for American and French historians. In the United States it refers to the contemporary mass culture, generally considered as a poor, manipulated and alienating culture. In France—and perhaps in Europe—the term 'popular culture' evokes at first a lost culture, lively in the ancien régime societies, a culture different from and resistant to the legitimate culture that the Church and the State tried to impose. To distinguish clearly between these two contradictory meanings of the same expression seems important in order to avoid ambiguities and misunderstandings as much as possible. This said, I want only to stress some general questions raised by the paper and to propose some reflections on the ways in which the history of books and publishing can be used as an entry into the study of popular culture. I want to agree with Mr. Grimsted's criticism of the dominant and classical understanding of popular culture, either in America or in France. This understanding is based on three assumptions: first, that popular culture can be defined by contrast to what it is not; secondly, that it is possible to characterize as popular—in a strictly social sense—the public of particular cultural productions; and thirdly, that cultural artifacts can be considered as socially pure, popular in and of themselves.

These three characteristics, recognized as basic in the American theories of popular culture, were also central in the classical

This article, in slightly different form, was read at the conference on the history of the book in American culture as commentary on the paper delivered by Mr. Grimsted.

works done in France on popular literature, that is to say, the chapbooks printed in such provincial cities as Troyes, sold by peddlers, and generally known as the *Bibliothèque bleue*. According to the traditional hypothesis, it was suggested that these books were intended for the people of the countryside, and that their texts were anonymous works, based on oral traditions and folk culture. But it is now clear that these two assumptions are dubious. All the texts of the French chapbooks had already been printed before their popular editions, and all have a learned origin and circulation previous to or parallel with their diffusion by the *Bibliothèque bleue*. And it is now possible to say that the chapbooks did not have a specific public but constituted a reading matter for different social groups, each approaching it in ways ranging from a basic deciphering of signs to fluent reading. This French example fits very well with the remarks made by Mr. Grimsted on the audience of the opera in the United States in the 1840s, or on the readers of James Fenimore Cooper and Walter Scott.

I believe, therefore, that we must replace the study of cultural objects or productions considered as socially pure with another point of view that recognizes each cultural form as a mixture, whose constituent elements meld together indissolubly, whose public in the modern and early modern societies is always cross-class and mixed.

Perhaps it is pointless to try to identify popular culture by some supposedly specific distribution of cultural objects, for example, by some genres of printed materials. Their distribution is always more complex than it might seem at first glance, as are their appropriations by groups or individuals. A sociology of distribution, implying that the classification of social groups corresponds strictly with a classification of cultural products or practices, can no longer be accepted uncritically. It is clear that the appropriation of texts or codes or values in a given society may be a more distinctive factor than the always illusory correspondence between a series of products and a specific sociocultural level. The popular cannot be found ready-made in a set of texts that merely needs to be identified, listed, analyzed. Above all, the popular indicates a kind of relation, a way of using cultural products, or ideas and attitudes that are shared by all of a society but used in styles that vary. Such an argument evidently changes the work of the historian because it implies identifying and distinguishing the different ways in which cultural sets are differently appropriated.

For a history of the book, such a point of view as that suggested by Mr. Grimsted has several consequences. In the first place, it requires one to recognize and to differentiate the contrasted ways of reading that exist in a given society. Perhaps we could characterize popular reading as a mode that needs texts broken into numerous segments, articulated on a small set of narrative schemas, with many repetitions, summaries, and titles. That is to say, popular reading can be described as a unique form of reading that differs from learned reading, in which the reader is able not only to grasp the texts in their overall meaning, but also to classify immediately each text in a canonical repertory of genres, and to understand texts that have very different structures.

Secondly, to define culture as a plurality of appropriations forces one to focus upon the implied readers and/or reading that each publisher inscribes in his editions. If we accept the idea that the same text can circulate in different social groups, it is necessary to describe closely the physical, material, sometimes textual differences that exist between the printed objects that make that text available to different publics. Surely, Fenimore Cooper belongs to elite and popular and middle class culture, *but* his text reached these different milieus through various printed forms. The case is clear for the *Bibliothèque bleue*: the texts of the series were learned works, mainly religious or literary, but the popular publishers adapted their presentation for readers who were not learned. They reduced the original texts, and simplified them in order to permit a process of reading that avoids any memorization of numerous characters or episodes. They divided the chapbook, creating new chapters, multiplying paragraphs, adding titles and summaries, in order to facilitate a process of reading that required short and closed sequences. Therefore, to study popular literature is, in this case, to study how the publishers tried to make a learned or shared text compatible with specific cultural abilities.

From this perspective, a topic very important for me—and now to other French colleagues—is the problem of the relationship between visual images and written words in the prints published for a public that is not, or not only, the public of the *virtuosi* of reading. The different possible relationships between text and image, from inclusion in the same space to complete separation, create various possibilities for decoding the visual message or understanding the text itself. It seems to me that when images and texts appear side by side, the printed material in which they are located was more likely to be understood in the same or similar ways both by the fluent reader and by persons only capable of a rudimentary reading. All these kinds of printed materials (almanacs, broadsheets, posters, comic strips) *surely* played a great role in familiarizing the people of the early modern and modern period with printed and written culture. By contrast, when the image and the text are separated, the image, considered as an illustration, probably gave rise to different readings, some that understood all the dimensions of the relation between the two languages, and others that only made sense of the image and the text separately. But, however that may be, I think that the study of the placement, role, and form of images in those publications dedicated to a large public is one of the major issues in the reappraisal of popular printed culture.

On another point, I fully agree with the two-fold criticism made by Mr. Grimsted of the opposed theories of mass culture, considered either as powerful manipulation or direct expression of popular myths and desires. These two views seem to obliterate the reality of cultural consumption. Cultural consumption, such as reading, is always a form of production that creates ways of using that cannot be limited to the intentions of the producers or manipulators. Cultural consumption is not passive, or dependent, or submissive, but a creative activity, an 'art of doing' and 'doing with' imposed materials. In no way can the user's or reader's intelligence be reduced to a soft wax on which the ideas, representations, and models of the mass culture, or of the culture for the mass, could be inscribed with absolute legibility. For too long, the acculturating force of messages manipulated by dominant groups has been overestimated, whether in the case of mass culture in the twentieth century or the culture imposed by the absolutist state and the religious reformations—Catholic or Protestant—in early modern Europe. For too long, the history of culture has been written as a succession of golden ages of popular culture and of dark ages in which it is repressed, disintegrated, destroyed. This schema has been used to understand the cultural changes before and after the thirteenth century, before and after the mid-seventeenth century, before and after the modernization of fin-de-siècle Europe, before and after the development of a canned and Americanized mass culture in the 1950s.

Contrary to this habit, which always locates popular culture in a world we have lost, in a golden time, a history of the printed materials intended for a large public must consider all the traces of the different uses of these materials, all the cultural and social practices through which the printed matter is appropriated. For example, in early modern Europe, between the practice of private, individual and silent reading on the one hand, and passive listening to a printed text read aloud by an oral mediator on the other hand, there exists a wide range of attitudes toward printed culture, collective and utilitarian attitudes, rooted in the basic social experiences of the popular classes, developed in the workshops, the festive confraternities, or the religious conventicles. I suppose that the same kind of relationships to books existed too in America between the seventeenth and the nineteenth centuries. In his paper Mr. Grimsted suggests that the term *neglected* might be better than *popular* to qualify this 'other' culture which is not the canonized one. It is possible to agree, provided that the opposition is seen as a process that is constantly at work, determining the boundary between the neglected and the canonized. Let me take the example of early modern France. The diffusion of the chapbooks on a large scale had two consequences. First, it led to a contrast between two sets of texts: those that aimed to feed the curiosity of the popular classes, i.e., texts abandoned by learned readers, and the texts that constituted a renewed high culture. But, as I said before, the texts shared by all the society are very numerous. In this case, the chaptooks created another difference: between two kinds of printed materials, with forms, circulations, and uses that are no longer one. The material aspects of books indicate clearly this contrast: on the one hand, a book can be seen as a noble object, refined, bound, and preserved; on the other hand, a book can be defined as an ephemeral, rough, and cheap object. Hence, the texts published in this manner were progressively stigmatized and became in the eyes of the elite unworthy reading because they were immediately recognized as belonging to another culture. Hence, the neglected culture is not fixed once and for all, but results from complex processes that qualify as distinctive, or disqualify as vulgar, certain texts and objects.

I think that when the differences in book diffusion were attenuated, when the printed work was no longer a rare possession, the distinction between popular and elite concerned above all the *manner* of reading—whether recommended or spontaneous, praised or condemned. This is why the study of popular printed culture implies for me a study of the successive and contradictory representations of the different uses of books.

The propositions listed by Mr. Grimsted at the end of his paper are very impressive and suggestive. They lead one to choose different series of printed materials and to study them as texts, as objects, as commodities.

Roger Chartier

The Bibliography and Textual Study of American Books

G. THOMAS TANSELLE

I

THE WORDS one reads on a printed page are the product of a complex process of transmission, reaching ultimately back to the author's mind—a process affected both by mechanical factors (the physical routines associated with pen and type) and by more intangible social and economic pressures. What a text says is forever linked to the mundane realities underlying the physical product that gives the text a material embodiment. For this reason, the interdependence of all approaches to the study of the history of books is nowhere better exemplified than in the fields of bibliographical and textual scholarship. Those interested in tracing the textual history of a printed work and assessing the authority of variants in its text must take into account all evidence they can find relating to the printing and publishing history of the work—the clues present in copies of the printed books themselves, as well as information from printers' and publishers' records, from letters and journals, and from previous scholarly studies that serve to suggest norms and contexts in regard to printing and publishing practice and indeed to society at large. Conversely, those pursuing broad historical questions raised by the existence of books—the influence of books on the social and intellectual life

This paper was prepared for a needs-and-opportunities conference on the history of the book in American culture, held at the American Antiquarian Society November 1–3, 1984, and funded in part by a grant from the National Endowment for the Humanities, with a matching grant from the Earhart Foundation.

of a particular period, for example—must be concerned with the ideas in those books and therefore must take note of textual matters and of the connections between textual content and printing processes. The impact of a specific work cannot be properly examined without a knowledge of the textual differences among copies of that work, since obviously a difference in text may make a difference in readers' interpretations.

Once one understands how physical processes affect text and recognizes that all the copies of an edition, being separate physical objects, are separate pieces of evidence, one sees that intellectual history and bibliographical analysis are indissolubly tied. The emphasis in some recent scholarship on the changes in social and cultural life wrought by the coming of the printed book has perhaps made it somewhat less easy for us to keep in mind the similarities between books and manuscripts. We expect the texts of manuscripts to differ one from another; but we often expect printed texts—copies of a single edition, at least—not to vary. Obviously it is unscholarly to assume that objects one has not seen or examined are identical. I cannot think of any other area in which responsible scholars are so careless in their handling of historical evidence. The printed sheets of an edition are produced one by one, and therefore changes can enter, either intentionally or inadvertently, at any point in the process. It is naive to think of a text as being stable in print: a text not only varies, almost always, from one edition (that is, typesetting) to another; it also can vary—and often does so, in all periods, not just the early centuries of printing—from one copy of an edition to another. Such variations, along with other physical evidence, can increase one's knowledge of the bookmaking process, even as they increase one's understanding of the text.

These points are obvious. And yet, remarkably, they have not been heeded to any significant extent in the study of American books. Of course, the study of the book in America is a much larger subject than the study of American books; and to the extent that one is concerned with imported English books, the situation is not so depressing, for a great body of work devoted to the bibliographical analysis of English books has been produced in this century—work that not only illuminates the printing and textual history of particular books but also provides techniques and procedures of wider applicability. Yet however important British imports have been in the American book trade—and they have been very important indeed—the full story of that trade, and of the book in America more generally, must clearly take the native product into account as well. One of the primary tasks for the future is the careful scrutiny, the page-by-page examination, of multiple copies of American books, followed by the analysis of the physical evidence obtained thereby. The results would enrich, as well as revise, the story of American book production and would simultaneously enable us to comment in a more informed way on the texts that were made available to American readers. At present, however, the analytical bibliography of American books, particularly of the seventeenth and eighteenth centuries, remains in a primitive state.

Criticisms of this situation are nevertheless seldom heard. David D. Hall, in his James Russell Wiggins Lecture, *On Native Ground: From the History of Printing to the History of the Book* (Worcester: American Antiquarian Society, 1984; also printed in the Society's *Proceedings* 93[1983]:313–36), echoes the sentiments of many historians when he comments on the undeniable strength of the tradition of local imprint recording in the United States and judges that by the 1930s 'a distinct maturity had been achieved' (p. 10). He does not proceed to point out how immature in general that work was in comparison with what had by then been accomplished for English books, nor does he suggest how inadequate much of that work is by present-day standards of bibliographical research. There is no question about the quantity of work that has been done: my *Guide to the Study of United States Imprints* (Cambridge: Belknap Press of Harvard University Press, 1971) devotes sixty-seven pages to recording imprint lists and bibliographies, most of them regional in scope, and another ninety-four pages to enumerating works that list American imprints by genre. But we have no grounds for complacency in the face of all this work, for most of it shows no understanding of the fact that enumeration, even if that is the sole aim, must eventually rest on analysis. Naturally, we should be grateful for the devotion of scores of workers who have retrieved obscure printed items from their places of hiding and who have patiently pieced together a record of local printing; but we also have to recognize that this work is only a start and that it does not, by itself, put our national bibliography on a sound footing. Charles Evans, who undertook the more ambitious task of recording all American imprints to 1820,[1] certainly deserves our gratitude; but the genuine debt we owe him should not prevent our recognizing how amateurish and unsophisticated he was in bibliographical matters, compared with the scholars in England who, in Evans's time, were focusing on the bibliography of incunabula and pre-1640 British books.

Since then the record of early American printing has been substantially improved, largely through two efforts associated with the American Antiquarian Society: first, Clifford K. Shipton and James E. Mooney's *National Index of American Imprints through 1800* (1969), an offshoot of the production (also supervised by AAS) of the Readex Microprint set devoted to early American imprints; and second, the recataloguing of AAS's holdings of pre-1801 American imprints, as the first phase of the North American Imprints Program (one goal of which is to contribute the American entries to the Eighteenth-Century Short Title Catalogue project). These newly catalogued entries for AAS copies certainly surpass previous listings; nevertheless, they constitute a catalogue of a collection, not a bibliography, as long as the descriptions are based on the

[1] I shall not provide full citations of works, such as this, that are listed in my *Guide.*

examination of single copies.[2] It is the second phase of NAIP that will provide the opportunity for the emergence of a bibliography, for that phase is to consist of obtaining reports on copies in other libraries. Determining when the multiple reports of a given title refer to the same edition, or to different editions, or to different issues of a single edition, requires the analysis of physical evidence; and the contribution made by the resulting bibliography will rise in proportion to the amount of direct comparison of copies that can be managed. The English tradition of bibliographical analysis has kept the work on English books a step ahead: Katharine F. Pantzer, in revising the *Short-Title Catalogue* of pre-1640 English books (London: Bibliographical Society, 1926), has had the rich body of previous analytical work on these books to draw on and also has often engaged in further analysis herself, identifying issues and noting variant formes. One does not expect a work of this scope to present the quantity of physical detail that would be possible in a more specialized study; but one is continually impressed by how much intensive investigation does in fact underlie the entries in the new *STC* (1976–). The four-page table devoted to the *Book of Common Prayer* (16267 ff.), providing signature collations and identifying states, is of course exceptional, but it dramatically illustrates the necessity of examining bibliographical evidence. Many other, more routine, entries draw concisely on similar research, as when they cite variants in headlines (as in 21254 ff.) or particular reset sheets (as in 18282a) to distinguish editions. Without such analysis, an inventory of printed output does not fulfill its function, for its aim is not simply to record titles of works but to identify editions of those works.

This contrast in the treatment of the early printing of England and the United States is reflected in other comprehensive

[2] For further explanation of this point, see G. T. Tanselle, 'Descriptive Bibliography and Library Cataloguing,' *Studies in Bibliography* 30(1977):1–56; reprinted in *Selected Studies in Bibliography* (Charlottesville: Bibliographical Society of the University of Virginia, 1979), pp. 37–92.

bibliographies as well. There is the obvious contrast, for example, between David Foxon's exemplary *English Verse, 1700–1750* (Cambridge: Cambridge University Press, 1975), which includes signature collations in every entry, and Lyle Wright's *American Fiction* (covering 1774–1900; published 1939–69), which records only the number of pages of each item.[3] Lack of attention to physical evidence has unfortunately been a characteristic of much bibliographical work on Americana, even in studies of lesser scope than those of Evans and Wright. Among the best of the state imprint bibliographies to have appeared in the last twenty-five years are Robert Greenwood's for California (1961), Marcus A. McCorison's for Vermont (1963), Cecil K. Byrd's for Illinois (1966), George N. Belknap's for Oregon (1968), Evald Rink's for Delaware (1969), and Robert D. Armstrong's *Nevada Printing History* (Reno: University of Nevada Press, 1981); yet, excellent as these works are in many respects, none of them includes signature collations. Nor are signature collations to be found in such earlier prominent works of this kind as Winkler, Streeter, and Friend's for Texas (1949–63), Bristol's for Maryland (1953), Byrd and Peckham's for Indiana (1955), and Crandall's and Harwell's for the Confederate states (1955, 1957). The presence or absence of signature collations is a revealing touchstone of bibliographical approach, for those collations, by indicating the structure of each successive gathering of a book or pamphlet, provide the most basic record of physical makeup, to which any further bibliographical analysis must refer.[4] Failure

[3] Rather, it normally cites the last numbered page, in order 'to afford an idea of the length of the contents' (2d rev. ed. of vol. 1, 1969, p. x). Wright's essentially unbibliographical approach is further shown by his statement that 'rarely' has he 'examined more than one copy of a title' (p. ix).

[4] Early in the century Victor Hugo Paltsits, an accomplished bibliographer of Americana, issued 'A Plea for an Anatomical Method in Bibliography,' *Papers of the Bibliographical Society of America* 1(1904–7):123–24, calling for 'a more scholarly method in American bibliography,' which would entail 'an analysis of each volume by its component parts, by its pagination, by its signatures, and by the location of its plates and maps.' He complained, 'The mere lumping of pagination and plates falls far short of usefulness; it is, indeed, a source of irritation and annoyance.' His plea went largely unheeded in the field of Americana.

to include an element of such fundamental importance would seem to suggest a lack of understanding of the significance of what the analytical bibliographers of English literature have been discovering over the last century about the connections between text and physical structure.[5] In any event, the truth is that signature collations have had little role to play in the development of the form of the peculiarly American genre of state imprint bibliographies.

Douglas C. McMurtrie, whose voluminous production of imprint lists in the 1930s and 1940s helped establish as standard a form of entry without collation, stated explicitly in his *Manual of Procedure* for those employed in the American Imprints Inventory (Chicago: Historical Records Survey, 1938) that 'we want as a final record the equivalent of a good library catalogue card, which also constitutes a sound title for inclusion in a bibliography' (p. 20); he thus provided some instructions on recording pagination (pp. 31–34) but said nothing about signatures. (Of course, it might not have been feasible to instruct WPA workers in the rudiments of bibliographical analysis; but apparently McMurtrie saw no necessity for including signature collations in his own bibliographies.) Neither did the Bibliographical Society of America insist on signatures in the series of four imprint bibliographies it sponsored at McMurtrie's urging (on the Dakotas, Arkansas, Rhode Island, and Oklahoma, 1947–51); John E. Alden, however, who prepared the one on Rhode Island (1949), did include a signature collation in a few entries and complained in his preface, 'It is regrettable that in the collation the methods of the American Imprints Inventory did not permit the recording of signatures' (p. xi). A more significant statement than McMurtrie's *Manual*, by a more important scholar, was Lawrence C. Wroth's

[5] This lack of understanding can also be revealed by bibliographers who do give signature collations. Charles F. Heartman, for example, in his *American Primers, Indian Primers, Royal Primers* (1935) normally records signatures; but sometimes he says simply 'Irregular signatures' or 'No signatures'—as if the signatures themselves, rather than the gatherings, were of primary interest.

Rosenbach Lecture on 'Early Americana,' printed in *Standards of Bibliographical Description* (Philadelphia: University of Pennsylvania Press, 1949). Wroth, who had provided signature collations in *A History of Printing in Colonial Maryland* (1922), did recommend that standard entries for Americana should contain a 'summary statement of signatures' (p. 118), but he immediately added that his proposed 'minimum' would not be 'altogether acceptable to many careful bibliographers of today'—among whom he had in mind were presumably Curt F. Bühler and James G. McManaway, who contributed the essays on 'Incunabula' and 'Early English Literature' to the same volume. He was clearly departing from their recommendations: after registering his respect for 'a minute analysis of the make-up of a book,' he asserted that 'in the treatment of Americana the reward of this procedure seldom compensates for the pains required to carry it through' (p. 118). What he advocated for Americana was 'a shift from elaboration in the description of the physical form of a book to the consideration of its meaning in relation to its time and subject' (p. 112). That his suggestion of a 'summary statement of signatures' had little influence on bibliographers of Americana can therefore no doubt be explained by the context in which it was set. Wroth was in fact reaffirming a tradition that did not put great weight on physical analysis, as the juxtaposition of his essay with Bühler's and McManaway's made all the more evident.

The reasons for this situation make it an interesting episode in the history of scholarship, for they underscore the harmful effects of the lack of communication between fields. Modern analytical bibliography has developed largely in connection with literary study and the establishment of literary texts; and historians, dealing with what in general is thought of as 'non-literary' writing, have therefore often felt that they need not look closely into the matter of analytical bibliography, believing it to be more related to the concerns of literary scholars than to their own. The earliest important work in analytical and descriptive bibliography was in fact not literary in orientation, for it emerged from the examination of incunabula (many of which could scarcely be called 'literary' in content) in the late nineteenth century by such men as Henry Bradshaw, Robert Proctor, and A. W. Pollard. But the more direct impetus for the great elaboration of the field during this century was the work on Elizabethan and Jacobean drama undertaken in the early years of the century by Pollard, R. B. McKerrow, and W. W. Greg. They came to realize that an essential part of their preparation for understanding the textual history of a work and thus for making informed textual decisions was as thorough a knowledge as possible of the page-by-page printing history of the relevant editions. Their influential writings illustrated a new approach to the study of printed texts, based on the recognition that much important evidence relating to the production history of printed books remains accessible in the finished products.[6] This important insight is obviously applicable to all books of all periods; but the vast body of analytical work resulting from it has been largely devoted to English Renaissance drama, following the lead of Pollard, McKerrow, and Greg, with some attention being paid to other English books of literary content through the eighteenth century. When people speak of an Anglo-American tradition of bibliography, they are referring to the fact that American as well as British scholars have made notable contributions to the study of the physical evidence in books; the term does not refer to research on American books, for the bulk of the books examined in this way has been English. One can understand, of course, given the importance of the literature that appeared in English books of the sixteenth, seventeenth, and eighteenth

[6] I have offered some further reflections on the historical development of analytical and descriptive bibliography in 'Physical Bibliography in the Twentieth Century,' in *Books, Manuscripts, and the History of Medicine: Essays on the Fiftieth Anniversary of the Osler Library*, ed. Philip M. Teigen (New York: Science History Publications, 1982), pp. 55–79; and in 'The Evolving Role of Bibliography, 1884–1984,' in *Books and Prints, Past and Future: Papers Presented at the Grolier Club Centennial Convocation* (New York: Grolier Club, 1984), 15–31.

centuries, why those books have been subjected to intense scrutiny. But the neglect of the physical evidence in pre-nineteenth-century American books does not spring solely from the nature of their contents. It is largely the result of two fallacies that have been fostered by the historical circumstances under which analytical bibliography has grown: the notion that such analysis is tied to textual criticism and scholarly editing and the belief that it is a tool more appropriate for research on literature than on other kinds of writing. Neither of these positions is tenable; yet they have been accepted as true by many historians who are thoughtful in other respects.

Wroth's essay on 'Early Americana' is a prominent case in point. Although it makes a number of valuable peripheral observations, the argument at its center is seriously defective. In attempting to support his view that bibliographers of Americana should emphasize historical context rather than physical form, he sets forth a dubious distinction between belles-lettres and Americana: 'Works of the creative imagination—plays, poems, and novels—are subjective in origin, proceeding from within, from the mind and spiritual experience of the author. The normal work of Americana, on the other hand, is an objective work, brought into being through the impact upon the author of some event or movement or set of circumstances outside himself' (p. 111). The line separating belles-lettres from other writings, if there is one, has never been adequately defined, and Wroth's effort is clearly superficial; but for present purposes the important matter is what this division (however arrived at) leads to. It presumably provides the theoretical basis on which Wroth rests his statement, a few pages later, that the 'historian is less interested in minor textual differences than is the student of literature' (p. 118). But if historians are interested in what texts say, how can this be? Wroth's next sentence only confuses the issue: 'Such differences often are important, but the cost of discovering them and making them known is immense when it may be achieved only by the most intensive physical analysis of a volume.' If textual differences are 'often' important, one might expect a scholar to feel an obligation to uncover them, regardless of the arduousness of the process. Indeed, even if they were seldom important, the fact is that they obviously can be so, and one cannot know which is the case until one discovers and studies them. Wroth's elaboration of his point does not serve to lessen the fuzziness of the argument:

> Extraordinary results have been attained in the field of letters through this sort of bibliographical procedure, for in creative writing every textual difference, whether a radical revision or simply the change of an adjective or the cadence of a line, is or may be important to the student of taste or feeling. But I repeat that in my experience with Americana the discoveries made by these exhaustive procedures are so seldom important as to make their general adoption of no avail. Better to use that physical effort and cerebration in the study of the history and significance of the text in its relationship to subject and to other texts. (p. 119)

The double fallacy I spoke of underlies this passage, with its assumption that physical analysis must serve textual ends[7] and that a knowledge of textual variants is peculiarly relevant to literary study. There is no hint of recognition here that physical evidence is important in its own right, even if one had no interest whatever in textual matters; it is, after all, the primary evidence out of which the history of printing in a given time and place is built up, book by book. Nor does this passage suggest any understanding of the fact that all texts, literary or not, pose problems of interpretation and that a knowledge of textual variants is of interest not merely to 'the student of taste or feeling' but to all readers who wish to understand, as fully as they can, what a work is saying. Wroth's lapses here are sur-

[7] Wroth states flatly, 'The first and most important affirmation is that the end of bibliographical analysis is the elucidation of the history of texts' (p. 105). He calls this an 'accepted' definition; if so, it is a widespread misconception. Textual study, of course, is but one of the uses to which bibliographical analysis may be put.

prising, but I cite them because he is not the only scholar to have fallen into a similar line of thought. I have no doubt that many scholars even now would be inclined at first to agree with Wroth, until they stopped to examine more closely what is being said. If so, their first reaction is testimony to how little understood are the connections between the process of textual transmission and the intellectual content of the work transmitted, even among those accustomed to examining documentary evidence.

One hopeful recent sign is Hall's statement, in his Wiggins Lecture, that a task for the future is the incorporation of the findings of analytical bibliography into the more socially oriented history of the book (p. 27). Hall is not entirely free, however, of the misconceptions we have been considering, as his remark about 'the work of analytical bibliographers and their holy of holies, the text,' shows. Furthermore, he comments only on textual study directed toward establishing the texts intended by their authors.[8] But a related point worth adding is that for historical study one also is interested in less authoritative forms of a text if they were the ones that influenced people. If, for example, an unauthorized and carelessly produced edition of a work—one that had no connection with the author—was widely circulated, the historian cannot dismiss it, since many people would have encountered the author's ideas in this form. To attempt to establish the author's inten-

[8] He points out—what is obviously true—that it 'may be impossible to arrive at a text that corresponds exactly to the author's intention'; but the reasons for that situation are not what Hall implies in his ensuing discussion. 'Certainly the American printer and the American reader,' he says, 'were quite indifferent to this issue, content as they were to publish and to read the most extraordinarily corrupted editions. The very concept of a perfect text is an invention of the twentieth century, and cannot be imposed upon the past.' There is no doubt that readers of all places and times, not just early America, have generally been unconcerned about the reliability of the texts they read; and unquestionably some writers wavered among several intentions at various points in their work (textual scholars do not speak of 'perfect' texts). But these facts do not invalidate the scholar's attempt to uncover whatever can be learned about an author's intention and the extent to which it was realized in the published texts available to contemporary readers. The problem exists, whether or not much attention was paid to it in the past.

tion is certainly a basic task; but one must also recognize that the author's reputation, contemporary or posthumous, may have been based on an edition that in various ways subverted that intention. The importance of textual study for the historian is not simply to set matters right (that is, to ascertain just what the writer meant to say); it is also to put one in a better position for understanding what the contemporary audience *perceived* the writer to be saying. What may appear at first to be a contemporary misunderstanding of an author's point of view on a given point may actually have resulted from the correct interpretation of an incorrect text. Since the process of textual transmission leading to publication can so easily result in corrupt texts, it is perhaps not going too far to suggest that corrupt texts have in general been more widely read and have had a greater impact than accurate texts—with various concomitant distortions, both major and minor, in how those texts have been interpreted. The process of establishing accurate texts—which necessarily involves analysis of the physical bibliographical evidence, the clues present in the printed product itself—is therefore one that all historical scholars (in any field: literature, or music, or political history) have an obligation to be familiar with, whether or not they are preparing editions. It is simply part of the equipment necessary for historical investigation.

II

Any survey of what has been accomplished along these lines must deal to a considerable extent with work focusing on British or continental books. Because so little bibliographical work of an analytical nature has been devoted to American books, historians of the book in America must turn for basic instruction to studies that at first may seem unrelated to their concerns, particularly the large body of scholarship focusing on the physical evidence in the early editions of the plays of Shakespeare and his contemporaries. The most famous and influential book in the field of analytical bibliography is R. B. McKerrow's *An Introduction to Bibliography for Literary Students* (Oxford: Clarendon Press, 1927), which is still the best starting place. Written by one of the founders of the field, it effectively conveys the importance of, and the attitude of mind necessary for, the pursuit of bibliographical evidence. The last three words of the title should be ignored: McKerrow was addressing students of literature, but what he has to say is crucial for all who use printed books. For technical details—that is, for an account of the processes of typefounding, papermaking, printing, binding, and so on in various periods—McKerrow has been superseded by Philip Gaskell's *A New Introduction to Bibliography* (Oxford: Clarendon Press, 1972), which is the other book to start with. McKerrow's classic work, however, has not been superseded as a statement of an approach.[9] Armed with a point of view from McKerrow and a body of factual information from Gaskell, one can begin to examine physical features of books with some understanding of their significance. Although not intended as a textbook, Charlton Hinman's great work, *The Printing and Proof-Reading of the First Folio of Shakespeare* (Oxford: Clarendon Press, 1963), does serve as an introduction to the various techniques that have been developed for extracting information from physical evidence in Renaissance English books, since it makes skillful use of those techniques. Another similarly useful large work, which applies the techniques to quarto rather than folio printing, is the first volume of Peter W. M. Blayney's *The Texts of "King Lear" and Their Origins* (Cambridge: Cambridge University Press, 1982). A theoretical underpinning for the field is provided by Fredson Bowers's *Bibliography and Textual Criticism* (Oxford: Clarendon Press, 1964). Five years later D. F. McKenzie criticized the field for its incautious use of inductive evidence, in 'Printers of the Mind: Some Notes on Bibliographical Theories and

[9] I have elaborated on this point in a review of Gaskell in *Costerus*, n.s. 1(1974): 129–50.

Printing-House Practices,' *Studies in Bibliography* 22(1969): 1–75, which stressed the importance of research in printers' records. No one would defend the careless work that has sometimes been produced by analytical bibliographers whose enthusiasm outran their judgment, and no one would deny the importance of studying any surviving evidence in archival documents; but one must face the fact that the books themselves are part of the total body of evidence, and we have to continue to seek ways of deciphering and using the evidence in them.[10]

Hinman's book builds on a large body of work by many scholars, and the work has not stopped with Hinman. The literature of the analytical bibliography of Renaissance English books is so large that I shall not attempt to do more here than cite some outstanding examples of different techniques, which will serve to show the kind of thinking involved in the search for clues in physical evidence. Perhaps the most obvious technique is the examination of spelling differences throughout a volume to see whether they reflect the habits of different compositors and whether one can then assign specific sections of the book to each compositor; on this matter, see, for example, Charlton Hinman, 'Principles Governing the Use of Variant Spellings as Evidence of Alternate Setting by Two Compositors,' *Library*, 4th ser. 21(1940):78–94, and T. H. Hill, 'Spelling and the Bibliographer,' *Library*, 5th ser. 18 (1963):1–28. (Other features that might help to distinguish compositors—such as punctuation, contractions, and the typographic handling of stage directions, scene headings, and speech prefixes in plays—have also been studied in this way.) One of the most powerful techniques is the analysis of the recurrence of recognizable types: when pieces of type become damaged so that they are recognizable, their reappearances

[10] I have made these points in more detail in 'Bibliography and Science,' *Studies in Bibliography* 27(1974):55–89 (reprinted in *Selected Studies*, pp. 1–36); and I have also tried to show how analytical bibliography has contributed facts to general printing history, in 'Analytical Bibliography and Renaissance Printing History,' *Printing History* 3, no. 1(1981):24–33.

throughout a volume can be tracked, providing evidence as to when the type from a given forme was available for reuse, a fact that has a bearing on a number of matters, among them the determination of the order in which pages were set and how many were standing in type simultaneously. The detection and analysis of type shortages (signaled by a compositor's substitution of italic for roman, small capitals for large, and so forth) is similarly useful. These points are clearly set forth by Robert K. Turner, Jr., in 'Printing Methods and Textual Problems in *A Midsummer Night's Dream* Q1,' *Studies in Bibliography* 15 (1962):33–55, and in 'Reappearing Types as Bibliographical Evidence,' *Studies in Bibliography* 19(1966):198–209. Recurring types have been put to effective use in proving that certain books were set by formes (that is, according to the pages that would be on the press at one time) rather than seriatim (that is, in the numerical order of the pages); setting by formes, in turn, required 'casting off copy' to estimate how much text would fit on each page (a process that, when inaccurate, could obviously affect the text itself). The pioneering article in this area is William H. Bond's 'Casting Off Copy by Elizabethan Printers: A Theory,' *Papers of the Bibliographical Society of America* 42(1948):281–91; and one of the classic showpieces of bibliographical analysis is Charlton Hinman's 'Cast-Off Copy for the First Folio of Shakespeare,' *Shakespeare Quarterly* 6(1955):259–73.

In addition to establishing the history of the composition (typesetting) of an edition, the bibliographer can sometimes also work out the precise sequence of the formes through the press by observing the patterns of recurrence of particular settings of running titles (which are identifiable not only by damaged types but by peculiarities of spacing): see Fredson Bowers's 'Notes on Running-Titles as Bibliographical Evidence,' *Library*, 4th ser. 19(1938–39):315–38, and his 'The Headline in Early Books' and Charlton Hinman's 'New Uses for Headlines as Bibliographical Evidence,' in *English Insti-*

tute Annual 1941, pp. 185–205, 207–22. Evidence from paper is of course central to determining format and thus to the arrangement of the type-pages in the forme, and anyone who examines paper should understand the points made by Allan Stevenson in a series of ground-breaking articles: 'New Uses of Watermarks as Bibliographical Evidence,' *Studies in Bibliography* 1(1948–49):151–82; 'Watermarks Are Twins,' 4 (1951–52):57–91; 'Chain-Indentations in Paper as Evidence, 6(1954):181–95; and 'Paper as Bibliographical Evidence,' *Library*, 5th ser. 17(1962):197–212. There are other important articles on related questions of format, such as Kenneth Povey's 'On the Diagnosis of Half-Sheet Impositions,' *Library*, 5th ser. 11(1956):268–72; and discussions of cancels, such as R. W. Chapman's *Cancels* (London: Constable, 1930), are likely to make use of evidence from paper. The fact that stop-press alterations occurred routinely in the printing of seventeenth-century books provides a great body of textual variants that can shed light on proofreading procedures. Attempting to evaluate the significance of the various combinations of corrected and uncorrected formes that can occur has resulted in some of the most sophisticated pieces of analytical bibliography, such as Fredson Bowers's 'An Examination of the Method of Proof-Correction in *Lear*,' *Library*, 5th ser. 2 (1947–48):20–44, and his 'Elizabethan Proofing,' in *Joseph Quincy Adams Memorial Studies*, ed. James G. McManaway et al. (Washington: Folger Shakespeare Library, 1948), pp. 571–86.

These techniques, developed for the study of Renaissance books, are often applicable, sometimes with adjustments, to books of later periods. Compositor analysis, for example, is worth trying on later books, though the features that might vary from compositor to compositor may naturally be different at different times; and running-title analysis is productive for some eighteenth-century books, as David L. Vander Meulen demonstrates in 'The Printing of Pope's *Dunciad*, 1728,'

Studies in Bibliography 35(1982):271–85. (He also uses an eighteenth-century book to make a major contribution to the examination of paper: 'The Identification of Paper without Watermarks: The Example of Pope's *Dunciad,*' *Studies in Bibliography* 37[1984]:58–81.) In addition, new practices enter into book production in successive periods, leaving their mark on the finished books and thereby offering a new kind of evidence for investigation. A feature unique to eighteenth-century books is press figures, those numbers (not signatures) that often are present, one to a forme, in the lower margins. Of the many discussions of press figures, some of the most important are Philip Gaskell's 'Eighteenth Century Press Numbers: Their Use and Usefulness,' *Library,* 5th ser. 4(1949–50): 249–61; William B. Todd's 'Observations on the Incidence and Interpretation of Press Figures,' *Studies in Bibliography* 3 (1950–51):171–205; and Kenneth Povey's 'A Century of Press Figures,' *Library,* 5th ser. 14(1959):251–73. The literature of analytical bibliography focusing on the eighteenth-century is not large, however, and that devoted to the nineteenth-century is quite sparse. Among the most interesting of what has appeared are Oliver L. Steele's series dealing with the complicated question of format in machine-printed books (see, for example, 'A Note on Half-Sheet Imposition in Nineteenth and Twentieth Century Books,' *Gutenberg Jahrbuch 1962,* pp. 545–47) and Peter L. Shillingsburg's articles on the problems of books printed from plates (such as 'Detecting the Use of Stereotype Plates,' *Editorial Quarterly* 1, no. 1 [1975]: 2–3, and 'Register Measurement as a Method of Detecting Hidden Printings,' *Papers of the Bibliographical Society of America* 73[1979]:484–88).

The kind of analysis of books reflected in the titles cited here is a natural part of the research underlying a descriptive bibliography: without such analysis, a bibliography would be deficient in its account of the production history of the books covered and very likely in its classification of their impressions and issues as well. Analytical bibliography and descriptive bibliography are obviously complementary, and the historian of American books should be acquainted with the standard practices of descriptive bibliography, developed (like the analytical techniques) in connection with European books—in such monuments as A. W. Pollard's first volume of the *Catalogue of Books Printed in the XVth Century Now in the British Museum* (London: British Museum, 1908–) and W. W. Greg's *A Bibliography of the English Printed Drama to the Restoration* (London: Bibliographical Society, 1939–59). The great codification of these practices is Fredson Bowers's *Principles of Bibliographical Description* (Princeton: Princeton University Press, 1949), which starts from the position that a bibliography is a historical study and that it is based on the detailed examination of physical evidence.[11] His book remains the primary one in its field.[12]

Textual scholarship, too, in its search for all relevant evidence, must take physical evidence into account; the research required for a descriptive bibliography and for an edition overlap so considerably that both are often planned as a single undertaking. Anyone who wishes to study the role of the book in America is perforce concerned with the texts of the books that have circulated there and thus needs to be aware of the principal issues raised in recent years by editorial theorists. Debates about establishing texts have of course existed for centuries, and in some respects the issues remain the same. But just what those issues are and how they may have been

[11] It uses American books as examples from time to time, including one of 1669 (p. 222).

[12] Readers can decide whether it should be supplemented by studies since that time of bibliographical arrangement (*Studies in Bibliography* 37[1984]:1–38), the concepts of *issue* and *state* (*Papers of the Bibliographical Society of America* 69[1975]:17–66) and *ideal copy* (*Studies in Bibliography* 33[1980]:18–53), tolerances (*Library*, 5th ser. 23[1968]:1–12), title-page transcription and signature collation (*Studies in Bibliography* 38[1985]:45–81), typography (*Papers of the Bibliographical Society of America* 60 [1966]:185–202, paper (*Studies in Bibliography* 24 [1971]:27–67), inserted plates (*Studies in Bibliography* 35[1982]:1–42), and publishers' binding patterns and colors (*Studies in Bibliography* 23[1970]:71–102, and 20[1967]:203–34).

affected by the growth of analytical bibliography are matters that the student of book history, not merely the prospective editor, cannot afford to ignore. Much of the debate in the English-speaking world in the last thirty years has stemmed in one way or another from W. W. Greg's celebrated essay 'The Rationale of Copy-Text,' published in *Studies in Bibliography* 3 (1950–51):19–36, and reprinted in his *Collected Papers*, ed. J. C. Maxwell (Oxford: Clarendon Press, 1966), pp. 374–91. I have tried to provide a critical history of this debate in two pieces in *Studies in Bibliography:* 'Greg's Theory of Copy Text and the Editing of American Literature,' 28(1975): 167–229 (reprinted in *Selected Studies*, pp. 245–308), and 'Recent Editorial Discussion and the Central Questions of Editing,' 34(1981):23–65. Two brief introductions to modern editorial thinking are Fredson Bowers, 'Textual Criticism,' in *The Aims and Methods of Scholarship in Modern Languages and Literatures*, ed. James Thorpe (2d ed.; New York: Modern Language Association of America, 1970), pp. 161–88; and G. T. Tanselle, 'Textual Scholarship,' in *Introduction to Scholarship in Modern Languages and Literatures*, ed. Joseph Gibaldi (New York: Modern Language Association of America, 1981), pp. 29–52. The suggestions for further reading appended to the latter essay need not be repeated here; but perhaps in this context I should call attention to my effort—in 'The Editing of Historical Documents,' *Studies in Bibliography* 31(1978): 1–56 (reprinted in *Selected Studies*, pp. 451–506)—to show the illogic of treating 'historical' writings differently from 'literary' writings.

The books and articles I have named here are only a small selection from a voluminous literature, but I believe they form a reasonable introduction to bibliographical thinking—to the kind of thinking that should underlie all study of book history. When we look for what work, built on such a base, has been done specifically on the book in America, there is little to point to, other than a small number of bibliographies and the growing shelf of CEAA editions. A few complaints about this situation have been voiced over the years, along with suggestions on how to proceed. In 1968, for instance, in 'The Descriptive Bibliography of American Authors' (*Studies in Bibliography* 21:1–24), I attempted to explain the deficiencies in the bibliographical treatment of American writers. Four years later Edwin Wolf, 2nd, published a far more important essay, 'Historical Grist for the Bibliographical Mill,' *Studies in Bibliography* 25(1972):29–40. Deploring the 'wall separating bibliography as applied to literary works from bibliography as applied to historical or political works' (p. 37), he demonstrated—through an impressive assemblage of telling examples, all American—that bibliographical analysis is as essential for 'nonliterary' books as it is for 'literary' ones. He noted that most Americanists 'have opted bibliographically and textually for the simplicity of an accurate, but not intensive, description of the single copy at hand' (p. 38), and he ended by asking, 'Isn't it time for a change?' There has been no more eloquent and forceful plea for reforming the bibliographical approach to Americana. It is depressing to recognize, more than a dozen years later, that the situation has scarcely changed.

We can, however, point to a few isolated bright spots. For eighteenth-century studies,[13] the one that stands out is C. William Miller's great work, *Benjamin Franklin's Philadelphia*

[13] One work that might have been expected to offer some bibliographical analysis of a seventeenth-century book is the two-volume set on the Bay Psalm Book that Zoltán Haraszti published in 1956 (University of Chicago Press), one volume a facsimile and the other Haraszti's commentary (*The Enigma of the Bay Psalm Book*). But his chapter on the printing of the Psalm Book does not draw on physical evidence, and the one on 'The Extant Copies' limits its discussion of differences among copies to whether or not they are 'perfect,' nowhere suggesting the value of collating the texts or examining the paper of those copies. His facsimile is largely of one of the Prince copies, but several pages are substituted from the other Prince copy. He does, somewhat tentatively, recognize that he should provide a record of these pages: 'In his Introduction [to the 1903 facsimile], Wilberforce Eames, the foremost American bibliographer of his time, did not specify the pages prepared from the Lenox copy. . . . Yet the noting of substitutions may be useful.' Nevertheless, in his own facsimile, Haraszti has allowed 'blemishes' to be 'removed by careful opaquing.' To his credit, it must be added, Haraszti understood that, in proofreading, a facsimile must be 'compared, letter by letter, with the original pages.'

Printing, 1728–1766: A Descriptive Bibliography (Philadelphia: American Philosophical Society, 1974). Although Miller has to deal with 856 items in the main part of this bibliography, he provides in every entry (among other things) a signature collation and information on type, paper, binding, and (when applicable) running-titles, catchwords, ornaments, and plates. These details, furthermore, are based on the examination of multiple copies whenever possible, often a dozen or more and sometimes as many as twenty-eight (for the first book, 1728) or even sixty-four (for the *Cato Major* of 1744). The 453 large double-column pages of descriptive entries (along with the appendixes showing types, ornaments, and binding decorations) provide a major monument for other students of eighteenth-century American books to look to. (Miller's work shows how far bibliography has advanced since that earlier landmark of seventeenth- and eighteenth-century bibliography, Thomas J. Holmes's series of bibliographies of the Mathers, published 1931–40—which did, however, include signature collations.) On a lesser scale, but nevertheless significant as an instance of the detailed scrutiny of a piece of eighteenth-century American printing, is Frederick R. Goff's *The John Dunlap Broadside: The First Printing of the Declaration of Independence* (Washington: Library of Congress, 1976). Goff was able to assemble at the Library of Congress seventeen of the twenty-one known copies of the Dunlap broadside for side-by-side comparison; his report tabulates damaged type, offset (from folding when the ink was wet), watermarks (with three beta-radiograph illustrations), and chainlines, as observed in each copy. The discovery of two states of the imprint, as it happens, could have been made without the Hinman Collator and without bringing the copies together; but that fact does not mean that the effort of bringing them together was futile. This investigation was rightly based on the recognition that direct comparison of originals may (indeed, often does) turn up details not likely to be detected in any other way; one cannot know the outcome in advance. Perhaps it is not surprising that Franklin and the Declaration are the first to receive this attention; the next step is to see to it that the methods employed here are applied to more routine printed items of eighteenth-century America.[14]

For the nineteenth century, the situation is somewhat better, but almost all the activity has been concerned with literary figures. Nevertheless, a great deal of information about nineteenth-century bookmaking and publishing is present in the pages of the *Bibliography of American Literature* (New Haven: Yale University Press, 1955–), begun by Jacob Blanck, continued by Virginia L. Smyers and Michael Winship (vol. 7), and soon to be completed (vol. 8) by Winship.[15] The descriptive entries in this extensive work, though they do not contain the amount of detail that one might wish (even allowing for the scope of the work), do include signature collations and are based on the examination of multiple copies. They are the product of bibliographers who understand book structure and its significance, and they are ordered and classified with the help of physical evidence. Because many of the authors treated are minor, one cannot help but think of the more important

[14] Another notable, if less detailed, study is Thomas R. Adams's *American Independence: The Growth of an Idea* (Providence: Brown University Press, 1965), which records American Revolutionary pamphlets printed 1764–76. Although the entries are not descriptive of physical evidence in most respects, they do include signature collations; and in his introduction Adams recognizes that the pamphlets deserve 'an exhaustive bibliographical analysis that includes a close comparison of all available copies' (p. xviii), even though he has not chosen to undertake the task himself. I append here another reference to a piece of mine because it sets forth some physical evidence from what might be regarded as routine eighteenth-century American books: 'Press Figures in America,' *Studies in Bibliography* 19(1966):123–60, which calls attention to the presence of press figures in American books and tabulates their occurrence in thirty-seven volumes.

[15] On the basis of his experience in examining large quantities of nineteenth-century American books, Winship has drawn some conclusions about the physical evidence left behind by printing from plates: see 'Printing with Plates in the Nineteenth Century United States,' *Printing History* 5, no. 2(1983):15–26 (esp. 22–23). Two earlier standard surveys of bibliographical problems in nineteenth-century American books are Rollo G. Silver, 'Problems in Nineteenth-Century American Bibliography,' *Papers of the Bibliographical Society of America* 35(1941):35–47; and Jacob Blanck, 'Problems in the Bibliographical Description of Nineteenth-Century American Books,' 36(1942): 124–36.

'nonliterary' writers that have never been examined at all in a truly bibliographical way. But of course it is important to have the minor writers covered, for one learns about the printing and publishing process from unimportant books as well as important ones, and the *BAL* is a storehouse of information about a sizable cross-section of nineteenth-century American books. When it began in 1955 there were no thorough descriptive bibliographies of any major nineteenth-century American author; it provided the first serious attention for many authors, but its coverage was not intended to preclude fuller treatment in separate bibliographies. We now have a few of them, the products of the Pittsburgh Series in Bibliography (University of Pittsburgh Press): *Nathaniel Hawthorne* (1978) by C. E. Frazer Clark, Jr.; *Henry David Thoreau* (1982) by Raymond R. Borst; and three by Joel Myerson, *Margaret Fuller* (1978), *Ralph Waldo Emerson* (1982), and *Emily Dickinson* (1984). The standards maintained in this series are generally high, the principal entries containing signature collations, descriptions of type, paper, and bindings, and records of copies examined.[16] One can find fault with them in several respects, but only because one sees that they are more sophisticated than previous bibliographical treatments of nineteenth-century American books, and one feels it appropriate to hold them to the highest level of achievement. Historians who deal with 'nonliterary' writers are usually aware that bibliographies of this kind exist for literary figures and believe that such treatment is somehow not necessary for other writers. As long as this notion persists, the record of bibliographical achievement will remain as it now stands, with little of note outside the area normally called 'literature.' One must give credit, however, to Robert H. Becker, whose recent rewriting of the Wagner-Camp work *The Plains & the Rockies* (San Francisco: John Howell—Books,

[16] In some of these bibliographies it is not clear how many of the copies listed as 'located' were actually examined.

1982) is based on a fresh examination of multiple copies of editions of 690 works and does provide signature collations; although his descriptions are not extensive,[17] his work obviously represents a step in the right direction in the treatment of Americana.[18]

Other than descriptive bibliographies, the principal repository of physical evidence about nineteenth-century American books is the series of editions that have been produced under the auspices of the Center for Editions of American Authors (CEAA), now the Center for Scholarly Editions (CSE), of the Modern Language Association of America. These editions, though they differ among themselves in a number of ways, are descended from the main line of English bibliographical scholarship[19] and therefore are alike in being based on a firm understanding of the essential role that physical evidence plays in textual study. Because the task of elucidating the publishing history of the works to be edited, sorting out the editions and impressions of them and analyzing the physical characteristics of the volumes, had not previously been undertaken, or accomplished satisfactorily, the CEAA editors had to do this work before they were in a position to assess the authority of variant readings turned up in collation. What they did, in other words, was the research for descriptive bibliographies, and many of the results are set forth in essays and lists incorporated in the

[17] One may also question his listing of copies. He says, 'I have cited the location of these [examined] copies, or others whose presence has been factually confirmed, in italics in the location notes' (p. ix). The distinction should not be blurred between copies examined by, and those reported (however 'factually') to, the bibliographer.

[18] Another example of a work that pays attention to, and records, physical evidence is Richard J. Wolfe's *Early American Music Engraving and Printing* (Urbana and New York: University of Illinois Press and the Bibliographical Society of America, 1980), in which an appendix lists 'Watermarks on American Music Sheets, 1793–1830.'

[19] Fredson Bowers's 'Some Principles for Scholarly Editions of Nineteenth-Century American Authors,' read at a conference in 1962 and published in 1964 (*Studies in Bibliography* 17:223–28), suggested the applicability to American writings of the approach Greg set forth in his 'Rationale'; and in 1963 the CEAA was founded on principles deriving from Greg. The resulting editions have since become a focus for theoretical debate about the editing of modern literature.

volumes of their editions.[20] For example, the editions of Hawthorne (Ohio State University Press, 1962–), Stephen Crane (University Press of Virginia, 1969–76), and Charles Brockden Brown (Kent State University Press, 1977–) include signature collations and other elements of formal bibliographical descriptions. The *Scarlet Letter* volume uncovers and analyzes the duplicate setting of the last two pages of the first edition of that work; the *Wieland* volume investigates the half-sheet printing of the first edition and offers two tables setting forth possible printing schedules, the whole discussion advancing our knowledge of the important printing shop of T. & J. Swords; the *Typee* volume of the Melville edition (Northwestern University Press and The Newberry Library, 1968–) uses an imposition diagram for duodecimo to propose a physical explanation for a textual variant. These are random examples, which could be multiplied from other volumes of these editions, or from the editions of Howells (Indiana University Press, 1968–), Irving (University of Wisconsin Press [later Twayne], 1969–), William Gilmore Simms (University of South Carolina Press, 1969–), Emerson (Harvard University Press, 1971–), Thoreau (Princeton University Press, 1971–), Mark Twain (University of California Press, 1972–), Harold Frederic (Texas Christian University Press, 1977–), James Russell Lowell (Northern Illinois University Press, 1977–), and Cooper (State University of New York Press, 1980–).

Following the pioneering lead of the edition of John Dewey (Southern Illinois University Press, 1969–), several editions of this kind in the field of American philosophy are now under way (the William James edition [Harvard University

[20] There have been a few separate articles of analytical bibliography devoted to nineteenth-century American books, such as Oliver L. Steele's 'On the Imposition of the First Edition of Hawthorne's *Scarlet Letter*,' *Library*, 5th ser. 17(1962):250–55, which analyzes the patterns of rough edges of leaves in untrimmed copies to determine format. But most such discussions relating to American books occur in the editorial matter appended to scholarly editions.

Press, 1975–] is well along); and it is to be hoped that scholars in other disciplines begin to see the necessity for such editions in their fields.[21] All these CEAA/CSE volumes are naturally important for the texts they provide, but they should not be overlooked as a source of printing and book-trade information: one can find in them the fullest bibliographical analyses and descriptions available for certain books; the discussions and lists of variants provide some of the data for refining our conception of what nineteenth-century American publishers did to the texts of the works that passed through their offices; and the essays are filled with details that help one to understand the international copyright situation and other aspects of the business of publishing in nineteenth-century America. The number of books covered by these CEAA/CSE editions is not yet sizable enough to support large generalizations; but the volumes are impressively demonstrating the inseparability of physical bibliography, publishing history, and textual criticism.

III

It is clear that the examination of the physical evidence in American books has scarcely begun. Despite all that has been written on the book in America, the vast body of printing evidence that lies embedded in the physical product itself has hardly been touched. But it is there, waiting to be extracted, in every book we pick up. There is thus a multiplicity of important tasks that need to be undertaken. Any interested scholar will find here a wide-open field, in which it is still possible to be

[21] There has of course been great activity in the last thirty years in the editing of the writings of nineteenth-century American statesmen and other historical figures. Most of the texts in these editions have come from manuscripts of letters and journals; but occasionally a printed text had to be dealt with, and in those instances the editors, accustomed to handling manuscripts (how well is not at issue here), frequently did not understand what the editing of printed texts entailed. Cf. Edwin Wolf's remark (in the essay cited above) that Julian Boyd and Leonard W. Labaree (editors of Jefferson and Franklin) 'never questioned the validity of the text of only a single copy of any printed work' (p. 29). These editions do not generally make a contribution to printing and publishing history.

a pioneer. Those who become analytical bibliographers of American books, though they will be working in the shadow of the bibliographers of English literature, will make discoveries that will affect the thinking of all who have occasion after them to be concerned with American printing history. The tasks to be performed are not necessarily different in general terms from those that have long been recognized: we need more regional imprint bibliographies, more bibliographies of genres and of authors, more histories and bibliographies of individual printers and publishers, more essays setting forth in detail the production history of a single volume, more studies of the textual history of particular works. An understanding of the importance of physical evidence, however, will cause these standard tasks to be approached in a new way, and the resulting scholarship will be qualitatively different.

Consider national and regional imprint bibliographies, which provide the basic record of printed output. The eighteenth-century catalogue resulting from NAIP, when completed, will certainly be the foundation for bibliographies covering smaller areas; but those bibliographies will still be needed to provide fuller detail than the comprehensive catalogue can be expected to include. For the nineteenth century, state (or, in some instances, city) imprint bibliographies have traditionally been fundamental, since there was no counterpart to Evans, and they will continue to be so. The checklists produced by Shaw and Shoemaker and their successors are, as their compilers recognize, very tentative and preliminary (but nonetheless essential) efforts; and when more sophisticated catalogues of nineteenth-century imprints appear, they are likely at first to be simply union catalogues of library holdings. (The Nineteenth Century Short Title Catalogue project, under way at Oxford, will in its first phase go only to 1815 and include the holdings of six libraries.)[22] For the entire period,

[22] See G. Averley and F. J. G. Robinson, 'The Nineteenth Century Short Title Catalogue,' *Library Association Rare Books Group Newsletter*, no. 22(November 1983): 15–20.

both before and after 1800, there will continue to be a need for regional bibliographies of imprints that take up manageable enough units of material for bibliographical analysis of some depth to be made. Many of the earlier state imprint bibliographies have long been recognized as unsatisfactory, and many segments of the total record have never been attempted at all. Work to remedy these deficiencies should obviously proceed, but it should proceed with an understanding of physical evidence and the role of analytical bibliography in the study of book history. At a minimum, entries should be based on an examination of multiple copies, with the aim of detecting and reporting issues, printings, and editions; they should also include a signature collation, even if other physical facts, such as information about type and paper, are not noted in detail. There has been a tendency to exaggerate the importance of title pages and to undervalue other aspects of the physical book. (Bibliographers of Americana—I should in fairness point out—are not the only ones guilty of placing excessive reliance on title pages.) Books are made up of parts, and a title page is not sufficient identification for a whole book. Fredson Bowers's advice that one should describe books as if they had no title leaves is worth heeding.[23] What I am suggesting, therefore, is that regional imprint bibliographies of the future should carry through more consistently the line of thinking that underlies their basic structure. The idea of assembling a record of the printed output of a particular area during a particular time emphasizes production history, not the intellectual content of the items produced; but many imprint bibliographers, having taken that initial step toward production history, take few additional steps in that direction, proceeding instead to treat the material from what might be called a literary, rather than a bibliographical, point of view. The imprint bibli-

[23] 'Purposes of Descriptive Bibliography, with Some Remarks on Methods,' *Library*, 5th ser. 8(1953):1–22; reprinted in his *Essays in Bibliography, Text, and Editing* (Charlottesville: Bibliographical Society of the University of Virginia, 1975), pp. 111–34.

ographies we need in the future will differ from those of the past not in the way they divide the total body of material but in the approach they reflect. As they increasingly recognize and exploit bibliographical evidence, they will become livelier and more rewarding as pieces of historical scholarship.

Bibliographies arranged according to such other principles as genre (fiction, almanacs, statutes, primers, and so on) or author will also continue to be useful, and they, too, will become more valuable as they emerge from this process of seeking and recognizing the evidence inherent in printed artifacts. From the point of view of printing and publishing history, however, such organizing principles are not as basic as an arrangement by region, for they emphasize the intellectual content of books, whereas regional lists bring together books produced by the limited number of printers and publishers working within a particular geographical area and thus enable one to search for characteristics of an individual firm or of a number of firms situated in proximity to one another. This point was perceived by Robert Proctor nearly a century ago in his epoch-making work on incunabula: he saw that grouping books (in chronological order) by printer and then assembling those printer-lists by town ('Proctor order,' as it came to be called) would place each book in the context that would best illuminate its production. Facts learned in connection with one book might be relevant to understanding the production history of others close to it in origin; and printer and date might be assigned to books previously lacking such identification. This principle is as valid for more recent books as it is for incunabula. Certain kinds of physical facts, it must be granted, do emerge from other arrangements; for instance, the conventional formats for poetry or fiction or drama in particular periods might be more readily discernible from bibliographies of those genres. But this information could also be made available through indexing, when the basic arrangement emphasizes printing history. Debates about the relative merits of different arrangements are rather futile, in any case, in the age of the computer. If descriptions are entered into a data-base and intelligently provided with a wide range of access points, one can always procure a print-out of whatever category suits one's purpose at the moment. The emphasis is ultimately, therefore, on the amount of information given in individual entries; and there is no getting around the fact that studying a book in the context of others produced in the same shop and the same area will be most revealing. Studies of the output of particular printers or publishers—a subclass of regional imprint bibliographies—are thus what our hopes for the future must rest on, for they can be pursued to a depth generally not feasible for the broader regional studies. Whether they take the form of bibliographies or of narrative histories is fundamentally of little moment. We do need to have bibliographies with discrete entries for ease of reference and for manipulation in data-bases; but the form that bibliographies take should not blind us to the fact that they are indeed histories, involving the same questions about emphasis, selection of detail, and evidentiary standards as other scholarly histories.[24] Bibliographies of printers and publishers, like the best modern author bibliographies, are forms of biography.[25] They can vary in the fullness of their details; but whatever outward shape they take—whether continuous narrative prose or a series of formulaic statements—they will be deficient if the details they provide do not spring from a truly bibliographical point of view, a recognition that a bibliographical enterprise entails the use of bibliographical evidence.

As detailed studies of individual printers and publishers, incorporating the results of the analysis of the physical evidence found in the books they produced, begin to line up on the shelf

[24] See G. T. Tanselle, 'The Arrangement of Descriptive Bibliographies,' *Studies in Bibliography* 37(1984):1–38.

[25] One indication of the growing recognition of this point is Dan H. Laurence's Engelhard Lecture, *A Portrait of the Author as a Bibliography* (Washington: Library of Congress, 1983). See also the essays cited in note 6 above.

(and we are a long way from having a substantial shelf of them), they will form the foundation for various additional kinds of work. They will make possible, for example, new generalizations that will cause the broader accounts of American printing and publishing to need revision. One sort of generalization that will be greatly facilitated is the description of physical features common to the printed matter of a particular area at a given time—the range of papers and typefaces used, the wording of imprints and title pages, the placement and style of signatures, page numbers, and footnotes, the presence or absence of running titles, and so on. A brilliant example of what can be done along these lines, though it is concerned only with British and continental books, is R. A. Sayce's 'Compositorial Practices and the Localization of Printed Books, 1530–1800,' in the *Library*, 5th ser. 21(1966):1–45 (reprinted as a pamphlet, with additions and corrections, by the Oxford Bibliographical Society in 1979). Sayce's work provides only a start, but no comparable start has been published for American books.[26] The kinds of generalizations that grow out of physical evidence are not, however, limited to physical points. Analytical bibliography can uncover—with greater or lesser fullness and certainty, depending on the evidence in each case—such details of the printing process as how many compositors set type for a particular book, whether they set type-pages in consecutive numerical order or in the order needed for the press, what the procedure for proofreading was, and how many copies were in the edition. Generalizations about such matters are naturally important for printing history, but they have been scarce in most historical studies of American books, because the available underlying work has focused more critically on archival documents (such as printers' ledgers) than on the printed products. Recognition that the

[26] The *BAL* could have served as a reasonable basis for such a survey if it had recorded more physical details. Even as it stands, a thorough index to the *BAL*, including references to bibliographical points, would provide a worthwhile start on study of the localization of American books.

latter constitute the primary evidence will add a new dimension to printing history, which will then deal with the process of printing as well as the business of printing.

Indeed, it will be able to explore more fully than in the past the relation of the two. For considerations arising from the examination of physical evidence lead directly into the broadest concerns of economic, social, and intellectual history. Compositor analysis, for instance, enriches what can be learned from external sources about the work force, just as details of proofreading practice reflect economic as well as intellectual standards. When bibliographical analysis helps to assign responsibility for a textual alteration to the author or to the publisher, it is contributing to a knowledge, in the former case, of the writer's process of thought or, in the latter, of the publisher's motivation and perceived audience. The analysis of textual variants is important both for the history of ideas and the history of reading. Such analysis, it is worth emphasizing, need not be preparatory to the publication of an edition. Although we do not by any means have in progress scholarly editions of all the works that deserve such editions, we should also recognize that there are thousands of works of insufficient stature or interest to warrant republication in scholarly editions. Nevertheless, study of the textual history of all these works would indeed be useful. Every published work takes its place, however modest, in intellectual history; and every study that helps to reveal how the text of a particular work reached its published form and how it changed in later editions is a contribution to our understanding of intellectual history and is part of the groundwork for broader historical generalizations. On the list of desiderata for future research, it is hard to imagine a more important category than essays of this kind, detailing the printing, publishing, and textual histories (necessarily intertwined) of individual works. The research is the same as what underlies a scholarly edition, but it is no less valuable for being pursued independently of any proposed edition. As such essays accumulate, we shall begin to have evidence (unavailable now in significant quantity) documenting not only printing history but also the rise of the entrepreneurial role of the publisher and the ensuing influence of the publisher in determining what works—and what texts of those works—reach the public.

Although physical evidence is the primary evidence for printing history, it must naturally be supplemented by any other reliable evidence available. Secondary documents may at times be proved incorrect by the physical evidence of the artifacts themselves. But those documents may also preserve information that one would have no way of ascertaining from the artifacts; indeed, they are the primary evidence for some aspects of the publishing operation that disseminated the printed objects. One obvious source of this kind is printers' and publishers' archives, and what is urgently needed in this area is a guide to the locations where such archives can be found—a guide that (one hopes) would stimulate more publications like those of the Ticknor & Fields and Carey & Lea cost books. The Bibliographical Society of America is looking into the feasibility of providing a guide along these lines. Another source, insufficiently used up to now, is the copyright records, the bulk of which is housed in the Library of Congress.[27] At present the Center for the Book in the Library of Congress is investigating the publication of the pre-1870 records in machine-readable form—another project that deserves the support of all historians of American books. A third source is contemporary lists of books such as catalogues of booksellers and of private or institutional libraries. Some use has already been made of such catalogues by students of the history of reading, and Robert B. Winans is producing an important checklist of this material through 1800,[28] which is bound to stimulate further study.

[27] See G. T. Tanselle, 'Copyright Records and the Bibliographer,' *Studies in Bibliography* 22(1969):77–124.

[28] The first segment of which has been published as *A Descriptive Checklist of Book Catalogues Separately Printed in America, 1693–1800* (Worcester: American Antiquarian Society, 1981). This work does, by the way, include signature collations.

Some of the difficulties of interpreting catalogues as evidence of what people actually read are well known; but there are other difficulties, not as often regarded, in determining precisely what the catalogue entries refer to. All too often, the historians who turn to these catalogues think only of the works mentioned in the entries but do not (because they have not been trained to) consider the specific physical entities, the particular editions, being cited. This problem arises to some extent in the use of any documents external to the books themselves, but it is particularly acute in connection with catalogues, for the entries in them may involve more unknowns (such as publisher or printer and date) than is generally the case with printers' archives or copyright records. A more widespread understanding of how books were produced in the past and how bibliographical evidence can be analyzed will significantly affect future studies of intellectual history. Book catalogues of all kinds obviously have much to offer the historian of reading tastes and the intellectual historian who must know what ideas were current in a given place at a given time. Such historians, however, have been known to accept entries in lists or catalogues without asking whether those items really ever existed, or, if they did exist, what form—or, more likely, forms—of the text they contained. But these documents must be approached critically: one cannot simply use the titles listed in catalogues without being prepared to examine what happened to those books in the stages that preceded publication, what their presence in the catalogues means, and whether apparently distinct editions of a listed title are in fact different editions.

This point deserves some elaboration, for the relation of textual investigation to cultural history has been neglected. Even historians who have recognized the need to identify the editions referred to in catalogue entries have sometimes been guilty of inadequate discrimination. It is not sufficient, for example, simply to segregate abridgments from complete texts. Not every abridgment of a given work is identical, obviously; neither, for that matter, is every edition that purports to contain the full text. If a crucial passage is mangled or omitted in certain popular abridged editions, that fact would be important in assessing just what kind of influence the work would have. Furthermore, children's abridgments should not be underestimated: it is well known that children's books have a profound influence. And one cannot assume that the audience for them is only children. Adults do read children's books—if only to their children—and the abridged form of a classic prepared for children may be the only form certain adults know and may have a greater influence in a particular society than the original text. Similarly, it is often recoginzed that the texts of translations must be scrutinized if one is to examine the influence of particular works in foreign countries. But the point is that any text of a work must be looked at carefully before one can assess its role: one cannot talk about the impact of *works* without knowing what *texts* of those works are involved.[29]

What I have been saying, in commenting on these several kinds of research, is simply that they need to be informed with a new point of view. And at the heart of that view is the recognition that a critical approach to physical evidence is as crucial for dealing with printed matter as with manuscripts. Many historians recognize that to read a manuscript properly they must take into account its paper, its ink, and the process of its inscription;[30] but it appears to be more difficult for some of

[29] Another instance of the general point: one cannot take the recurrence of the same titles in booksellers' lists as a sign of popularity without knowing what editions are referred to. It may rather be a sign of unpopularity, indicating that the books were not selling and were still on hand. Of course, when it can be established that the references are to separate editions, there is some ground for thinking that a certain demand for those works may have existed, but even then the relative size of the editions is an important factor, though often such figures are not known very precisely. In any case, it is unquestionably true that some books remained in stock many years. For these reasons I think that the term 'reading tastes' is not always what the historians who use it are really talking about. Both words may be wrong: the 'reading' of books may not be the subject so much as the availability of books; and 'tastes' may exaggerate the degree of choice involved and the extent to which readers' interests dictate the kinds of works that are made available.

them to see printed items as documents whose physical features are similarly essential for an informed reading of the texts they contain. It is ironic that Lawrence Wroth should have advocated curtailing the record of physical evidence in order to concentrate on the meaning and significance of texts, as if the one were an alternative to the other. Although he maintained that historical texts did not demand the editorial labors that literary texts did, he nevertheless argued for a 'shift of emphasis' from 'minutely exact transcription and elaborate physical description of the book' to 'research into textual history and relationships' (p. 111). Description of form, he said, is only half the job; the rest concerns the text, 'the treasure which the earthen vessel contains'—'the circumstances which brought the text into being; the relationship between circumstances, author, and composition; the publication progress of the book; subsequent editions or issues; or, its passage into oblivion' (p. 106). Everyone would agree that these are important matters. But what Wroth seems, strangely, not to have understood is that 'elaborate physical description' furthers the investigation of such points. The more one learns about the 'earthen vessel' the more one understands the 'treasure' within it. Indeed, one has access to the treasure only because it has been preserved in the vessel, and a prerequisite for assessing the contents is an investigation of how they have been affected by the particular manner of their transmission. The relationship between physical description and what Wroth saw as a shifted emphasis is not dissimilar to the recently debated opposition between bibliographical analysis and the history of books in society. The comment one must make on the former applies equally to the latter: the analysis of the physical object is not a narrow or limited pursuit, since it opens the way for soundly

[30] Although there are many others who seemingly do not understand even this, judging from the number who are content to rely entirely on photocopies of manuscripts and to go into print without ever having examined the originals. (This group includes, shockingly, some of the editors of statesmen's papers.)

based studies of the intellectual contents of those objects and their influence. A great body of evidence stands ready to be tapped: practically every time that I have compared two or three copies of an early American book, or traced such features as press figures or running titles through even a single copy, I have found some variation or problem worthy of further analysis. Because problems of this kind in American books have not been tackled over the years, the approach of a great many historians to American printed artifacts is still naive and essentially uncritical. The fundamental task for the future is the development of a more bibliographically sophisticated view, one that recognizes the necessity for applying to printed artifacts the critical scrutiny that scholarly inquiry presupposes.

To examine the impact of printed matter on society—the effect that the printing press, through its products, has had on the course of events—is a principal element of the approach to the history of books often referred to as *histoire du livre*. It is not usual, however, for historians in this general tradition to be concerned with examining the physical evidence present in books or with collating texts and analyzing textual variants.[31] But book-production history and textual history, themselves intimately related, are integral to cultural history. The effort to understand how printed matter has affected society cannot divorce itself from the evidence that emerges from a study of the manufacturing and textual history of each book. I hope it is clear I am not claiming that literary scholars in general understand these points and historical scholars do not. Certainly many literary scholars do not understand them, and I am simply suggesting that there should be more recognition of the need to discuss these questions among scholars in all fields. It just happens that certain literary scholars are the ones who

[31] See John Feather, 'Cross-Channel Currents: Historical Bibliography and *l'Histoire du Livre*,' *Library*, 6th ser. 2(1980):1–15; and G. T. Tanselle, *The History of Books as a Field of Study* (Chapel Hill: University of North Carolina, 1981).

have taken fullest advantage thus far of the fact that the texts of books are affected by the physical means through which they are transmitted. But this insight is one that applies equally to all written and printed communication. There is no reason why belles-lettres require more attention to textual matters than any other form of communication. Anyone serious about understanding what a work says must be interested in any evidence that bears on determining what words and punctuation the text of that work contained in specific appearances, and on judging what words and punctuation it was meant to contain by its author. Establishing these matters normally involves knowing the printing and publishing practices of the time, and knowing therefore how to evaluate the primary evidence preserved in the printed items themselves. Studying the role of printed matter in society is a complex process requiring many different approaches; surely the establishment of texts, and the analysis leading to that establishment, are central elements in this basic task of historical understanding.

A Comment on Mr. Tanselle's Paper

G. THOMAS TANSELLE'S EXCELLENT essay divides naturally into two major parts. On the one hand, he offers suggestions and exhortations for strengthening research on the history of the book in America. All that he has to say on this subject seems to me hardly debatable and certainly should be heeded without hesitation. Several of the papers yesterday urged us to look at the individual book, to study the output of printers in detail, etc. On the other hand, Tanselle introduces some general strictures about procedures or methods in the use of sources in historical study, and this part of his paper is perhaps more open to question, at least for the sake of argument. I will say a few words first about his recommendations for furthering *l'histoire du livre* and then move on to some of the 'juicier' questions implicit and explicit in his essay that in fact extend to matters beyond the aims of this conference, strictly defined.

The paper in general is a cogent and eloquent plea for the uses of bibliographical analysis, for the close study, that is, of the physical characteristics of individual copies of books. When performed on an extensive scale, by many researchers, this task may lead to surprising findings and new insights into the history of the book in America. This kind of study, Tanselle urges, is 'a wide-open field, in which it is still possible to be a pioneer.' Such bibliographers of American books will be working 'in the shadow of the bibliographers of English literature,' but the result will be 'discoveries that will affect the thinking of all who have occasion after them to be concerned with American printing history.' 'As detailed studies of individual printers and publishers . . . begin to line up on the shelf,' Tanselle

This article, in slightly different form, was read at the conference on the history of the book in American culture as commentary on the paper delivered by Mr. Tanselle.

writes, studies, that is, based on close analysis of the books these printers and publishers produced, they will form a 'foundation for various additional kinds of work.' In one of the strongest statements of his essay, one that constitutes almost an article of faith, Tanselle writes, 'Considerations arising from the examination of physical evidence (of individual books) lead directly into the broadest concerns of economic, social, and intellectual history.' We all know, however, that such has not always been the case, yet I do believe that the imaginative scholar can make it so. The same would apply even more, as Tanselle notes, to studies arising from the printing, publishing, and textual histories of a particular work, as opposed to the study of an individual book.

I did not prepare specific examples of the worth of this concrete approach, but my instincts are that it is sound advice. There will be many frustrations and dead ends, of course, when the leads that are buried in the physical book cannot be followed up because so many records of printing, publishing, and distribution have been lost. But, as often happens in historical study, a small beginning with a set of concrete cases or documents—in this case, the surviving copies of a book are the documents—can widen out exactly as Tanselle has presented the case, bringing surprisingly rich and broad results. At the risk of being trendy, I see here an instance in which the methods of the archaeologist, anthropologist, and the historian can be utilized together to study an object or a series of objects—the book as an artifact of the past enmeshed in a culture. We are more accustomed to speaking of books in general as cultural artifacts. It is less common to do the same with individual titles, to ask, Where does this particular book come from? How is it constructed? How was it used?

The techniques to be employed to make such discoveries are essentially those that have become standards for bibliographical study, as described by Philip Gaskell, for example. But what can carry this kind of study beyond the merely bibliographical—forgive the 'merely'—is the alertness and imagination of the historian of the book who is determined to study this object in its broadest cultural setting. Thus, for the *historian of the book*, Tanselle's paper can only be regarded as a great encouragement and a great guide and stimulus, one of the most persuasive such statements that we have.

We come, however, to the larger claims of Tanselle's paper, where my enthusiasm lessens slightly. Tanselle has become in recent years a formidable—even a terrifying—critic of the methods of textual editing generally practiced by historians, and in this paper I see the same *ideal* standards being carried over to historical method in intellectual history, or even to history in general. This kind of criticism, by one so clear-minded, firm, and learned as Tanselle, leaves me unnerved and trembling for my sins—I know I could be more fastidious about my use of printed sources, and I know I could know them better, as we all could. But I am also left a bit divided. I end up oscillating between the ideal that Tanselle upholds and the practical, realistic, 'cost-effectiveness ratio' that we are in fact usually guided by. In reading Tanselle's critical essays on method, such as the one at hand, I am moved both to protest and cheer at the same time. I want to protest because there are occasions, we all know, when the pursuit of the ideal, of the best and the purest, can delay or even destroy practical progress; I wish to cheer because none of us should tolerate methodological laxness either in textual editing or in our application of the principles of bibliography to printed sources.

I am moved to protest especially when Tanselle takes issue with the statement by Lawrence Wroth which, on the surface, seems so eminently sensible: 'In the treatment of Americana the reward of this procedure [a minute analysis of the make-up of a book] seldom compensates for the pains required to carry it through.' It is undeniably a prime rule of historical method that we must be skeptical of our sources. Let us suppose, for example, that I set out to write an article on an eighteenth-century event involving polemics or the transmittal of ideas. I need to read an essay or sermon or treatise by one of the personages involved with the event, and I find a copy in a rare book library—or maybe on an Evans microcard. My whole argument may revolve around a few paragraphs or sentences found in this book, and yet I have looked at only one copy, or worse, perhaps a microform version of a single copy. That copy could well be corrupt. I know it. A whole paragraph could have been dropped, or a paragraph added. I may not even know whether I have an earlier or later printing that does or does not contain some crucial passages. I may assume that I am working with the first printing, but there may be earlier unrecorded printings. The work as a whole could be a plagiary from an earlier book by another author.

I will cite one famous example. In each of the first four printings of Locke's *Essay Concerning Human Understanding*, the great philosopher changed the text, sometimes in fundamental ways. The modern editions of Locke all make this perfectly clear, so the historian is duly warned. But let us suppose that no bibliographical analysis has been performed on the work I am using, and I naively write my article at a level of generalization that is entirely flawed because of my own inattention to bibliography. Clearly, this is bad method, and the result will be bad history. When Tanselle says, in reference to bibliographical analysis, that 'I cannot think of any other area in which responsible scholars are so careless in their handling of historical evidence,' we hear words that truly should make historians reproach themselves for their frequent lack of caution about the exact nature of their sources.

In an essay written a few years ago that has become an instant classic, sometimes referred to as 'the Tanselle massacre' Tanselle brilliantly exposed the inconsistencies and the potential dangers in the 'modernizing' methods of textual editing used by virtually all of the great *historical* documentary projects of the post-war period—the Jefferson, Adams, Madison, and Franklin papers among others. Could Tanselle also, if he had the time and energy, similarly review the best historical monographic literature of the past fifty years and show that the absence of bibliographical knowledge or bibliographical sensitivity has resulted in false conclusions again and again? Perhaps such a review would not find serious errors. Most historians, I think, are sufficiently suspicious of their sources, when those sources are being called upon to play crucial roles in their arguments, to take the time to discover something about them. But the warning is well made. Certainly, much more attention should be given in graduate school to bibliographical analysis as an essential component of historical method. I think it is generally true, as Tanselle observes, that 'intellectual history and bibliographical analysis are indissolubly tied.' One of the ways we can determine how influential a book was, for example, is to note the number of printings it had. But even that, in itself, can be a difficult bibliographical problem.

For all this, however, the common sense of the matter is on the side of Lawrence Wroth. Our rule must be to use the method in each case that is appropriate to our purposes. Here is where I think Tanselle is in error in practical terms, if not in principle, and this applies to his strictures regarding textual editing as well as bibliography. It is Tanselle's apparent insistence on *uniform* method—as opposed to *appropriate method*—that we may quibble with.

There are occasions, certainly, when attention to the physical character of an individual book or the printing history of a work is of the utmost importance. But there are many more occasions when one can safely play the odds and trust, for example, that there are no significant variations from copy to copy. Every researcher must gamble this way; otherwise, we would never get our research done. Of course, such casualness is especially appropriate when a work is being used only in a very general way, as is often the case in historical rather than literary, research. When a whole book is being reduced to a few paragraphs of summary in the historian's narrative, who cares about variant editions?

Tanselle has persuasively made the case more than once that there is no way one can distinguish consistently between the treatment that so-called *literary* works deserve, both in textual editing and bibliographical analysis, and the treatment that 'other', 'non-literary' historical documents deserve. Yet this blanket identification can be questioned. It appears sometime that Tanselle would have every book and every text subjected to the same minute analysis as that applied to Shakespeare folios. I personally do not think this is an unworthy goal. Indeed, I believe it is the kind of interesting, delightful, and possibly fruitful task that scholars will be assigned to in the eternal afterlife. But on earth we must assign priorities.

Hence, the two alleged fallacies that Tanselle identifies in his paper I do not regard as truly being fallacies. Tanselle argues, first, that it is a fallacy to believe 'that analytical bibliography is tied only to textual criticism and scholarly editing.' He also argues that it is a fallacy to believe 'that analytical bibliography is a tool more appropriate for research on literature than other kinds of writing.' These statements, rather than being fallacies, describe certain essential links that will always be strong. In my opinion, analytical bibliography is *primarily* tied to textual criticism and scholarly editing, although not only to these, and secondly, analytical bibliography is a tool *usually* more appropriate for research on literature than other sorts of writing, although not exclusively so. And one could add that analytical bibliography is important in intellectual history, but not as consistently so as in textual criticism.

In conclusion, I want to make a general point. Ironically, the professionalization of textual editing that has occurred in the United States in the course of the past thirty years may not be all to the good. It is true that we have gone far beyond the textual mutilations that were characteristic of much nineteenth-century documentary editing, but the standards of documentary editing have now risen so high that the kind of useful 'quickie' transcribing and publication of documents that formerly was commonplace has now nearly come to an end. Scholars have grown timid, fearful of criticism; every editing project must now follow the high and time-consuming standards endorsed by the NHPRC or by the Center for Editions of American Authors. Where would we be if E. B. O'Callaghan or John Russell Bartlett in an earlier era had been so fastidious? It is an undeniable fact that for many of the purposes of writing history, although not necessarily literary history, corrupt texts serve well enough. The quality of the textual editing simply has to be good enough to suit the purpose at hand—*a method appropriate to the purpose.* Often, that purpose is quite broad, and a poorly edited document is good enough. I do not want to encourage sloppy work, but this pragmatism is a way in which literary study and historical study differ.

By extension, the same approach applies to bibliographical analysis. How often do we need it? For the most part, I would shift the burden of proof on this matter to scholarly reviewers and critics. I hope we will be ready to pounce when a sloppy historian fails to do the bibliographical work he or she should have done and fails to learn what *must be* learned about the printing history of the work or the individual copy in question. But the burden of proof is on the critic or the reviewer.

It will not do, surely, for the critic of the future to feel emboldened to dismiss a monograph out of hand because there is no evidence in the notes that the author examined all nine or all twenty-five extant copies of the principal source he is using. If such a state of mind did take hold, we may find there is as much timidity and consciousness of vulnerability in historical writing as there now seems to be in scholarly editing. Is this the direction we want to go in?

In the end, the extent of bibliographical research will be guided primarily by vested interest, as most other things are, and not by ideals. Scholars who are adopting *l'histoire du livre* as one of their fields, and who are going to speak about books as objects, had better do their homework. Tanselle's paper will undoubtedly prod descriptive bibliographers to include signature collations and similar details. Intellectual or cultural historians, too, should know whereof they speak when they cite a printed text.

In one area of research the vested interest in bibliographical analysis is of overwhelming importance, and in this area such analysis goes on daily. This is the rare book world, where the failure to realize the general truth that no two books are exactly alike can cost a dealer, or a collector, or a library thousands of dollars. It is for this reason that I think Lawrence Wroth was a poor choice of a foil by Tanselle. When it came to buying books for the John Carter Brown Library collection, I am certain that Wroth did not assume that painstaking and time-consuming study of the physical book failed to compensate for the pains required to carry it through. Any good curator of rare books wants to know everything that can possibly be known about each individual volume in his collection. Now, because what is known about a book is essentially comparative or relative to other existing copies, one is immediately confronted with the problem of the inadequacy or the absence of descriptive bibliographies that will provide just that comparative information. So here we have a nice convergence of interests among librarians, bibliographers, book dealers, and historians, each contributing according to his interest. The money that rare book libraries—or special collections divisions of libraries—are now regularly pouring into the cataloguing of rare books according to AACR II bibliographical standards, which are quite high, eventually ought to serve *l'histoire du livre* very well, somewhat along the lines that Tanselle has outlined.

I want to make one final remark. Despite the seeming contentiousness of this paper, I would like to use this public forum to acknowledge the extraordinary achievement of Thomas

Tanselle in the two fields of textual editing and bibliography. His accomplishments and contributions in these areas seem to me to be nearly unrivaled in this country and it gives me pleasure to say so.

Norman Fiering

Notes on Contributors

Roger Chartier is maitre assistant at l'École des Hautes Études en Sciences Sociale, Paris.

Norman Fiering is director and librarian of the John Carter Brown Library, Brown University.

James Gilreath is American history specialist in the Rare Books and Special Collections Division at the Library of Congress.

David Grimsted is associate professor of history at the University of Maryland.

David D. Hall, professor of history at Boston University, is chairman of the Society's Program in the History of the Book in American Culture.

John B. Hench is associate director for research and publication at the American Antiquarian Society.

William S. Pretzer is a member of the staff of the Edison Institute, Henry Ford Museum and Greenfield Village.

G. Thomas Tanselle is vice-president of the John Simon Guggenheim Memorial Foundation.

Michael Winship is editor of the *Bibliography of American Literature.*